REFLECTIVE TEACHING AND LEARNING IN THE SECONDARY SCHOOL

Developing as a Reflective Secondary Teacher series

The core textbooks in this series provide practical guidance and support to student teachers through their training and beyond. These comprehensive guides help trainee teachers develop a more reflective and critical approach to their own practice.

The series offers students:

- An introduction to national subject frameworks
- Support on all aspects of subject teaching, including planning creative lessons, how to improve classroom performance, classroom management, differentiation and teaching strategies
- Examples of good practice and teacher commentaries
- A research-based section demonstrating M-level work
- Critical and analytical reflection on practice
- A comprehensive companion website www.sagepub.co.uk/dymoke, which includes video clips of lessons, and a range of activities and exemplar material and weblinks.

They are essential reading for student teachers following PGCE, GTP, Teach First, or undergraduate routes into teaching.

Teaching Mathematics in the Secondary School, 2nd edition (forthcoming, Spring 2013)
Paul Chambers and Robert Timlin
Teaching English
Carol Evans, Alyson Midgley, Phil Rigby, Lynne Warham and Peter Woolnough
Teaching ICT
Carl Simmons and Claire Hawkins
Teaching History
Ian Phillips
Teaching Science
Tony Liversidge, Matt Cochrane, Bernie Kerfoot and Judith Thomas

Second Edition

REFLECTIVE TEACHING AND LEARNING IN THE SECONDARY SCHOOL

Edited by
SUE DYMOKE

Los Angeles | London | New Delhi
Singapore | Washington DC

Los Angeles | London | New Delhi
Singapore | Washington DC

SAGE Publications Ltd
1 Oliver's Yard
55 City Road
London EC1Y 1SP

SAGE Publications Inc.
2455 Teller Road
Thousand Oaks, California 91320

SAGE Publications India Pvt Ltd
B 1/I 1 Mohan Cooperative Industrial Area
Mathura Road
New Delhi 110 044

SAGE Publications Asia-Pacific Pte Ltd
3 Church Street
#10-04 Samsung Hub
Singapore 049483

Editor: James Clark
Assistant editor: Monira Begum
Production editor: Thea Watson
Copyeditor: Neil Dowden
Proofreader: Mary Dalton
Indexer: Martin Hargreaves
Marketing manager: Catherine Slinn
Cover design: Wendy Scott
Typeset by: C&M Digitals (P) Ltd, Chennai, India
Printed in India at Replika Press Pvt Ltd

Library of Congress Control Number: 2012933091

British Library Cataloguing in Publication data

A catalogue record for this book is available from
the British Library

ISBN 978-1-4462-0714-7
ISBN 978-1-4462-0715-4 (pbk)

CONTENTS

2 An overview of learning   47
Sue Dymoke

3 Learning and teaching contexts   73
Ingrid Spencer and Sue Dymoke

FIGURES

TABLES

ACTIVITIES

You will find Critical reading at Master's level boxes on the following pages:

ABOUT THE AUTHORS

About the Editor

Sue Dymoke is a Senior Lecturer in Education at the University of Leicester where she leads the Secondary English PGCE course and the Master's in Teaching and Learning (MTL) programme. In 2011 she was awarded a National Teaching Fellowship in recognition of her teaching excellence. Previously she taught English in secondary schools for 16 years, eight of these as a Head of English. She is a published poet with a particular interest in researching the processes of writing poetry and how these are taught in schools.

About the Authors

Jennifer Harrison was Senior Lecturer in Education at the School of Education until her retirement from the University in September 2010. She was formerly a biology teacher in two UK secondary schools, until she entered higher education as a teacher educator. At the University of Leicester she led the Science PGCE course, subsequently became leader of the Secondary PGCE course, and then Director of Research for a number of years. She co-edited the successful first edition of *Reflective Teaching and Learning* (Sage, 2008). Her research interests have included induction into teaching, the role of the mentor and reflective practice and, more recently, beginning teachers' professional learning. She has continued to write in this last area and has contributed nationally and internationally to academic seminars.

Tony Lawson is a Senior Lecturer in Education and a Governor at a Leicester sixth form college. He has held various responsibilities in advanced level examining, from Chief Examiner to member of the Standing Advisory Committee at AQA. He was President of the Association for the Teaching of the Social Sciences for 12 years. His main research focus is information and communications technology. He was a Co-Principal Investigator on a series of nationally funded projects on the use of videoconferencing in primary and secondary schools. He is currently involved in a collaborative research project on the classroom practicum experiences of teacher trainees in Britain and Turkey.

Joan Smith is a Lecturer in Education and has co-ordinated the Secondary PGCE programme, leading the core Teacher Development Course. Joan taught in urban, 11–18 comprehensive schools for almost 20 years. Initially a teacher of English as a second language, she subsequently taught modern foreign languages, and held a range of middle and senior leadership posts before moving into higher education. Her research focuses on women teachers' careers, gender issues in education, feminist theory and research methodology, teacher identity, educational leadership and social justice.

Ingrid Spencer is a Lecturer in Education at the University of Leicester where she works on the Secondary PGCE English/English with Media Studies and the Primary PGCE English and Primary Teach First programmes. She spent five years teaching English in Japan and also worked at a 14–19 community college in Leicestershire for nine years specializing in teaching A Level Communication and Culture and Film Studies. Her research interests include teachers as writers and the use of storytelling and drama strategies as vehicles for deep learning.

Chris Wilkins is a Senior Lecturer in Education. He was Head of Primary PGCE for five years, and has served as Director of Teacher Education at the University of Leicester for three years. His research is in the area of the social contexts of schooling, looking at social justice issues (particularly into issues of 'race', gender and social class) and citizenship education. He has published widely in this field.

Phil Wood has been Programme leader of the PGCE Secondary course at the University of Leicester and co-ordinates the PGCE Secondary Geography programme. He also leads the Pedagogy Pathway specialism on the Master's in International Education and supervises doctoral students. Previously he worked at a large comprehensive in South Lincolnshire where he was subject leader for Geography and an advanced skills teacher. He is a member of the Collaborative Action Research Network, and the Geographical Association, bringing both areas of interest together to investigate innovative approaches to learning and curriculum.

ACKNOWLEDGEMENTS

The writing team wishes to thank Clive Sutton and Mel Vlaeminke, who originated the University of Leicester Secondary PGCE Teacher Development Pack, together with past and present colleagues Jane Adams, Richard Aplin, Denise Burn, Wasyl Cajkler, Chris Comber, Hilary Cremin, Wendy Curtis, Karen Garland, Ian Godwin, Morag Gornall, Roy Kirk, Roger Knight, Sylvia McNamara, Marlene Morrison, Tony Mummery, Mike Price, Sarah Raynes, Gabby Ramos, Rosemary Sage, Hugh Starkey, Adrian Stokes, Alan Sutton, Megan Thirlaway, Angela Wortley and David Whale, who have all contributed to the development and revisions of the pack since its inception. Thanks are also due to Steve Woods for his help during the first edition final draft stage.

Sue Dymoke would like to thank the University of Leicester for granting her a period of study leave in 2012 during which the final edit of this 2nd edition was completed.

Publisher's acknowledgements

SAGE gratefully acknowledges the contributions of the following reviewers who read the proposal and draft chapters along the way:

Andrew Connell, Keele University
Anne Guilford, Manchester Metropolitan University
Bernadette Fitzgerald, University of West England
Cathie Holden, University of Exeter
Sue Wood-Griffiths, University of Worcester

The tables used in chapter 6 are reproduced with permission from Teacher's Pocketbooks.

Table 6.2 has been used with permission from Taylor and Francis:

Holmes, Elizabeth, *The Newly Qualified Teacher's Handbook*, 2nd edition, © 2002 Routledge.

Activity 7.10 has been used with the permission of and derived from Gaine, 1989.

Table 7.13 has been reproduced with permission from Trentham Books:

Miriam Steiner, *Developing the Global Teacher: Theory and Practice in Initial Teacher Education* © 1996 Trentham Books.

ABBREVIATIONS AND ACRONYMS

ADHD:	attention deficit hyperactivity disorder
DARTs:	Directed Activities Related to Texts
EAL:	English as an additional language
E-Bacc:	English Baccalaureate
ECM:	Every Child Matters
EiC:	Excellence in Cities
EOC:	Equal Opportunities Commission
EWO:	Educational Welfare Officer
GCSE:	General Certificate of Secondary Education
GTCE:	General Teaching Council of England
HLTA:	Higher-level Teaching Assistant
IB:	International Baccalaureate
IEP:	Individual Education Plan
LA:	Local Authority
MI:	multiple intelligences
NGO:	non-governmental organization
NLP:	Neuro Linguistic Programming
PDA:	personal digital assistant
PLTS:	personal learning and thinking skills
PoS:	programme of study
SATs:	Standard Assessment Tasks

SEN: Special Educational Needs
SEF: Self-Evaluation Form
SENCO: Special Educational Needs Co-ordinator
SMART: Specific, Measurable, Attainable, Realistic, Time-based
SSP: systematic synthetic phonics
VAK: visual, auditory and kinaesthetic
VLEs: virtual learning environments
ZPD: zone of proximal development

INTRODUCTION

Sue Dymoke

Content, organization and underpinning approach

This book has been written for beginning teachers who are preparing to teach in secondary schools. It covers a range of core professional studies which all graduate teachers need to address, whatever their subject or **curriculum** specialism or form their initial teacher education takes. It acknowledges that the impact of national government policy to raise educational standards in England, and the wider academic research that informs and underpins new approaches to teaching and learning, are *both* contributing to new developments in secondary schools and initial teacher education.

The organization of the book is as follows. Chapter 1 aims to develop your understanding of **reflection** as a critical activity, provides opportunities for focusing on core competences such as communication skills, and examines the relationship between 'reflective practice' and professional learning.

Chapter 2 introduces you to theories of learning and explores the implications of these for your preparation for teaching and learning along with related issues including the development of thinking skills and the place of creativity and risk taking in education.

Chapter 3 considers the way learning and inclusive environments can be structured in secondary schools. It also explores how educational policy has shaped teaching, curriculum content and the qualifications framework, as well as some of the impacts of **e-learning**.

Chapter 4 covers the many aspects of managing learning within classrooms (and other learning places) both in and out of school. It provides you with the chance to

reflect upon the dynamics of classroom life and the ways in which you can influence learning through systematic planning and evaluation of your practice.

Chapter 5 focuses on key issues concerning monitoring, **assessment**, recording, reporting and accountability. It provides some of the theoretical background to assessment and the terminology you will need to use, and provides ways for you to reflect on your early experiences of assessing your students.

Chapter 6 opens out a range of issues to do with the pastoral care and the many tutorial responsibilities of all teachers. It examines the links between pastoral tutoring and the academic and personal, health and social education curricula, and provides you with a chance to think critically about your own tutorial roles in the future.

Chapter 7 considers some of the important social contexts in which schools operate and the complex, often contentious, issues that lie behind them. It provides opportunities for you to explore your statutory duties with regard to diversity and social justice issues and to reflect on how your own 'world view' might impact on your work in the classroom.

Each chapter provides an academic approach to these same studies that teachers need to address in order to reach Master's (M) level. While this book complements the separate subject studies that form part of all secondary initial teacher education (ITE) courses, each author in the writing team for this book is from a different subject specialist area and working on a postgraduate certificate course. Each author has been able to bring to the separate chapters of this book some particular perspectives from their subject area. This should help you, also, to make the bridges or connections necessary for integrating your knowledge and understanding of both professional and subject studies.

We believe this book, and the reflective approaches embedded within it, will find a place in the various routes for initial training, in induction and the early professional development of new teachers. It provides a flexible learning resource for use by beginning teachers in private self-study, when working in group seminars (tutor-led) at the university, when working with mentors during school placements, or in more informal groupings in twos or threes.

Teaching is a professional activity. In learning how to teach we need to explore three important questions in becoming a teacher:

- What do teachers do?
- What affects what they do?
- How do they do it?

However 'knowing about teaching' is much more than acquiring a set of skills and accomplishing technical expertise. It is about asking a further question:

- How do teachers improve their practice?

In exploring this question, beginning teachers have to exercise originality of thinking and critical judgement, use educational research strategies, draw on educational theories, and develop professional values and practices to support professional learning and development. These are rooted in the several forms of 'enquiry learning'.

When we ask the very important question 'What *kind* of teacher do we want to be?', we have to recognize four core characteristics of teaching. The first is that teaching is an *intellectual activity.* This includes the **ability** to process knowledge and understanding, together with a capacity to communicate it effectively. A second characteristic is forging and maintaining effective *personal interactions.* A third area is the forming of *ethical judgements.* The fourth characteristic is the *social significance* of teaching. The book incorporates reading and activities and attempts to take account of all of these areas of teaching within each chapter.

Reflective practice as a dynamic developmental process in initial teacher education is at the heart of the book. We have incorporated a first chapter to explore what is meant by 'the reflective practitioner'. Although reflective practice has been an assessed standard in initial and continuing professional education, it is actually a state of mind as well as an educational approach for all professionals to examine both non-critical and critical incidents in our working lives. We present it as a pedagogical approach – one in which you can begin to learn through **professional enquiry**.

Reflective practice provides a way of examining your personal experiences in the workplace. Thus, it is psychologically useful but, more than this, it is situated within the wider political and social structures of education. Therefore we believe that, through reflective practice, you can be encouraged to examine the values that underpin all your practice in teaching.

This book should also help to raise a beginning teacher's awareness of the particular role of their teacher–mentor. A mentor helps you to step 'outside of the box' of your job and personal circumstances, and look in at it together. Clutterbuck and Megginson describe this as 'like standing in front of a mirror with someone else, who can help you see things about you that have become too familiar for you to notice' (1999: 17). A mentor can contribute to your learning in a number of ways: as teacher, coach, encourager, supporter, enabler, role model or critical friend. A mentor should be able: to offer empathy and non-judgemental critique; to challenge your behaviour (not you); to challenge your assumptions (not your intellect); to challenge your perceptions (not your judgement); and to challenge your values (but not your value). They should be able to help you evaluate the available evidence from your practice. Many of the activities in this book can involve other teachers and mentors with you and can stimulate the wider professional discussions that are so important in your early training.

Terminology

We have adopted the term 'beginning teacher' to describe the trainee or student teacher, or new entrant to the profession, who is learning how to teach. We have therefore chosen to avoid the use of the term 'student teacher' in order to distinguish clearly the term 'student'. The word 'student' in this book, therefore, refers always to the young person, pupil or child whom the beginning teachers will teach.

We have used the word 'mentor' in relation to the **designated** teacher in your own subject or curriculum area who is likely to have been given a particular *supporting* and *mentoring* role in relation to you and your initial training in the school. In some cases the mentor may be the same person as the school 'tutor' and therefore have multiple roles in connection with your training and its assessment.

There is much jargon used in education and there is terminology that often has specialized meaning in educational settings and which differs from its everyday use. These are emboldened at their first appearance in the book. A glossary of key terms and a list of abbreviations and acronyms are provided to give you extra referral points for important terminology.

Ways of using the book

This book has been written in such a way that it should allow you to read and think more widely about education and teaching, and to work with other beginning teachers and tutors in higher education institutions (HEIs) and in schools and colleges. You are encouraged to read the early parts of each chapter as an introduction to the seven professional areas of study. As you read further into each chapter you will find an extension to the area of study, and the references to wider reading and associated activities for the most part will become more complex.

Reading and using a textbook can be a rather passive and lonely experience, with the expectation that you will assimilate all the ideas within it. We sincerely hope that this will not be the case with this book. It has been written in such a way that it allows you to read and think more widely about education and teaching, and to work with other beginning teachers and tutors in higher education institutions and in schools and colleges. A wide variety of activities and links to web-based materials are embedded within each chapter. We hope these approaches will challenge and stimulate you to think for yourself about teaching, and in ways that will provide you with opportunities for direct 'conversations' with yourself and with others.

Companion website

A companion website containing a range of supporting material can be found at www. sagepub.co.uk/dymoke. Links to companion website resources can be found throughout the book – these are indicated by a globe icon in the margin at appropriate points.

Postgraduate certificate in education (PGCE) M level

Study at Master's level requires a level of critical reflection which is not always achievable by the already packed programmes of most PGCE courses. This book should go a long way towards providing you with some independence in learning, particularly if you are embarking on this route. For example, it provides flexible materials and tasks so you can use your non-contact time effectively. Each chapter provides you with references to high-quality, current theoretical literature, some of which can be accessed through online links. University libraries should have access to key texts as well as a range of e-journals. Your institution's **virtual learning environment (VLE)** may also provide you with valuable opportunities for beginning teachers and tutors to share and develop ideas, and to communicate with each other in discussion forums. This book can be used to assist and inform critical reflection in preparation for assessed units of work.

The range of tasks in each chapter has been selected to provide explorations of topics at both Higher and Master's levels. All the tasks address *general pedagogical issues*. We have recognized the progression that will be needed to move towards M level. There is at least one substantive task which allows for a more in-depth 'professional enquiry' within each chapter together with a critical reading at Master's level activity, which is located, in most cases, towards the end of each chapter. Tutors and teachers in both school-based work and taught sessions will have a role to play in helping you relate your M-level study to your work in schools, and thereby link theory, research and practice. The Master's level work in our book is integral to all elements of the general or professional part of a PGCE programme – it has not been conceived as a 'bolt-on' to the traditional PGCE course structure.

Sue Dymoke
31 January 2012

Reference

Clutterbuck, D. and Megginson, D. (1999) *Mentoring Executives and Directors.* Oxford: Butterworth-Heinemann.

CHAPTER 1

PROFESSIONAL LEARNING AND THE REFLECTIVE PRACTITIONER

Jennifer Harrison

By the end of this chapter you will have

- developed your understanding of reflection and critical thinking
- gained an overview of the relationship between the reflective practitioner and professional learning
- been introduced to the core competences and skills of the reflective practitioner
- developed your understanding of the role of professional learning conversations and the mentor in deepening reflection on practice

An introduction to the reflective practitioner

Perhaps, by the time you open this book, you have already come across ideas such as *reflective writing* or *evaluation of teaching and learning* or *problem-based learning*. You may have discovered how reflective practice can widen your understanding of teaching in educational settings or, indeed, in other workplaces where you have been able to consider and evaluate an aspect of your work. Some of us, as keen promoters of reflective practice, can point to its particular role in professional activities and value how reflective practice contributes to professional learning and development (Harrison, 2004). All the authors of the chapters in this book anticipate that it will help you to make sense of what you do and to help place value on the knowledge and experiences that you already have, and will gain, during your early professional years.

Some other professionals you meet may be rather more critical of the reflective process and may think that engaging in reflective practice can be a somewhat superficial activity – just another hurdle to jump across in the training process, or to be seen as a bit of a chore. If it does seem to have become a somewhat repetitive exercise in your training programme, then we hope that, by reading this chapter and engaging in some of the activities, you will be helped to re-focus on its benefits.

What is a reflective practitioner; what is reflective practice?

These appear to be simple questions and, initially, any answers might appear to be rather obvious to the reader. Surely all professionals think about what they do and adapt their ways of working as a result of such thinking? Certainly reflective practice is talked about in teacher education, as well as in other professional settings such as nursing and social work, so it has gained credibility as well as criticism as a much over-worked expression.

To support reflective practices, various strategies have been designed within many professional programmes, such as storytelling, learning journals, using metaphors, conducting analyses using videos of teaching sequences, modelling and using reflective frameworks. Thinking about *reflective practice* as a concept is crucial since we do need to be clear about what it means. Whether we are beginning teachers, university education tutors or school mentors involved in school-based training, it is important to have a chance to clarify what we understand by it and what we expect it to entail. The starting point in this chapter is that it is much more than simply *thinking about teaching*.

Asking questions
Reflective practice can be thought about in terms of asking searching questions about an experience. Most questions you are already asking do not form out of thin air. They come from the contexts in which you are working, or in response to situations in which you find yourself. Pause here and jot down some questions that have already occurred to you as a result of your work, or of your experience, in an educational setting. Here are some examples:

- For teachers (me) and for students (Year 9), what are the different ideas of what is fun or exciting in a science lesson on *climate change*?
- How can I make clear my expectations and guidelines for students to know how to act and learn?

- What are the different ways that I can plan for a (practical) lesson that takes account of the fact that some students have particular skills, and others do not?

Alternatively, many education headlines in the media lend themselves to the formation of questions. Look at some of the following taken from *The Times Educational Supplement* and identify a question for each headline:

- 'Diverse classes "can be less tolerant"' (15 April 2011)
  www.tes.co.uk/article.aspx?storycode=6077929 (accessed 3 November 2011)
- 'Ofsted brands careers advice for girls "weak"' (15 April 2011)
  www.tes.co.uk/article.aspx?storycode=6077927 (accessed 3 November 2011)
- '"Stretch and challenge" A levels "too easy"' (8 April 2011)
  www.tes.co.uk/article.aspx?storycode=6076715 (accessed 3 November 2011)

Investigating

John Loughran (2002) describes reflective practice as 'a lens into the world of practice' (p. 33), recognizing that it offers a chance for questioning of often taken-for-granted, assumptions. In other words it provides a chance to see one's own practice through the eyes of others. It is through both questioning and investigating that reflection has the potential to lead to a developing understanding of professional practice. Brookfield (1995) talks about our 'assumption hunting' (p. 218) as we learn about and experiment with, different approaches to our teaching practices.

Being a reflective practitioner at any stage of teacher development involves a constant, critical look at teaching and learning and at the work of you, the teacher. Some of this investigation might be done through your reading of the relevant literature (for example, when you are asked to produce a review of the professional or academic literature in a chosen area, resulting in a written critical summary). This activity can help highlight important gaps in your professional knowledge. Some investigation might be done through your talk with expert teachers and so comparing different sorts of evidence of practice (for example, you might be expected to present your learning orally to your peer group in a small group seminar on the chosen issue). Some investigation might be done individually through your private framing and reframing of episodes of teaching (learning journals/diaries can assist with this process), or more publicly by inviting someone into the classroom to view the experiences using another set of eyes (professional conversations which enable further analysis to take place are important part of this way of working).

What does this mean for beginning teachers?

Reflecting on aspects of teaching practice is usually fairly instinctive for most beginning teachers. You focus mentally on particular problems or dilemmas that are to do with how a particular teaching session went. Perhaps with the aid of a lesson evaluation form, you identify what went well during the teaching session, and what did not go according to plan. You are then encouraged to go on to think about what might need changing in the next teaching session, or to identify what could be tried out in other types of teaching sessions. This process takes you from an essentially routine kind of reflection towards a more technical/*practical reflection*, in which you begin to examine the interpretative assumptions you are making in a particular situation or aspect of your work. The focus for your reflection shifts *from* what you as teacher might be doing *towards* what your pupils might be doing, and why. In exploring a situation, you become more open to consider new ideas and you actively seek the views of your peers, the pupils or others. A deeper, *critical* level of this hierarchy of reflective practice (van Manen, 1977) is where, as your teaching career develops, you begin to critically reflect on broader societal, ethical or political dimensions of your work and to consider its wider educational goals. There may be in time a reframing of your perspective with a more fundamental change in your practice. These ideas are developed further in this chapter.

The practical and critical levels are less instinctive to most beginning teachers. Indeed you may feel frustrated that, while you are being encouraged to discuss theoretical issues, you have a more immediate need to master the day-to-day aspects of teaching: for example, how to get your students to listen to you, how to establish authority, how to teach about *cells* as the basic unit of life in a meaningful and engaging way, and so on. This is why we want to encourage you to try the activities in this particular chapter and consider critical reflective practice as part of your professional study. The practical levels of reflective practice, and the sorts of skills and attributes we would wish you to develop at the beginning of your teaching career, are explored later in this chapter.

Reflective practice and professional knowledge

It is in its relationship with professional knowledge and practice that deeper reflection becomes such an important feature of reflective practice. If reflective practice stays at a technical level, restricted to the evaluation of teaching and learning strategies and classroom resources, it would be difficult to stress its overall importance in teacher development. However as reflective practice is used to explore more *critically* the underlying assumptions in our teaching practices, then we can begin to build our understanding of learning and teaching and add to our professional knowledge. Teachers who are unreflective about their teaching tend to be more accepting of the everyday reality in their schools and 'concentrate their efforts on finding the most effective and efficient means to solve problems that have largely been defined for them by some collective code' (Zeichner and Liston, 1996: 9). In other words, such restricted ways of thinking do not allow problems to be framed in more than one way. A fuller rationale for critical reflection and teacher professional learning is given in Harrison and Lee (2011: 200–201).

There are a number of eminent writers and researchers who have contributed to the complex thinking that surrounds reflective practice. Dewey's (1910) book *How We Think* was seminal and clearly influenced the later work of both Schön and Kolb. Dewey's view was that reflective action stems from the need to solve a problem and involves 'the active, persistent and careful consideration of any belief or supposed form of knowledge in the light of the grounds that support it' (1910: 6). He proposed a five-step model of problem-solving, which included suggesting solutions, posing questions, hypothesizing, reasoning and testing. Together these form a sequential process for reflective thinking.

Dewey's work has been extended by others. Van Manen, as we have noted, highlighted, at the highest level of reflection, a moral dimension to reflective action in which the 'worth-whileness' of actions can be addressed (1977: 227). Carr and Kemmis also speak of this higher-level reflection as involving teachers as the central actors 'in transforming education' (1986: 156). More recently Pollard has stated, 'reflective teaching implies an active concern with aims and consequences as well as means and technical competence' (2005: 15).

There are clearly particular skills and dispositions associated with being a reflective practitioner. Dewey drew attention to particular qualities that could be linked to ways of thinking. These include open-mindedness, responsibility and wholeheartedness (1933). Others such as Brookfield (1987) tried to describe critical thinking in relation to **pedagogy** and have advocated ways of provoking critical thinking.

Brookfield (1995) coined the term 'critical lenses' and identified four perspectives that such lenses might provide when reflecting on practice:

- the practitioner (you, the beginning teacher)
- the learners (your students)
- colleagues (for example, your mentor)
- established theory (as found in the educational and other academic and professional literature)

Brookfield explored all those things that we do, the things that influence what we do, and the things we never stop to think about or ask questions about, and asked that we should try to unpack the assumptions about what we do in the classroom. Through such critical reflection on practice we should then be able not only to examine the *technical* aspects of our teaching, but also look *critically* at issues, both within the school as a whole, and outside, that might impact on the quality of teaching and learning in the classroom.

Some forms of **action research**, professional enquiry and **self-study research** have grown from these roots of reflective practice. As beginning teachers you might wish also to observe your own university tutors in their work as teacher educators. How do they create experiences for you to gain access to their thinking about, and to their practice of, teaching?

Alternative conceptions of reflection

Schön (1983, 1987) recognized that professional knowledge lies in the *doing* of the job. Many experienced teachers cannot actually articulate what they know – they just *do it*.

Schön argued that in these situations professionals use their knowledge and pa⟨t⟩ riences as a frame for action – it is a form of 'knowing in action' which come⟨s⟩ experience, and therefore it differs from Dewey's conception of routinized ⟨a⟩ Schön argued that if professionals can begin to separate out the things they know they do them, then they become more effective in their work. Part of this re-fra⟨mi⟩ng involves *setting* as well as *solving* problems, 'a process in which interactively we name the things to which we will attend and frame the context in which we will attend to them' (Schön, 1983: 40). He proposed two sorts of reflection: reflection-in-action and reflection-on-action. It is useful to explain these terms further.

Reflection-in-action is the almost unconscious, instantaneous reflection that happens as a more experienced teacher solves a problem or dilemma. Schön described this as drawing on their *repertoire* of knowledge, skills and understanding of a situation so that he or she can change direction and operate differently in the classroom. In other words, rather than randomly trying any other approach, the teacher is using the accumulated experience and knowledge to seek alternatives in the classroom in response to the needs of the pupils.

Reflection-on-action takes place after the event or teaching session and is a more deliberative and conscious process. There is more critical analysis and evaluation of the actions and what might have happened if a different course of action had taken place. Since it involves looking back at an event it is a form of retrospective reflection. It can involve the actual writing down of what happened and why (critical analysis and evaluation) as, for example, on a lesson evaluation form.

However, in attempting to separate *thinking* from *doing*, Schön gained a number of critics. Day (1993) and Solomon (1987), with others, have pointed to his lack of attention to the role of conversation or dialogue in teachers' learning, arguing that reflection is also a social process requiring the articulation of ideas to, and with, others to allow the development of a critical perspective. The importance of detailed conversation with a mentor in order to jointly analyse and evaluate what happened provides further opportunity to examine professional knowledge and theories-in-use. Time is also needed for separate reflection *on* action. Carr and Kemmis (1986) argued that Schön's narrow focus on the *individual* neglects any consideration of wider social settings. Thus we need to find ways of tapping into, and supporting, time available for such learning conversations and the improving the quality of these.

Experiential learning and the role of a mentor

There are several theoretical approaches which have been used to try to explain the relationship between experience and learning – sometimes referred to as *experiential learning*. One of the best-known models is that of the experiential learning cycle (Kolb, 1984), which has formed the basis of several mentor training manuals (see Moon, 2004; Harrison et al., 2005). Kolb's theory is that people learn from their experience, and the way this happens is through (1) reflection on the things we do (concrete experiences); and (2) experimentation (action) in similar situations at another time, in order to gain further experience; reflect again, and so on. It is this cyclical process of reflection that allows us to learn from experience.

Experiential learning also acknowledges that much informal learning takes place outside formal educational settings and this is as true for learners in initial teacher education as it is for students in schools. In this way reflective practice allows the learner to make sense of all learning, both formal and informal, and to organize and evaluate it.

The knowledge and theories that beginning teachers learn in the workplace (in this case, schools and colleges) are as valid as the knowledge gained through more formal qualifications (such as in a first degree in a specialist subject area, or a professional qualification). In saying this, Argyris and Schön (1975) argued that there are two types of theories that professionals use in their workplace and distinguished the two as follows. First, there are the *official* theories of the profession, to be found in text books, codes of practice and so on. There are plenty of these examples in the subsequent chapters of this book. Such theories gain an established place and are endorsed by professionals – the teachers, and others. Then there are the theories-in-use – the *unofficial* theories of professionals, which are the ideas and concepts that professionals actually draw on. They are the professional's own ideas and theories about learning and teaching.

Activity 1.1 'Official' and 'unofficial' theories in education

Work on this within a small, mixed curriculum group of beginning teachers. Look at the *theories* listed as bullet points below:

(a) First, each of you should work on your own. Try to annotate each theory with either 'U' or 'O':

- 'U' is an 'unofficial' theory of a teacher
- 'O' is an established 'official' theory in education

(b) Then, compare your annotations and the reasons for your choices, with other members of the group.

- Boys don't enjoy writing as much as girls.
- People with dyslexia are lazy and don't attempt to overcome the difficulty of acquiring and using **literacy** skills.
- Teachers don't eat in the classroom in the presence of the boys and girls – it gives the students the wrong idea.
- The parents I need to see most at parents' evening are the ones that stay away. They lack the motivation or skills to support their children's education.

- The main point of '**constructivism**' is that humans actively construct their knowledge rather than receive it fully formed from external sources.
- Children learn in different ways. That is why we need different ability 'sets' for subject teaching. Mixed ability classes just don't work.
- Intelligence is fixed and is something that can be measured.
- Caring relationships in a classroom are an important medium for supporting students' learning and socio-emotional development.
- Collaboration is essential for an inclusive climate in school.
- The '**zone of proximal development**' is the difference between what the child can do by himself or herself and the more he or she can do with assistance from an adult, or a more knowledgeable peer. There are sensitive periods in a child's development for learning particular skills.
- Vocational courses are for students who are ill-equipped for academic courses.

Thus, it is through reflective practice that teachers can begin to tease out the different types of theories, select and apply them to advantage. The pedagogy of constructivism (see Chapter 2 for more on this concept) forms an important part of most teacher education courses and professional expectations are that 'knowledge is … created rather than received, [is] mediated by discourse rather than transferred by teacher talk, [and is] explored and transformed rather than remembered as a uniform set of positivist ideas' (Holt-Reynolds, 2000: 21). This acquisition of knowledge is similar to the process of building or construction and Vygotsky's work (1962, 1978) is important, not only in identifying the particular role of discourse of practice, but also in pointing towards the particular importance of mentoring or learning conversations in support of experiential learning (see also Chapter 2). Structured suggestions for ways of exploring and transforming ideas and promoting critical reflective practice during formal mentor conversations can be found in Harrison et al. (2005).

There are many issues raised in the rest of this book which should provide you with opportunities for critical reflection in this widest sense. For example, you might start with your own classroom practice and examine how well your students responded to your use of *small group* activities within a particular lesson (see Chapters 3 and 4 for more on grouping). Afterwards ask yourself some specific questions such as:

- To what extent did the activities empower independent learning or a more democratic approach in the classroom?
- Did all students respond in the same way?
- Was your class briefing satisfactory?
- Were all students ready for a lesson that was less structured and expected independent learning?

Identity matters for teachers

Looking in the *looking glass*

Teaching is a public practice which bears some similarities to the process of acting. This is because teaching involves constant vigilance of the audience, with the teacher making regular efforts to imagine how he or she is coming across, and regular evaluations on-the-job of whether attempts at communication are being understood by students as intended. This comparison with acting stresses the *looking glass* nature of teaching. It is one in which Cooley, as early as 1902, emphasized the essentially reflective nature of identity in his articulation of the *looking glass self*. You will find yourself reflected in a variety of mirrors: your colleagues, your learners, their parents, the government and media, all of whom provide multiple, often idealized, images of teachers' professional identities. These images may compete frequently with your personal identity, may distort your self-image, and bring about a need for self-reflection. It is now recognized that identity in the workplace is not fixed and singular but is multiple, changing and provisional in nature (Weick, 1995). Identity construction is always a social activity; it involves a continual constructing and re-constructing of relationships with others in the workplace.

Nias (1989) has also made important contributions to debate about teachers' developing identity. In her longitudinal study of primary school teachers' lives and identities, she identified a distinction between the personal and the professional elements. She found that incorporation of the identity of 'teacher' into an individual's self-image was accomplished over long periods of time. It follows that it is highly likely that you, as a beginning secondary school teacher, are experiencing a *substantive identity* (that is, your stable, core identity – *you*) as relatively independent of your presentation of yourself within professional setting such as a school (that is, your *situated identity*, or professional self – *teacher*). You may be into your second decade of teaching before you will have fully incorporated your professional role into your self-image and can identify your substantive identity as *teacher*. Nias concluded that being yourself in school was less to do with the practical aspects of teaching young learners, skills and information, and more to do with generating a sense of community and integrating personal and professional connections between teacher and learner.

Thus the central idea is that constructing identity (here, your professional or situated identity) involves you, first, in *making a pattern of experiences* that have consistency over a period of time. You gradually acquire, and accept, characteristic patterns of decision which, in turn, determine your choices and decision-making in the workplace. This second process of *integration* which Nias describes is very challenging particularly to beginning teachers because there are so many mirrors available in which to examine your professional identity. While each of these mirrors may have a distorting effect in terms of providing competing messages about teachers' professional lives, it is important to begin the process of describing each new professional self throughout the training process. The third part of the process involves a *disruption* or *inconsistency* in identity (see Warin et al., 2006). There will be plenty of instances that you, and your peer group, will experience, in your learning of how to teach, where your own pedagogical beliefs (for example, about the importance of learner-centred education) may not coincide with another teacher's beliefs in more teacher-centred methods; or where your perceptions about your subject's status may differ from those of teachers of other subjects.

For further reading, you might look at some publications arising from the VITAE project, a four-year study conducted by the Universities of Nottingham and London. The book *Teachers Matter* by Day et al. (2007) presents strong evidence of the complexities of teachers' work, lives, identity and commitment in relation to their sense of agency, well-being, resilience and student attitudes and **attainment**.

Self-awareness

The humanistic psychologist Carl Rogers noted that, 'if I can form a helping relationship to myself – if I can be sensitively aware of and acceptant towards my own feelings – then the likelihood is great that I can form a helping relationship toward another' (1967: 57). Developing your self-awareness is therefore an essential tool for teachers and is central to developing your reflective practice. At this early stage let us think about the **reflexive** practitioner as the teacher who is attentive to him- or herself in practice.

Activity 1.2   Developing your self-awareness as a new teacher

This is an individual/small group activity.

(a) You are very new to the teaching profession.

After some very early experiences in the classroom, think about your answers to the questions below. Then share your thoughts with other beginning teachers after attempting to answer the following questions:

- What kind of status does teaching have?
- What does it mean to you, personally, to take on the mantle of 'teacher'?
- What public images are there of teachers with which you can identify?
- How might new teachers begin to combine their personal and professional identities? (Accept that, for some, this might be experienced as the inability to be oneself.)

(Continued)

(Continued)

- What is your overall philosophy of teaching and learning?
- What assumptions (implicit or explicit) about the nature of students' learning are inherent in your approaches to teaching?

(b) Try to return to the final two questions in three and, then, six months' time and answer them again.

- What changes to your philosophy and your assumptions have taken place?
- Specifically, have there been any changes to your general approach to teaching and learning, for example in terms of you 'reaching out' to *all* the students in your classes?

To begin developing your self-awareness, try using metaphors in your *storytelling* about your teaching experiences, or in your journal writing. You could start this with a sentence which begins, 'Teaching is like …'

Francis (1995) provides examples from her beginning teachers' reflective journals which illustrate the mismatch for some, between their espoused theories of practice and their choice of metaphor. Here is one from a beginning teacher who claimed to have adopted a constructivist approach to teaching and learning:

> I see myself as a teacher who is like the current flowing through an electric circuit. Each student causes a resistance and a subsequent withdrawal of energy from the teacher …. The source of energy which the teacher relies on eventually runs down and needs to be recharged if the light bulbs are to continue to glow brightly … (Francis 1995: 238)

The flow, or movement, metaphor used here is clearly at odds with notions of constructivism. Thus, by constructing such metaphors, beginning teachers can become more aware and be helped to examine any inconsistencies between their teaching beliefs and their actual practice.

Some beginning teachers struggle to understand teaching and to know how to work in realistic ways. Schools, as workplaces, often provide complex contexts that can produce confusion and stress. They can generate, very quickly, feelings of vulnerability. There is an urgent need for you to learn about yourself and how to best engage with your students and their difficulties and there will be many questions about the precise role of schools, for example within multicultural communities. Activities (such as 1.2) can provide a bridge between feelings and realities, and can open up questions about difficult experiences. This is reflective practice. The place of emotional intelligence is as important in teacher education as it is in student learning. To learn more of the concept of emotional intelligence and how it is developed in secondary schools go to www.tes.co.uk/teaching-resource/KS3-4-PSHE-Emotional-Intelligence-6047708. (accessed 3 November 2011).

The following exercise grows out of the work of Luft and Ingham in the 1950s. They created the 'Jo-Hari Window' for their work on group process (1963). The Jo-Hari Window is a technique that allows people to understand themselves better, and to learn more about themselves from feedback given by other people and from the types of information communicated to others. It is a four-section window that helps the person to map out different aspects of the self in the categories shown in Figure 1.1.

The first area is the *open* area. These are the things both you and others know about you; these are public and are also obvious to you. Where there is a lot of feedback from others, together with sharing with others, this window would be large in proportion to other three areas.

The second area is the *blind* area. These are things that others know about you, but things of which you may not be aware. The blind spot can be reduced by asking others for more feedback.

The third area is the *hidden* area. These are things that you know about yourself, but that others do not know about you. The hidden area can be reduced by letting others know more about yourself.

The fourth area is the *unknown* area. Neither you nor others are aware of these things here. Some things in an unknown area can be reached by offering more feedback or providing for more disclosure among people; group interaction often brings up old memories and experiences that were forgotten. However, there will always be some unknown and secret area of ourselves.

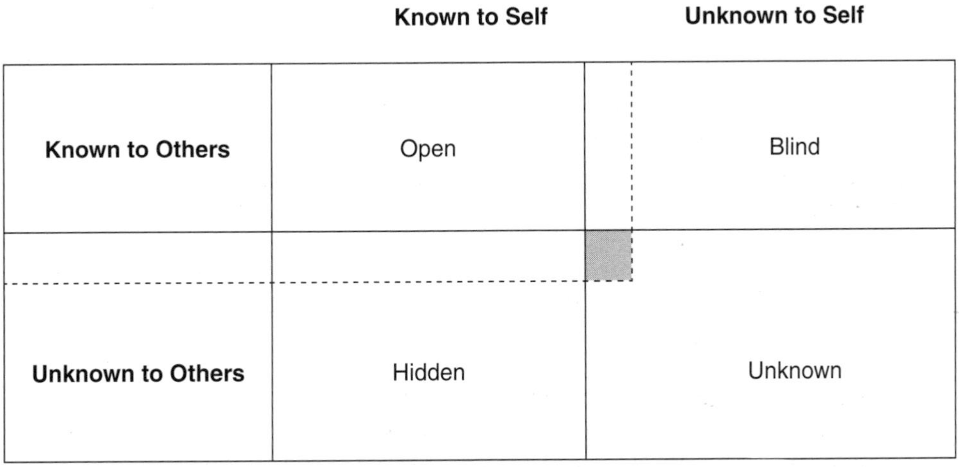

	Known to Self	Unknown to Self
Known to Others	Open	Blind
Unknown to Others	Hidden	Unknown

Figure 1.1   The Jo-Hari Window (based on the original work on group processes of Luft and Ingham, 1963)

Activity 1.3a   Representing your Jo-Hari Window

This part is an individual activity.

(a) On paper, create an intuitive map of your own Jo-Hari Window. Arrange the squares as they appear in Figure 1.1, but adjust their actual sizes once you have explored part (b).

(b) Think about yourself and ask yourself if you have a large open (public) area or hidden area. Give some general proportions to your own window, and consider what it indicates about the public and private aspects of your life.

If you have a large *unknown* area, this clearly offers you the least potential for self-awareness, since you may not be accustomed to much interaction with others. Conversely, a large *open (public)* area offers great potential for self-awareness that is based on your open sharing and receiving feedback that has happened in the past.

Activity 1.3b   Examining your Jo-Hari Windows

This is best carried out with some beginning teachers who tried Activity 1.3a. Work with more than two, but not more than five peers.

(a) First, have a look at the four types of personality types listed below, which reveal themselves when working within a group.

Open area: *Open and attentive* (i.e. gives and takes feedback)
Blind area: *Bull-in-a-china shop* (i.e. gives, but does not take feedback)
Hidden area: *Interviewer* (i.e. takes, but does not give feedback)
Unknown area: *Ostrich* (i.e. does not give or take feedback).

A personality type is represented by each window (as shown in Activity 1.3a). Some people characterize each area as a set of *attitudes* that will show up when a group is interacting.

(b) Referring to your own representation of the *size* of each of your windows (based on Activity 1.3a), work out the degree to which *you* are capable of exhibiting each one of these four types of personality. Share your thoughts with others in the peer group.

(c) This should follow any further group discussion. On your own, you should try to explore the degree to which you are willing to know and learn things about ourselves from others. Distinguish between your willingness to learn from *giving* feedback, and the willingness to learn from *asking for* feedback. Consider the importance of the intention behind feedback (here, sharing information for a professional learning process), and how it can be done directly, honestly and as concretely as possible. Remember, too, that feedback is not final and absolute. Further feedback can always be sought later as part of your developmental learning process.

This initial representation of your framework of windows is not static. The general proportions of your windows are likely to change with time, depending upon your actions. As you share more information with people, both the *hidden* and *unknown* areas should decrease. As you receive more feedback from people, the *blind* and *unknown* areas should decrease. The shaded area in Figure 1.1 represents the uncovered creative potential that you have. The aim would be to reveal as much of this as possible through self-disclosure and feedback from others.

It is worth noting at this point that the person-centred approach of Rogers (1980) has been very influential in education. His focus on the development of the learner led to a model of learning that places the learner at the centre of the learning and teaching process. The role of the teacher in this approach is to facilitate learning.

Reflective practice in workplace learning

Notions of reflection and reflective practice are now well established in a number of areas of professional education. As has been demonstrated in this chapter already, reflective practice is essential in the capacity to integrate and make sense of the on-going story of self in the face of the many images of the profession today.

Schön (1983) saw the risk that reflection-in-action could become stale and routinized and argued that *reflection–on-action* prevents this by revisiting previous judgements in a more analytical way designed to make hidden knowledge more explicit. It also allows for more deliberative judgement after the event: decisions (in your teaching) that were made quickly, in the heat of the moment, are revisited, and a wider range of options and theories can be considered.

Reflective practice has been readily accepted by many professional communities since the late 1980s because it provides for an individualistic view of learning and provides a useful framing device to help conceptualize some important processes in professional learning. The use of *individual action planning* involves a systematic *review* process with another, more experienced teacher, and ends with some agreed *plan* and target setting. It is a formal structured process which can provide the time needed for reflective practice. It forms the basis of our own initial teacher education course. It also forms the basis of termly review meetings with the Induction Tutor whom you should encounter during your first year of teaching (Induction year) in England. The Career Entry and Development Profile is a structure for you to make an Exit Action Plan ready for your first year of teaching (TDA 2011).

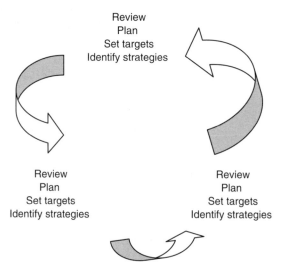

Review
Plan
Set targets
Identify strategies

Review
Plan
Set targets
Identify strategies

Review
Plan
Set targets
Identify strategies

Figure 1.2   Individual Action Plan (IAP) cycle

It is important to question the nature of professional practice, and in turn of the types of education and training that support developing professional practice. Dreyfus and Dreyfus (2005) provide a description of the several stages they have identified through which someone moves from being unfamiliar to becoming an experienced practitioner. Some professional educators wish to view reflection within the context of those settings that have more orientation towards a group, or a team of professionals. Think how you might collaborate with other staff inside a classroom, inside the whole school, or between staff, parents and other professionals in the community. For example, where students with 'special needs' are in regular classrooms, the regular teacher can begin to consider with these other staff (teaching assistants, support staff or other adults) how effective the system of individualized support for these children is in practice in this classroom.

As the contexts for professional practice change, teachers will rarely work alone. New teachers will be expected to be part of collective decision-making rather than making autonomous decisions in the classroom. New teachers will also be expected to work as part of an inter-dependent group of people, often containing participants from different professions or occupations. Cressey and Boud (2006) have described the particular concept of *productive reflection*. They argue that, on the basis of insights into what happened previously, productive reflection leads to interventions into work activity that change what is happening. In other words productive reflection leads to *organizational* as well as individual action.

In teaching, therefore, not only do professional practices change, as we shall see when working with other adults in classrooms, but also the professional identities of the partners in such settings are subject to change. As our professional identity shifts, we might also begin to regard our own students as involved in the co-construction of knowledge about themselves and their own situation (see Chapter 3 for more on personalized and student-centred learning).

In conclusion, as teachers in the next decade you will find yourselves increasingly working in mixed settings that change over time, and in groups that form and re-form for particular purposes related not only to the school but other organizational settings. These groups will require you to be able to work collegially with others, not simply as multidisciplinary groups but as groups that cut across traditional disciplines in an attempt to place children and young people at the very heart of everyone's practice.

What now follows in this chapter are four sections to help you develop the skills of reflective practice, each with Activities for you to try out. The first section explores what we might mean by professional identity with tasks to help you develop your self-awareness and engage in the use of *storytelling*. The next section provides tasks for you to consider five core competences for a reflective practitioner: **observation**, communication, judgement, decision-making and team working. Within the fifth competence (team working), there is also a brief introduction to forms of professional enquiry and action research. A further section presents particular features of critical reflection on practice and illustrates these as a two-stage process: (i) changes in awareness, followed by (ii) changes in practice.

The final section provides a summary of the whole chapter, with important words of caution about the use of reflection as a disciplinary regime, as well as identification of its potential emancipatory power as a form of learning in the workplace.

In summary we hope that, by engaging with the work in these next sections, you can gain the confidence to use critical reflective practice in your everyday work in classrooms, and can embed it in your wider professional training covered by the remaining chapters of this book.

Developing the skills and attributes of a reflective practitioner

The five core competences thought necessary for good practice as a reflective practitioner are presented in turn: observation, communication, judgement, decision-making and team working. All are important professional competences and are applicable to *all* stages of teacher learning, including initial teacher education.

Observation

The skills of observation take account of noticing your own feelings and behaviours (see also the section 'Self-awareness' in this chapter), and include *noticing*, *marking* and *recording* in order to distinguish some *thing* from its surroundings. You can find numerous practical exercises for developing these skills, designed for both individual and small group work, in Chapter 2 of John Mason's book (2002) *Researching Your Own Practice*.

Noticing involves recording brief but vivid details which allow you to recognize the situation for itself. There are various ways in which you might do this: through writing, drawing, or video- and audio-recording, and even photographing an artefact or product of your teaching. As Mason writes,

> … so all that is needed at first is a few words, literally two or three, enough to enable re-entry, to trigger recollection. Then the incident can be described to others *from* that memory, together with any significant further detail that may be needed. Brevity and vividness are what make descriptions of incidents recognisable to others. (2002: 51)

In learning how to teach, the noticing and recording of *critical moments* can be helpful in relation to developing the skills of reflective practice. Some practical suggestions are given in Activity 1.4 for you to try. One method may be more appealing to you than another. Try a few ways and then stick to ones that you enjoy and find useful.

Activity 1.4   Noticing and recording your critical moments – an autobiographical approach

Try this activity on your own.

(a) Describe a brief and vivid significant moment from your new life in teaching and learning your subject. Most people tend to record critical moments that are negative incidents. You don't have to choose one of these.

(b) If you plan to keep a *learning journal* the following guidance might be helpful to you. A *diary, a blog* or *electronic discussion forum* might also be used to contain isolated fragments of critical incidents.

When first asked to keep *personal accounts in a journal*, there are three standard formats that you might employ, in various mixtures and levels of detail:

- *Critical moments summarized in a few, rather generalized words*
  Remember, if you make a general summary, you might quickly lose contact with the incident itself. All that remains are generalities. Find a way to follow this up in a more detailed oral description to someone else.
- *Critical moments recounted in detail, including actions, feelings, thoughts*

Be wary, however, that excessive details, with attempts to justify or explain what actually happened, can block your further development. You should try to record immediate 'trains of thought'.

- *Critical moments recorded as conversations*
  If you record dialogues, you may be replaying 'talk in the head' after the event, often over and over. Bear in mind that there may be other important details to add, such as gestures, postures and tones of voice.

One frequently used activity in teacher-training programmes to encourage reflection is the use of the reflective-writing assignments. These allow you to draw from and enlarge upon examples of the critical moments which you might have recorded in your journal or diary. Sometimes these reflective assignments might involve the writing and analysing of a *teaching case*. You could be asked to identify a dilemma you are experiencing in the classroom and write a narrative or story about this event or situation. Its intention is to help you highlight the complexity of problem-solving and decision-making in learning and teaching. It also provides a way of observing and analysing your own teaching, rather than relying on relatively infrequent observations by others. Another purpose is to help you uncover beliefs and assumptions about teaching.

Written case-study accounts such as these might then be shared with others through a *case conference*. This allows a collaborative analysis and discussion of *the case*. A group of beginning teachers reflect together on the embedded dilemmas, identify the range of possible solutions and, in so doing, each can relate another's case to their own teaching experience. There is some research evidence (Lundeberg and Scheurman, 1997) to show that beginning teachers do benefit from a second reading of a case analysis in that it helps them connect theoretical knowledge with practice.

Another possibility is for you to stop a moment and step into another person's shoes (e.g. a student, parent, social worker) and consider how that person's perspective might be different from your own. What differences might there be? How does knowing about the differences change your own perspective on a situation or event? In this way you can start to consider the role of race, class, ethnicity and gender with regard to teaching dilemmas.

To encourage critical reflection you might identify two students on whom to focus your reflection – one for whom the lesson and being in school is a positive experience; one for whom the lesson content and being in school is a problem. In addition, one of the students could be of a gender, race or culture that is different from your own. Each student can then 'sit on your shoulder' and 'whisper' what went well and what did not.

You will find it helpful to audit your strengths and areas for further development from time to time during the training year. Such self-observation can be supported by systems such as the SWOT analysis or sentence completion – see Activities 1.5a and 1.5b for frameworks to support these approaches.

Activity 1.5a   Assessing your Strengths, Weaknesses, Opportunities and Threats (SWOT analysis)

This is an individual activity. Conduct a SWOT analysis for your own professional development.

Arrange on paper a table of four cells, labelling each as:

(S) STRENGTHS	(W) WEAKNESSES
(O) OPPORTUNITIES	(T) THREATS

You can do this analysis using bullet points to provide the key information. For each cell, try to identify at least one critical moment which has, in turn, provided you with evidence for your judgement. This activity also provides opportunities:

- to make explicit to yourself how you perceive your current state of preparation for the teaching to be done, with your goals, aims, desires and so on;
- for your self-assessment of the level of support and possible courses of action of which you are aware.

You will express your frustrations as well as noting things that appear to be hindering your progress.

Activity 1.5b   Assessing your likes, hopes and fears using sentence completion

Part (a) is an individual activity. Part (b) can form the basis of discussion with a mentor or peer.

(a) Complete a sentence for each of the sentence stems below:

What I most like to do (in my work) is ....

My biggest difficulties (in my work) involve ....

My greatest successes (in my work) are ....

My greatest pleasures (in my work) are ....

My greatest strengths (in my work) are ....

My biggest weaknesses (in my work) are ....

(b) You will need to be prepared to share the evidence you have that underpins each of your completed statements (remember, these are your judgements). Think of particular critical moments that will have provided you with evidence, insights and feelings that gave rise to your completed sentence.

Once you have made your own judgements and selected the evidence on which you have based these, you need to conduct a reality check with a teaching colleague or your mentor. For example, you could ask them to complete the same sentences in order to indicate their judgements about *your* progress. You can then compare how your perceptions of your own progress actually match another's perceptions of your work.

Finally, do ask yourself if you might be setting yourself too high a standard for 'good enough work' at this stage of your teaching career. Any gap between your current state and your personal and professional goals does provide the *window of opportunity* for further development. That gap needs to be wide enough to be sufficiently disturbing that you want to do something about it. However, it should not be so wide that it feels impossible to achieve.

Communication

Your communication skills in relation to reflective practice can be developed in a variety of ways: through the keeping of a personal learning journal or diary, or through a more formal professional portfolio, supported by a system of formal tutorials with a mentor.

Learning journal, diary or professional portfolio

Since critical reflection on practice is an active and conscious process (see Schön, 1983, 1987, 1991), you can start by asking yourself a series of open questions about a particular teaching episode or a critical incident within that episode, and jotting down your impressions using one of these ways of recording:

- What have I been doing/What am I doing?
- What has happened/What is happening?
- What led up to this?
- And why?

By doing this regularly you will be helped to reflect on and learn more about your practice. By sharing some of your reflections with others, you will learn more about yourself and your practice, your strengths and your limitations.

As we have noted already reflection can also be a *critical activity*. If you ask yourself 'How do I improve my practice?' you are actually questioning what you do, how you currently do things and the value of what you are doing. Asking a fundamental question like this will assist you in thinking more critically about why a particular practice of yours is a success (or a failure, or something in between). Remember that *being critical* is not a negative activity. It is about trying to see things differently and doing alternative things.

Formal tutorials with a mentor or university tutor

A key issue for a mentor, working in ITE, is how they can develop the beginning teacher's expertise in engaging in *reflective conversations* in more structured ways. In the past the **General Teaching Council of England (GTCE)** has referred more broadly to the role of the *Learning Conversation* in bringing about teacher development, claiming that it can 'encourage access to a diverse range of opportunities and activities … It is designed so that all teachers through performance management review and in other ways, may choose a route that matches their professional needs' (2004: 8).

We have seen that, through engaging with Activities 1.4 and 1.5, there is the opportunity for a follow-up dialogue to assist reflection on practice. Activity 1.4, with its focus on critical moments or critical incidents, provides a route in which professional development can be supported through a reflective conversation with a teacher, or mentor, who has a good working knowledge of the contexts or situations in which the described event has taken place. For Activities 1.5a and 1.5b, the dialogues might be more general and based on more open-ended questions such as 'How far are these observations … about what actually happened? … about your personal feelings? … about your personal and professional identities?'

A reflective conversation is therefore a process of bringing improvement forward. Crucially, it is the *quality of the conversation* that is important and so you and your mentor might need some structure for the best use of this conversation time. A 30-minute review meeting might be arranged along the following lines.

Guidelines for a structured reflective conversation with a mentor

- Looking back and reviewing significant features in a recent critical moment or event.
- Sharing some of your remarks in your own records of practice such as your learning journal, or diary.
- Celebrating some recent success.
- Identifying one thing that you could still improve whatever your level of **achievement**.
- Deciding together how best to bring the further improvement forward.
- Agreeing more precisely your next step.
- Ending by setting a date for your next review meeting.
- Aiming to keep your own brief record of the conversation and the main agreed targets.

All learning conversations are two-way dialogues where meaning is being constantly negotiated by both participants. At best they become learning and teaching situations for both parties. Sometimes, for the beginning teacher, the dialogue can be potentially both supportive and threatening since the power relations with the mentor may be imbalanced. Beginning teachers often feel that they would like more opportunities to explain their views and perceptions of a lesson, and that they prefer tutor's feedback to be constructive, and delivered in a friendly, supportive and encouraging way, rather than in a more challenging way. The dialogue will quickly close down if they feel powerless to intervene.

Tutor interventions may be thought of as either *directive* or *non-directive*. Table 1.1 illustrates these categories further. It can be a useful reflective exercise for mentors, occasionally, to record on tape or digital recorder (with your permission) their dialogues with you. This will allow them listen to recordings analytically, to ask to what extent the beginning teacher has been given a chance to make their own views known and to explore any other agendas of their own. In other words, reflection on practice is important for teacher educators too.

Although it is clear that different interventions can be used at different times and for different purposes, the *catalytic* category (see Table 1.1) has been shown to be crucial for professional learning. Heron suggests that 'it is the linchpin of any practitioner service that sees itself as fundamentally educational' (1990: 8).

Table 1.1   Types of (A) directive and (B) non-directive tutor interventions

(A) Types of directive intervention	Its purpose	Example of tutor intervention
Prescriptive (telling)	Directly informs beginning teacher about what to do; gives instructions or suggestions	'When you want the class to measure out the chemicals accurately, stop the class work. Ask them to watch you do a demonstration, focus on the careful use of the dropping pipette and use of the measuring cylinder ... That is why I asked you, "What are you trying to achieve?" If it is the development of the practical skill of measuring accurately, ask them to count how many drops they use to get 10 ml. of water into the measuring cylinder'
Informative	Provides information to the beginning teacher	'A double lesson is crucial for conducting some practical activities; you wouldn't be able to get the class to do these otherwise'
Confrontational	Challenges beliefs or behaviour of the beginning teacher; asks for a re-evaluation of some action	'I observed one task throughout that part of the lesson. It was just "question and answer", and it went on too long. I was expecting something else. What else could you have done on your plan to help bring about deeper learning?'

(Continued)

Table 1.1   (Continued)

(B) Types of non-directive intervention	Its purpose	Example of tutor intervention
Cathartic	Allows the beginning teacher a chance to express thoughts and feelings	'You let me see the lesson plans for that class for the whole week. You had some broad aims for the whole set of lessons. Some things did happen differently in the lessons. How do you feel now you have taught these lessons?'
Catalytic	Helps the beginning teacher become more self-aware and reflective	'We have agreed that managing behaviour in a practical lesson is very important. Is there anything else you could have tried, in terms of control?' 'What were some of the students doing while the others were taking the measurements? Did you notice, at each workbench, what was happening?'
Supportive	Tries to boost beginning teacher's confidence by focusing on what they did well	'I have noticed some crucial things in the lessons this week. You have dealt very well with some students when they give you certain answers. Shall we try together to summarize what was working so well?'

Source: adapted from Heron, 1990

Judgement

In order to analyse a classroom event or situation, we should try to be absolutely clear what that event or situation consists of. If we, too, are involved in that event or situation then this view of the event needs to be impartial. This is a difficult process – to see ourselves as others see us. Remember also that we often see in others what we dislike in ourselves.

Just describing what happens during the event can be problematic as well. We might, rather skilfully, combine details of the event with our judgement, or with additional explanations and theories. It would then be difficult for another person to begin to discuss our analysis and say whether they agree with the analysis, or not. Mason (2002: 40) has helpfully distinguished between an account *of* a situation and an account *for* it. Thus, if we wish to *account for* an occurrence, and particularly if we expect another teacher to agree with our analysis, we must first explain the thing precisely that we are trying to analyse (the *account of*). By doing this we can begin to recognize that when we give an *account for*, we are also giving a justification, a value judgement, a criticism, or an attempt at an explanation.

Accounting for means, first, asking 'why' and, second, providing an interpretation. Mason draws on an example from Tripp (1993: 18) and this note from Tripp's reflective diary, kept as a practising teacher, is useful to include here: 'John didn't finish his work today. Must see he learns to complete what he has begun.' What are the possible answers if we begin to ask why John is apparently not finishing his work today? That first sentence might have to be rewritten: 'John finished work on parts one and three whereas most others worked on parts one through seven; John was still working on part three when I stopped them working' (Mason, 2002: 42).

The crucial issue in the account above is about what constitutes 'finishing work'. Mason argues that, by asking further questions about how students see classroom tasks, and by thinking about the student experience of engaging in the given task (as opposed to the teacher's perceptions), then we are more likely to find out about the personal circumstances for a student such as John before we label him as a 'non-finisher'. Tripp (1993: 19) suggests asking the following line of questions:

- Why did John not finish his work?
- Why should he finish it?
- What was his view of the tasks demanded of him?
- Are the tasks of the right kind, quality, and quantity?

Activity 1.6   Developing your skills of judgement

This can be carried out with a small group of your peers (a maximum of three).

(a) Each chooses a recent segment of their teaching (such as the one about *John*, described on the previous page).

Use the prompts or questions given in columns one and two of Table 1.2. These will allow you to focus on the events that might have led up to the situation (before or during the lesson), to think about the judgements and actions you had to make or take, and to note what happened afterwards in any discussions about the situation.

Write in the third (blank) column of Table 1.2 your answers to the key questions given in column two.

(b) Join two other beginning teachers and, in turn, share what each of you has written. While one speaks (*Talker*), one other can use appropriate prompts to elicit meanings and thoughts which underpin your writing (*Critical Friend*). The third should keep brief notes of the key discussion points (*Observer–Scribe*) and share these for further discussion after all three have taken each role.

(c) **Plenary**. In your trio, draw some conclusions about the process you just engaged in:
  - How far were the conversations about 'what happened'?
  - How far were the conversations about 'feelings' and emotional reactions?
  - How far were the conversations about teacher identity and the extent to which you were able to distinguish between your personal and your professional identities in this situation?

e 1.2   Some key questions for 'Learning Conversations'

ea for exploration in a arning conversation	Key questions (for you to use to critically reflect with peers; or for your mentor to use to help your critical reflection on practice)	Your answers
Stimulus	What led you to make this judgement? What went on beforehand?	
Responsibility	Who made (or did not make) the judgement? Was it you, or was it made by a group?	
Ethical Issues	How far was your judgement made in someone's best interest? Did you take steps to safeguard their privacy, or gain their informed consent to share information?	
Information	To what extent was your judgement based on sound and valid data or information?	
Consequences	How far were the consequences of your judgement justified?	
Consensus	To what extent was there agreement on your judgement? Or was there disagreement, or conflict?	

Skills of decision-making

It is important to think about how you make sense of your learners and classroom events. From a constructivist point of view, Uhlenbeck et al. described teacher learning as 'organizing and reorganizing, structuring and restructuring a teacher's understanding of practice. Teachers are viewed as learners who actively construct knowledge by interpreting events on the basis of existing knowledge, beliefs and dispositions' (2002: 243).

There are, as we have noted already, several types of activities that can encourage reflective practice: reflective writing assignments form one of these. Another involves the writing and analysis of a *teaching case* (see earlier in Chapter 1). This, as we have discussed, has the potential to exert tremendous influence on your perceptions of teaching and learning. The following analysis is taken from a research study (Alger, 2006) in which the author classified six types of classroom-based *case* presented by her beginning teachers, and concerned with **behaviour management** in the classroom. The 56 solutions which the beginning teachers described in their cases were categorized as follows: 'teacher behaviours for seeking compliance' (28); 'curricular and pedagogical solutions for gaining student compliance' (15); 'help-seeking strategies to gain student compliance' (eight); and one 'other'.

Alger followed up her analyses by conducting interviews with these beginning teachers at the end of the year, in order to track the development of their reflection over time. The beginning teachers were asked to re-frame, or re-state, the original behaviour management problem they had described, and re-evaluate the strategies they had tried in order to solve the problem. She found that these beginning teachers' understanding of the solutions to the problems (that is, the way they made their decisions) had changed substantially, as did their nuances of the dilemmas. There were shifts:

- away from *behaviourist* approaches
- towards greater *relationship building*
- involving greater use of *effective classroom strategies* to manage behaviour

You will find more discussion on behaviourist approaches in education in Chapter 2.

For many of the beginning teachers in Alger's study reflection was a two-step process. The first step occurred at the planning stage when, for example, they tried to *visualize the lesson* based on the plan, asking themselves, 'What might work, what might not?' This process clearly involves drawing on previous teaching episodes to speculate on the effectiveness of the **lesson plan** in question. This is a form of reflection. A second step took place after the teaching, by asking oneself, 'What went well; what did not go so well?' This reflection might involve a mental review only, or recording in note form the evaluation, with further ideas for changes might be made on the next occasion.

Thus, these types of reflective practice strategies are important in that they should allow you to see, and cope better with, the complexities of teaching and help you make decisions for further actions. In addition the reflective practice itself is helped, through case analysis, to promote analysis and evaluation at a deeper level. The approach taken by Alger allows reflective practice to be both *deliberate and intentional*. Its power, as with other reflective practice strategies, hinges on the support provided by a mentor to help you probe the strengths and weaknesses of a lesson more deeply through dialogue and critical reflection on practice.

Team working

We know, increasingly, that schools as institutions and the individuals within them have to be flexible to respond to rapid changes of pace. Etienne Wenger, a socio-cultural theorist, focused on notions of networking in the workplace and developed a key concept with Jean Lave: **communities of practice** (Lave and Wenger, 1991; Wenger, 1998). As we have noted in an earlier section of this chapter on workplace learning we can no longer think about a teacher or a school existing in isolation.

It is now recognized that professional expertise has to be networked, integrated or joined up. As is explored in Chapters 3 and 6, you will find yourself working in a number of teams from the start of your teaching career: your subject or curriculum team, your pastoral team and cross-curricular groups working on particular issues such as **personalized learning** and aspects of assessment, and so on. The following sub-sections introduce you briefly to some collaborative ways of working in schools.

Co-teaching

This way of working provides experiences which revolve around collaboration and the sharing of ideas and perspectives on practice to help in the re-framing of earlier ideas (Schön, 1983). Co-teaching provides two teachers (mentor and beginning teacher; two beginning teachers) with access to possibilities for learning that are not so likely when working alone. This can have the advantage of providing a safer haven for more risk taking and experimentation, such as introducing new types of practical activities into a science lesson; managing a role-play; taking students for out-of-classroom activities. As Loughran has written, 'collaboration and teaming in ways that provide professional support for one another leads to improvements in practice as the sharing with, and learning from, one another offers meaningful ways of framing and reframing existing practice' (2006: 57). In other words all partners, experienced and inexperienced, can benefit. Co-teaching offers the opportunity to ask much of your partner:

- What is the purpose of this teaching session?
- How does what we do today link with last week's lesson?
- Why are you choosing to use that teaching strategy with this class?

Questioning one's own learning or thinking about one's own thinking is a form of **meta-cognition** (see Chapter 2). Co-teaching provides a vehicle for becoming more aware of one's thoughts and actions that influence the development of understanding of a situation. It also offers the possibility of insights into teaching and learning which might be very different from just being told what to do and how to think.

Collaborative practitioner enquiry

Enquiry is the response we make to a desire to find something out. Kelly (2006) has argued that teachers who identify closely with instrumental practices are likely to have cognitivist views of expertise and learning. In contrast, teachers with more reflective and discursive identities may, through an on-going conversation with their practice, adopt stances which respond to their learners' difficulties, and seek to collaborate with learners and colleagues. They *look for ways forward* in professional guidance and through research, using their learners and colleagues as starting points in their enquiry, and adopting complex measures of success.

There are some parallels here with the ways of conducting *academic research*. These also require systematic enquiry but are done less for oneself and more for reporting to other people so that conclusions can be criticized, challenged or taken up by others. This is a form of constructivism. For any research to be convincing the research questions have to be well formulated (these may be the hypotheses to be tested), and the chosen methodology (types of observations, other types of data collection and methods of analyses) has to conform to accepted standards.

Action research

This way of working tends to fall between 'academic researcher' researching other people and 'teacher practitioner' researching their own actions. *Action research* is an approach that has become widely used in research into education and schooling. It takes several different forms, one of which is systematic enquiry. Often beginning teachers, regular teachers and support staff work together and the enquiry is designed to produce practical results which can improve an aspect of, say, learning and teaching. It is a well recognized form of social science research.

Your choice of research topic with colleagues can be affected by your combined interests, values, any funding you have available, and so on. Using descriptive approaches, you might support, observe and study the effects of other people. In some cases you may be the *actor-researchers* using a more analytical approach to make a strategic change in your collective practices. You might start by asking, 'What can we do to improve our practice?' You could then pursue one of the action research routes illustrated in Figures 1.3a and 1.3b.

When you begin to research classrooms and schools in these ways, and small action research activities may start in your training year, you will probably need to read more widely about some of the concepts associated with these ways of researching classrooms. The *Handbook of Action Research* (Reason and Bradbury, 2005), *Learning and Teaching at M Level* (Bryan et al., 2010) and *Action Research: A Guide for the Teacher Researcher* (Mills, 2000) are good reference books for Master's students. By using action research approaches in these ways we are acknowledging the long-standing value of collaborative approaches to critical reflection on practice (Stenhouse, 1971, 1975) and teacher research in general (Elliott, 1991). Such approaches provide for close partnerships between schools and higher education institutions. On a more cautionary note, Kelly (2006) reminds us of government-led initiatives, such as the Best Practice Research Scholarships (DfEE, 2001; DfES, 2002) through which, he argues, the policy makers were exploiting the particular purpose of implementing some central policy. With a few exceptions, the wider research outcomes of such practitioner research do reside largely within the target school, and are not generally widely shared elsewhere.

It is also clear that, by enabling teachers and beginning teachers to work alongside each other, we can provide for shared knowledge and collaborative learning. All parties can benefit. Finally, it is possible through on-going initiatives for all teachers in their professional development to provide forms of support to develop teacher identities that are more rooted in reflective, discursive, collaborative ways of working, and which allow teachers to be more deliberate in their actions in their working lives.

Which?

e.g. Choose an episode of teaching to observe
that is attempting to implement a new strategy

Who? What? When? Where?

Provide a full description of the episode

Why? How?

Analysis and explore the reasons for your findings

Interpret

Consider what the impact was on the students.
What are the implications for your own professional learning?
How are these related to the particular goals of the new strategy?

Transform

Apply your (collective) insights to your own teaching practices.
What new goals and strategies will you now develop?

Figure 1.3a   An evaluative approach to action research (based on Levin and Camp, 2005)

You may prefer a more methodical, formal problem-solving sequence, such as:

Pose the problem ⇨   **Propose the method** ⇨

⇨ **Find a solution**   ⇨ **Look back**

Figure 1.3b   A problem-solving approach to action research (based on Polya, 1945)

Reflection as a critical activity

One pitfall with the idea of reflective practice is that it has tended to become a catch-all term. The terms *reflection* and *reflective practice* are now seriously over-used buzzwords, and are likely to mean different things to different people. Zeichner, in 1994, was already pointing out the separate and distinct interpretations of reflective practice, only some of which could be called *critical*.

The process of reflection can be in danger of reductionism – to a set of procedures; a skill to be learned. So far this chapter has tried to show what reflective practice can look like, but with a caution that it should not be reduced to some standardized competence. If that were the case, reflection would become an end in itself.

The questions that must remain are those concerning the purpose or focus of the particular reflection. It is these questions that are important for critical reflection. We have talked about reflection as a habit; one that is deliberative. Reflection and action run together if you wish to change the world around you. Therefore, critical reflection can create the conditions under which you as teacher, or your students as learners, can become more aware of the power of agency and the possibilities for action.

The sorts of questions that can progressively unearth deeper assumptions illustrate the process of critical reflection on practice. The process is transformative because it focuses on dominant assumptions which may influence our practice unwittingly (Brookfield, 2000: 12). From this perspective, critical reflection on practice enables an understanding of the way (socially dominant) assumptions may be socially restrictive, and has the potential to bring about more empowering ideas and practices. Critical reflection on practice provides a freedom to the individual and to groups to change the operation of the social environment at the level of their personal experiences. The process of critical reflection on practice can be thought of as a two-stage process, moving from changed awareness to changed practice. Activity 1.7 is designed to link with the sort of enquiry or action research approaches you might be using in order to reach M level.

Activity 1.7   Seminar to prepare for an Action Research project

(a) In a seminar setting (5–8 people) each participant brings a description of piece of their practice for reflection in two stages: a reflective stage, and a clear linking with the next stage with the intention of changing professional practice.

Example A:

Stage 1. How can I help my students improve the quality of their learning?
Stage 2. I would like the improvement to focus on the particular action.

(Continued)

(Continued)

Example B:

Stage 1. How can I respond to pupil diversity in my class?

Stage 2. I will present to the seminar a particular incident in my classroom experience as a new teacher which involved issues of diversity.

(b) Group members can help each person reflect on their chosen situation, by using a set of questions, such as selecting from those listed below:

- What does your current practice imply about ...?
- What are you assuming when ...?
- How do you influence the situation through your presence/your perceptions/your interpretations/your assumptions?
- What are your beliefs about power and where do they come from?
- What perspectives are missing?
- What types of language do you use and what do these patterns imply?
- What is your own thinking and what is the result of any power relations (e.g. gendered, cultural, structural)?

(c) Following this probing and discussion with others, work out in detail how you personally intend to bring about some changes in practice. Use the following example to help you.

To move to the next stage (that is, planning for changes in my practice) I decide to take the following steps through Action Research:

- *Focus on responding to the diversity of student strengths and needs as a teaching concern.* I will examine the positive and negative impacts of student diversity on their learning. I will aim to understand better the importance and skill of adapting the curriculum and the learning environment to include every student.
- *Develop ideas and skills during teaching practice.* I will plan ways of getting to know each student better and of adapting the curriculum to meet their particular needs. I will reflect on the various methods of learning and teaching that I try, and evaluate the impact that these have on the students' learning.
- During the process of implementing and reflecting, I will collect evidence of the effectiveness (or otherwise) of my particular attempts to respond to diversity. I will ask two key questions. How well are all the students engaged in the new lessons? What progress does each student make?
- *Critical evaluation using theoretical frameworks.* I will access and use wider academic reading on models of teaching and learning and research literature in connection with pupil diversity.

Fook (2000) has shown that, in a social work setting, this process of critical reflection on practice within a deliberatively reflective group structure is one of *critical acceptance*. It is conducted in a climate which balances safety and challenge. It is participatory, non-judgemental, and open to new and other perspectives. It involves the responsibility not to blame, the right to draw limits, and acceptance of multiple contradictory views. It provides a focus on the *story*, not the person, and on the *why*, not the *what to do*. It is non-directive.

Two very accessible texts for you to read further in this somewhat complex area are by Stephen Brookfield (1995) *Becoming a Critically Reflective Teacher* and Jennifer Moon (2004) *A Handbook of Reflective and Experiential Learning.*

A Reflection Framework for critical incident analysis

Brookfield (1995) and others recognize the unsettling and emotional demands that critical reflection can make in challenging your existing norms and assumptions. For some teachers this can lead to scepticism, anxiety, a loss of identity, fear, resentment or feelings of intimidation. You will be immersed in the fast pace of teaching situations and the overall demands of school as your workplace can leave little space for reflection, particularly with others.

Activity 1.4 provided you with an opportunity to record in detail a critical moment. Most people tend to record critical moments that are negative incidents. You can, however, choose a positive incident, and your narrative account should, in either case, highlight the dilemmas you faced and how you chose to act. Almost everything in the everyday life of school is a potential critical incident – even a basic routine like where you choose to position yourself in front of a class. If you can follow this writing with a dedicated professional conversation with an experienced teacher–mentor, you can be helped further to analyse your ideas of the particular *meaning* of the incident, rather than your experience of the incident itself. It is the critical analysis that makes the incident 'critical'.

Through such conversations, you should find that your emotional experiences in the construction of your understanding of teaching and identity provide an opportunity to reveal things in your own biography that you might otherwise be unable to recall.

The Reflection Framework shown in Figure 1.4 can be used as well, to help you monitor how critically you reflect. It includes opportunity to include aspects of your work outside the classroom as well as actual teaching experiences (see Harrison and Lee, 2011). You can apply the Framework to your piece of writing about a critical incident and judge your level of reflection (routine, technical, dialogic) across each of the three dimensions: focus, inquiry, change.

The following account is typical of many recorded by the author from beginning teachers when relating their early, significant experiences of classroom teaching. Try applying the Framework (Figure 1.4) to the following account of one particular critical

	LEVEL 1 Routine	LEVEL 2 Technical	LEVEL 3 Dialogic	LEVEL 4 Transformative
	Oneself is kept separate from the situation/change.	Practical response given to specific situation; little or no change in personal perspective.	Cycle of situated questions and action; active consideration of perspectives of others; new insights gained.	Fundamental questions asked; change in practice/ approach occurs.
FOCUS	How does this affect me? How do I get control? Have I been successful? XXX was to blame!	Focus is on specific teaching tasks/ professional actions. Re-adjustment of practice takes place – I can transfer learning to similar situations.	Focus is on my students/others, and how well they have been learning.	I am personally involved with fundamental pedagogical/ethical/ moral/cultural/ other wider concerns, and how these may impact on my students/others.
INQUIRY	My critical questions and analysis are generalized and limited to a critique of others. I have not asked questions about necessary personal change.	My questions relate to specific situations. I stop asking questions after initial problem addressed: there are no wider questions about routines or context.	My questions are situated and lead to new questions. Questions are explored with others, with open consideration of new ideas. I actively seek the perspective of my peers, pupils, or others.	There is long-term/ on-going enquiry including dialogue with my mentor, critical friend, pupils, and a careful examination of critical incidents. I ask questions that challenge my assumptions.
CHANGE	The analysis of my practice is done for its own sake, as if there were a gap between myself and the situation.	I personally respond to deal with a situation, but the situation is not used to change my perspective.	I synthesize the results of my enquiry, so I gain new insights into teaching/learning/ personal attributes; it results in changed/ improved practice.	There is a reframing of my perspective leading to a more fundamental change in my practice.

Figure 1.4 A Reflection Framework (Harrison and Lee, 2011: 202–204)

incident during a period of teaching in school. To what extent do you think it illustrates a low (level 1), an emerging (level 2) or a high level (level 3) reflector? As you read it think about the sort of questions you might pose if you were to act as the mentor to this beginning teacher to help them open up their practice and their thinking about actions and consequences.

I had a negative incident this week. I was teaching XXX (name of topic). I realize that, generally, this can be a boring topic for Year 12 students (no reason given). In fact my class teacher tutor says he no longer teaches this topic. In an attempt to make it more interesting I had planned a series of experiential and more 'practical' lessons (i.e. 'student-centred' lessons). In the first lesson, students were asked to collect some questionnaire data and then to perform a statistical analysis in their own time. (I thought) this went quite well. The second lesson was 'teacher-led' (no elaboration on its content or purpose is given here). In the third lesson I asked them to go out of the classroom and use a further test with some other students in the school (was this reinforcement of some key ideas?). During this particular (third) lesson, one quite outspoken student called out quite rudely just how boring she was finding this topic. I spoke calmly to her in front of the class, explaining that it is often the one topic students find dull, but that I had (tried to) made it interactive (so the practical tasks could be used to illustrate the theory). Because of her (reaction) and other chatter and moaning in the room, I was about to abandon the practical task and ask them to continue working on their posters from a previous lesson. I also explained that she has an examination (to pass) in January so it's crucial she does this (topic).

This seemed to strike a chord with her. She then explained the topic was boring (for her) because she was also studying it in (another subject). Eventually I got the class to carry out a rather quick and rushed version of the planned practical activity by testing each other. (I thought) they all seemed to enjoy this. After the lesson I talked to the girl again to explain that we needed an agreement if I was to get through other parts of the topic that she finds boring. She didn't seem enthusiastic about this conversation (why?), but I hope it started to make sense to her!

Although I think I handled the situation satisfactorily in the end, (I felt) it was a negative incident. It was challenging to stand in front of a class after being told that what you are doing is boring! I could have handled it more assertively and told her how rude she had been ... I shouldn't let the fact that she (seems to) feel comfortable in my class allow her to say whatever she wants.

In response to her comment, my class teacher and I agreed to make the next lesson very practical. I had planned this anyway. I am moving it (i.e. the planning) forward to appease them (the class) slightly!

Analysis

The *focus* is very much on 'me' gaining control of the behaviour problem – this is *routine* reflection (level 1).

In relation to *inquiry*, little or no critical questioning is revealed in this writing concerning the wider routines or context (*routine* reflection, level 1). Indeed, until there was a *conversation with the observing teacher later*, in which the mentor was able, through a well-structured learning conversation to shift the reflection towards the specific situation for the whole class rather than the girl in question (this illustrates movement on the part of the learner towards *technical* reflection, level 2).

- What were your assumptions about Year 12 behaviour in your class as you planned your teaching?
- Did these assumptions impact on your judgements in the course of recording your critical incident?

- Define what you mean when you talk about 'disruptive' and 'not on task'.
- What exactly was the 'critical incident' in the scenario that you have described?
- How did you feel when the students seemed to be ignoring you (and therefore not learning)?
- Did you consider at any stage being more assertive and addressing the whole class so they could consider why you needed silence so you could keep the lesson you had planned flowing towards the conclusion that you hoped for?

In relation to *change*, the extent of the focus on the students' (rather than on the teacher's) perspective seems limited in this account, and is revealed in the giveaway phrase 'to appease them [the pupils] slightly'. There is little evidence of a changed personal perspective (*routine* reflection, level 1).

Further questions for a professional learning conversation could aim to consider the overall professional learning more:

- Describe in detail how you felt at the end of that lesson. What impression do you think the girl student/the whole class has about you as the teacher?
- How important is it to build relationships with each student? How will you take forward what you have learnt from this critical incident into your next year of teaching?

Further re-writing of the critical incident and what was learnt through conversation could also provide opportunity for meta-analysis. It can provide more focus on the incident itself, increasing the existing details to make it all the more clear. It can also enlarge the picture of the incident, so we see much more of the picture in less detail. Chasing for further facts about a situation can contribute to the wider picture in order to make sense of it. In this way the analysis might extend over a longer period.

You can read more about reflective practice and professional learning (see Ward and McCotter, 2004), and find other examples of critical incident analysis and the learning conversation in Harrison and Lee (2011).

Critical reading at Master's level

You should now access and read the following scholarly article to prepare for this activity:

Kelchertermans, G. (2009) 'Who I am in how I teach is the message: self-understanding, vulnerability and reflection', *Teachers and Teaching, Theory and Practice*, 15(2): 257–272.

This individual activity is designed to further develop your critical reading skills. Your critical thinking and writing could also feed into a group seminar/discussion about the on-going process of professional learning (development). By working through the following questions you can summarize your developing understanding of the types of approaches to 'teacher thinking' research that form the basis of this paper:

1 Kelchertermans uses the metaphor of a 'pair of glasses' (p. 261) to explain how teachers develop a personal interpretative framework in their thinking about themselves and their teaching. Do you consider this to be a powerful metaphor in relation to reflective practice? What are its possible strengths and limitations?

2 Kelchertermans prefers the idea of 'self-understanding' (p. 261) rather than 'identity' (p. 261). What are his particular arguments for this preference? Briefly summarize the five components of self-understanding that he presents.

3 What have you learnt from Kelchertermans' presentation of 'subjective educational theory' (p. 263)?

4 A teacher's judgement is presented as a central feature of teaching, and in turn of reflection and professional knowledge: 'The process of judging remains essential (and for example deciding that in this particular situation the most appropriate action is to make an exception of what is normally is the rule)' (p. 264). Draw on one or more your own teaching experiences; for each, describe the process of judging which allowed you to link the 'what' (i.e. your perception of the task) with the 'how to' (the knowledge you used to achieve the particular goals and norms).

5 Summarize the three elements of teacher vulnerability that this author presents. Explain how these relate to his notion of 'broad reflection' (p. 267).

6 You can investigate the relationship between self-study and emotion in Kelchertermans and Hamilton (2004), and read further on understanding teaching and learning about teaching in Loughran (2006).

Conclusion: being a reflective practitioner

The notion of the reflective practitioner is an enticing one. It starts with messy, unpredictable practices, unpicks what is going on, generates **inductive hypotheses**, asks for analysis and attempts to reveal more about the nature of expertise within the professional setting and the judgements upon that. It provides an important counterbalance to current emphases in policy making on evidence-based practice, in which certainty and technical rationality are the ideals.

Reflective practice asks us all to weigh up the scientific evidence base against competing versions of events. Thus it can take account of the richness and creativity of our practice and lead to new notions of professionalism based on diversity and flex-ibility. At its heart is the unsettling of hierarchies (for example, the gendered nature of teaching) and traditional working practices. Loughran refers to this phenomenon as *disturbing practice* and argues persuasively that 'it does not divorce feelings from the actions associated with confrontation or challenge; it creates powerful learning episodes … Working with colleagues … [provides the opportunity] of gaining advice and feedback on such episodes and of continuing to push to make the tacit explicit' (2006: 57).

Reflection implies that you can see one thing in another – the external world in your mind and, as such, it provides a powerful metaphor which also deserves a word of caution. It describes and is performative, since the act of reflection can give back some improvement in professional practice (Biggs, 1999) – it may be expected that it leads to action and change. This is a persuasive feature of reflective practice. In addition, profes-sional portfolios can be used as vehicles for the assessment process in professional training and you can position yourself to present your material to make a convincing claim that you (as a professional) are competent. Reflection in this situation might become a self-measurement and provide for self-evaluation against standards or other appropriate performance measures.

In contrast to such highly instrumental practices in professional education there must be deeper forms of reflective practice as well as criticality in learning. These require freedom from the gaze, in the Foucauldian sense, of the institution in which we work (see Foucault, 1980: 155). Thus, research and autobiographical approaches in professional education do provide the freedom to think more about self in context, personally and socially, and in potentially radical ways. Truly reflective practice involves trust and relative autonomy; schools today are steeped in cultures of accountability and audits, involving measurements (for example, the number of students in school receiving free school meals) and managerialism (for example, through the publicity of league tables of performances). However, in today's rapidly moving society, the reflec-tive practitioner cannot and should not be seen as being freed of the constraints of the reality in which he or she practises. As Wenger's (1998) approach shows, professional work is influenced by participation and by the fixed and solid environment we all work in.

Very broadly, in workplace learning, professional development becomes the forma-tion of professional identity. It provides a process in which to translate the practices, values and attitudes of the *teacher* (the worker) with those currently part of *teaching* (the profession), and in some situations with the goals and mission of the *school or college* (the organization). However there are additional important words of warning. One of the current difficulties you will encounter with generic statements of **profes-sional standards** in teaching is that they allow for multiple interpretations of meaning. Professional (expert) teachers are presented in such a system as subjects who under-stand how the learner learns and how to support you as beginning teachers in your learning. If we are not careful, reflection could become simply a self-measurement and self-evaluation against these teaching standards. More than this, the rhetoric of technical expertise, competence and reflective practice is used to promote changes in professional practices and identities in particular ways, and can on occasions be used to identify certain practices and dispositions of the teachers as specifically *professional*.

Therefore in the remaining chapters of this book we anticipate that you will begin to recognize that workplace cultures can be very powerful and may be hidden from you in their operation (see Chapter 2 in Rogers, 2006, for an introduction to the nature of school cultures). The range of tasks we provide in each chapter should allow you to examine some of the assumptions implicit in all sorts of professional practices that you will encounter in your training year. By the end of your training period you should have a better understanding of what we might mean by a *teaching profession*, what we might mean by *professionalism* in teaching, and the range of *professional values*. In this way you can be helped to recognize the particular professional values and practices that are essential to developing competency in the classroom. Overall this book is designed to support what Yinger (1990) has described as 'the on-going conversation of practice' in which you are beginning to participate.

References

Alger, C. (2006) '"What went well, what didn't go so well": Growth of reflection in pre-service teachers', *Reflective Practice*, 7(3): 287–301.

Argyris, C. and Schön, D. (1975) *Theory into Practice: Increasing Professional Effectiveness*. San Francisco, CA: Jossey-Bass.

Biggs, J. (1999) *Teaching for Quality Learning at University*. Buckingham: Open University Press.

Brookfield, S.D. (1987) *Developing Critical Thinkers: Challenging Adults to Explore Alternative Ways of Thinking and Acting*. Milton Keynes: SRHE/Open University Press.

Brookfield, S.D. (1995) *Becoming a Critically Reflective Teacher*. San Francisco: Jossey-Bass.

Brookfield, S.D. (2000) 'Transformative learning as ideology critique', in J. Mezirow (ed.) *Learning as Transformation*. San Francisco: Jossey Bass. pp. 125–148.

Bryan, H., Carpenter, C. and Hoult, S. (2010) *Learning and Teaching at M Level: A Guide for Student Teachers*. London: Sage.

Carr, W. and Kemmis, S. (1986) *Becoming Critical: Education, Knowledge and Action Research*. Lewes: Falmer/Deakin University Press.

Cooley, C.H. (1902) *Human Nature and Social Order*. New York: Charles Scribner.

Cressey, P. and Boud, D. (2006) 'The emergence of productive reflection', in D. Boud, P. Cressey and P. Docherty (eds) *Productive Reflection at Work: Learning for Changing Organizations*. London: Routledge. pp. 11–26.

Day, C. (1993) 'Reflection: a necessary but not sufficient condition for professional development', *British Educational Research Journal*, 19(1): 83–93.

Day, C., Sammons, P., Stobart, G., Kington, A. and Gu, Q. (2007) *Teachers Matter: Connecting Work, Lives and Effectiveness.* Maidenhead: Open University Press/McGraw Hill.

Dewey, J. (1910) *How We Think.* London: D.C. Heath.

Dewey, J. (1933) *How We Think: A Re-statement of the Relation of Reflective Thinking in the Educative Process.* Chicago: Henry Regnery.

DfEE (2001) *Best Practice Research Scholarships.* Nottingham: DfEE Publications.

DfES (2002) *Best Practice Research Scholarships.* Nottingham: DfES Publications.

Dreyfus, H.L. and Dreyfus, S.E. (2005) 'Expertise in real world contexts', *Organization Studies*, 26(5): 779–792.

Elliott, J. (1991) *Action Research for Educational Change.* Milton Keynes: Open University Press.

Fook, J. (2000) *Social Work: Critical Theory and Practice.* London: Sage.

Foucault, M. (1980) *Power/Knowledge: Selected Interviews and Other Writings 1972–1977.* New York: Pantheon.

Francis, D. (1995) 'The reflective journal: a window to preservice teachers' practical knowledge', *Teaching and Teacher Education*, 11(3): 229–241.

GTCE (2004) *The Learning Conversation: Talking Together for Professional Development.* London: GTCE.

Harrison, J.K. (2004) 'Encouraging professional autonomy: reflective practice and the beginning teacher', *Education 3–13*, 32(3): 10–18.

Harrison, J.K. and Lee, R. (2011) 'Exploring the use of critical incident analysis and the professional learning conversation in an initial teacher education programme', *Journal of Education for Teaching*, 37(2): 199–217.

Harrison, J.K., Lawson, T. and Wortley, A. (2005) 'Facilitating the professional learning of new teachers through critical reflection on practice during mentoring meetings', *European Journal of Teacher Education*, 28(3): 267–292.

Heron, J. (1990) *Helping the Client: A Creative Practical Guide.* 4th edition. London: Sage.

Holt-Reynolds, D. (2000) 'What does the teacher do? Constructivist pedagogies and prospective teachers' beliefs about the role of a teacher', *Teaching and Teacher Education*, 16: 21–32.

Kelchertermans, G. (2009) 'Who I am in how I teach is the message: self-understanding, vulnerability and reflection', *Teachers and Teaching, Theory and Practice*, 15(2): 257–272.

Kelchertermans, G. and Hamilton, M. (2004) 'The dialectics of passion and theory: Exploring the relation between self-study and emotion', in J. Loughran, M. Hamilton, V. Lubler La Boskey and T. Russell (eds) *The International Handbook of Self-Study of Teaching and Teacher Education Practices.* Dordrecht: Kluwer Academic Publishers. pp. 785–810.

Kelly, P. (2006) 'What is teacher learning? A socio-cultural perspective', *Oxford Review of Education*, 32(4): 505–519.

Kolb, D. (1984) *Experiential Learning: Experience as the Source of Learning and Development.* New York: Prentice-Hall.

Lave, J. and Wenger, E. (1991) *Situated Learning – Legitimate Peripheral Participation.* Cambridge: Cambridge University Press.

Levin, B.B. and Camp, J.S. (2005) 'Reflection as the foundation for e-portfolios', www.adce.org/conf/site/pt3/paper_3008_455. pdf (accessed 3 July 2012).

Loughran, J. (2002) 'Effective reflective practice. In search of meaning about teaching', *Journal of Teacher Education*, 53(1): 33–43.

Loughran, J. (2006) *Developing a Pedagogy of Teacher Education: Understanding Teaching and Learning about Teaching.* Abingdon: Routledge.

Luft, J. and Ingham, H. (1963) *Group Processes: An Introduction to Group Dynamics.* Palo Alto, CA: National Press Books.

Lundeberg, M. and Scheurman, G. (1997) 'Looking twice means seeing more: developing a pedagogical knowledge through case analysis', *Teaching and Teacher Education*, 13(8): 783–797.

Mason, J. (2002) *Researching Your Own Practice: The Discipline of Noticing.* London: RoutledgeFalmer.

Mills, G.E. (2000) *Action Research: A Guide for the Teacher Researcher.* Upper Saddle River, NJ: Prentice Hall.

Moon, J. (2004) *A Handbook of Reflective and Experiential Learning.* London: RoutledgeFalmer.

Nias, J. (1989) *Primary Teachers Talking.* London: Routledge & Kegan Paul.

Pollard, A. with Collins, J., Simco, N., Swaffield, S. and Warwick, P. (2005) *Reflective Teaching.* 2nd edition. London: Continuum.

Polya, G. (1945) *How to Solve It.* Princeton, NJ: Princeton University Press.

Reason, P. and Bradbury, H. (eds) (2005) *A Handbook of Action Research.* London: Sage.

Rogers, B. (2006) *I Get By with a Little Help ... Colleague Support in Schools.* London: Paul Chapman Publishing.

Rogers, C.R. (1967) *A Therapist's View of Psychotherapy.* London: Constable.

Rogers, C.R. (1980) *A Way of Being.* Boston: Houghton Mifflin.

Schön, D.A. (1983) *The Reflective Practitioner: How Professionals Think in Action.* New York: Basic Books.

Schön, D.A. (1987) *Educating the Reflective Practitioner.* San Francisco: Jossey-Bass.

Schön, D.A. (ed.) (1991) *The Reflective Turn: Case Studies in and on Educational Practice.* New York: Teachers' College Press.

Solomon, J. (1987) 'New thoughts on teacher education', *Oxford Review of Education*, 13(3): 267–274.

Stenhouse, L. (1971) 'The Humanities Curriculum Project: the rationale', *Theory into Practice*, 10: 154–162.

Stenhouse, L. (1975) *An Introduction to Curriculum Research and Development.* London: Heinemann.

Teacher Development Agency (TDA) (2011) *Career Entry and Development Profile 2011/12.* Manchester: TDA. www.tda.gov.uk/about/publications/basket/tda0876.aspx (accessed 3 November 2011).

Tripp, D. (1993) *Critical Incidents in Teaching: Developing Professional Judgement*. London: Routledge.

Uhlenbeck, A., Verloop, N. and Beijard, D. (2002) 'Requirements for an assessment procedure for beginning teachers: implications from recent theories on teaching and assessment', *Teachers College Record*, 104(2): 242–272.

van Manen, M. (1977) 'Linking ways of knowing with ways of being practical', *Curriculum Inquiry*, 6: 205–228.

Vygotsky, L.S. (1962) *Thought and Language*. Cambridge, MA: MIT Press.

Vygotsky, L.S. (1978) *Mind in Society: The Development of Higher Psychological Processes*. Cambridge, MA: Harvard University Press.

Ward, J. and McCotter, S. (2004) 'Reflection as a visible outcome for pre-service teachers', *Teaching and Teacher Education*, 20: 243–257.

Warin, J., Maddock, M., Pell, A. and Hargreaves, L. (2006) 'Resolving identity dissonance through reflective and reflexive practice in teaching', *Reflective Practice*, 7(2): 231–243.

Weick, K. (1995) *Sensemaking in Organizations*. Thousand Oaks, CA: Sage.

Wenger, E. (1998) *Communities of Practice: Learning, Meaning and Identity*. New York: Cambridge University Press.

Yinger, R. (1990) 'The conversation of practice', in R.T. Clift, W. R. Houston and M.C. Pugach (eds) *Encouraging Reflective Practice in Education*. New York: Teachers College Press. pp. 73–96.

Zeichner, K.M. (1994) 'Research on teacher thinking and different views of reflective practice in teaching and teacher education', in I. Carlgren (ed.) *Teachers' Minds and Actions: Research on Teachers' Thinking and Practice*. Bristol, PA: Falmer Press. pp. 9–27.

Zeichner, K.M. and Liston, D. (1996) *Reflective Teaching: An Introduction*. Mahwah, NJ: Lawrence Erlbaum Associates.

CHAPTER 2

AN OVERVIEW OF LEARNING

Sue Dymoke

By the end of this chapter you will have:

- been introduced to theories of learning and the key figures who have researched, written and influenced theoretical developments in this field
- reflected on your own experiences as a learner
- explored the implications of learning theories for your classroom

Introduction

This chapter considers the nature of learning and learners. It explores theories of learning and the influence of key academic figures including Vygotsky, Bruner and Gardner. It also considers debates about the nature of learning including: learning styles, multiple intelligences, **accelerated learning** and thinking skills, creativity and risk taking, and the potential impact of these debates on classroom practice. This chapter leads you to reflect on your own learning in ways that can inform your developing classroom practice and awareness of the learners with whom you are working.

How do learners learn?

There are many contrasting and complementary theories about the ways in which young people and adults learn. These are constantly refined as new research is carried out and reported on. No single theory to date is able to describe neatly the complexities of the learning process. Learning is not just a discrete, school-based event. It occurs in many different contexts and is dependent on what Ileris (2009) describes as the integration of two processes, namely external interactions between learner and context and the 'internal psychological process of elaboration and acquisition' (2009: 8). Wood argues that the school environment engenders new and distinct forms of learning: school-based learning includes a series of 'contrived encounters' or 'social interactions that come about as a result of explicit educational goals' (1998: 16). Many different theoretical perspectives can inform the classroom practices you observe and begin to adopt for yourself during your training. Learning and teaching are, in many respects, closely allied. Successful teachers are those who want to continue learning and to reflect on and refine their practices throughout their careers. In exploring what it means to be a teacher, it is therefore vital for you to consider your own learning processes and what is understood by the term 'learner'. The learning theories introduced in this chapter do not constitute an exhaustive overview but they do include those theories which have influenced educational practices in the past hundred years and are frequently acknowledged within discussions of learning and teaching. Each is outlined in a simplified form. For more detailed information, you should consult the further reading and weblinks embedded within the activities together with the titles referenced on the reading list at the end of this chapter.

An introduction to the main learning theories

Learning theories developed in the twentieth century fit into two broad groupings – those concerned with behaviours (how people respond or react to different kinds of stimuli) and those linked with cognition (how people interact with stimuli and construct their own learning).

Behaviourist theories

Behaviourist theories have been developed through observation of how behaviours can change as a direct result of the learning process. **Behaviourism** is concerned with: modelling appropriate behaviours; creating environments that enable or condition students to respond in what are deemed appropriate ways; rewarding positive responses; and learning through repetition. A key figure in this field is Burrhus Frederic Skinner.

Skinner's laboratory-based experiments in the 1960s used small animals, under controlled conditions, and provided them with rewards (reinforcement) for any response that was near to the desired response. Gradually the desired behaviour was brought closer through the controlled use of stimulus–response associations, also known as *shaping*. Skinner extended his conclusions from this experimental work to consider the complex relationship between response and reinforcement in humans. He believed that learning was a process of conditioning centred on responding to particular stimuli and that reinforcement of learning (through use of an intermittently repeated schedule) and rewarding of positive achievements which resulted from this conditioned learning should be at the heart of teaching. Reinforcement made a particular response more likely to reoccur. Skinner (1968) argued that the education system favoured deficit models of teaching which were focused on punishment and exposed a learner's lack of understanding. He claimed that teachers did not shape students' learning effectively, with the result that the learning which did take place was inappropriate or of a temporary nature (see also Wood, 1998). Based on this behaviourist theory, Skinner even went to the extreme of designing teaching machines to provide further evidence to support it in human learning. These machines would break learning down into tiny error-free stages in which the learner would be uncontaminated by contact with the fallible human teacher. They were trialled in some schools but were never fully adopted.

The controlled (some would say rigid) approach to learning favoured by behaviour theorists can lead learners to take a very passive role in their own learning. It is increasingly perceived as presenting a limited view of how people learn as it does not embrace the different situations in which learning can take place or how people learn from new or one-off experiences without reinforcement. Nevertheless, elements of Skinner's research, particularly on the consequences of behaviour, have informed more recent whole-school policies and approaches to classroom behaviour management. For example, you may have already observed other teachers repeatedly using praise and positive feedback during an activity to draw as many students into a discussion as possible, or you might have reinforced previously taught expectations about putting up hands to answer questions or about how your own students should leave the room at the end of a lesson. All of these classroom events draw on aspects of behaviourism.

If you would like to know more about Skinner's research refer to Skinner (1968) and Wood (1998).

Activity 2.1 Repetition in learning

This can be carried out individually or preferably, in discussion with your mentor or another beginning teacher.

(a) Try to recall two occasions in your own childhood where you asked to:

- learn something through a process of repetition, reinforcement and reward;
- learn something through participation in a 'one-off' experience.

(Continued)

(Continued)

What precisely did you learn in each case? And what do you remember now? How did you feel about these experiences at the time? How do you feel about them now?

(b) Now focus on a specific topic within the subject that you are training to teach.

Are there aspects of this topic which might lend themselves to behaviourist repetition and reward strategies? Why do you think these methods might be appropriate? Share your ideas with another beginning teacher in the same subject area or with your mentor. Together, draw up a table with two columns to summarize the major strengths and weaknesses of applying Skinner's approaches to educational material and teaching strategies.

Constructivist theories

Constructivist theories are concerned with the social nature of learning: how learners create their own conceptual structures in order to make sense of the world. **Social constructivism** focuses on the **cognitive** processes that occur as people learn through social interaction, such as listening to and working with others. The relationship between learner and teacher is a crucial relationship to consider in this regard. These learning theories are often viewed as child centred and progressive. They have informed the development of many classroom practices currently used in schools. Key figures in this field are Jean Piaget, Lev Semonovich Vygotsky and Jerome Bruner.

Piaget was a psychologist. His theories were arrived at through observations of children in which he explored the qualitative development in their ability to solve problems as they reached different levels of maturity. In his view, maturation was the key influence on a child's cognitive development. He defined cognitive development as a sequential process of four phases: sensory-motor (0–2 years); pre-operational (2–7 years); concrete operational (7–12 years); and formal operational (12+ years but not attained by all). He discovered that children's modes of thinking are completely different from those of adults and they have different perceptions of reality. He argued that, as children matured, they became increasingly able to learn from their actions and to interact with other people and their environment. In turn, both of these increasing capabilities had an impact on their developing cognitive processes and their conceptions of reality. Piaget extrapolated universal statements about maturation through application of experimental psychological methods which used individual children as their subjects. His concept of four phases of maturation is now considered to be too fixed and inflexible. The phases do not, for example, acknowledge the possibility of children younger than seven years becoming logical and systematic in their thinking. They are also founded on an assumption that all young people mature at similar rates without regard to the impact of other extenuating factors such as culture, social class or well-being.

Vygotsky disagreed with Piaget's hypothesis that maturation would directly result in the development of higher level thinking skills. His own research on cognition took a different path. Work on language acquisition and development with deaf–blind children led him to conclude that speech preceded thought and, consequently, that language was the most significant factor in cognitive development. Vygotsky coined the term the zone of proximal development (ZPD) to define the distance which exists between the actual developmental level of learning and what potentially could be learned through problem-solving with guidance through that zone by a parent, grandparent, sibling, other adult such as a teacher or 'in collaboration with more capable peers' (1978: 86). Not everyone is educable in this way but Vygotsky's work has had a major influence on pedagogy in the latter part of the twentieth century. For examples, see the work of Barnes et al. (1972) and Britton (1974), all of whom applied Vygotsky's theories to classroom contexts and thus developed our understandings of the social functions of discourse, and the nature of co-operative learning. Nevertheless, Vygotsky's influence should still be explored with caution: his early death at the age of 37 meant that his research was underdeveloped; the English translations of his writings present different emphases. Gillen states that, in becoming fashionable, Vygotsky's research has been oversimplified. She questions why Vygotsky's work on ZPD has been 'so widely applied across pedagogic contexts' (Gillen, 2000: 193) when, in her reading, the original contexts of his research actually focused on assessment of learning and pretence play. In contrast, Levykh (2008) points to the significant contribution that Vygotsky's notion of learning can make to the cultural development of learners in a wide range of contexts.

Bruner has been influenced by Vygotsky's work and to some extent by that of Piaget. For Bruner, learning centres on the search for patterns within human communication. Each human is also perceived as having their own distinct cognitive processes which vary according to subject or environment. Bruner is particularly interested in the different processes and patterns which underpin creative problem-solving and the critical role which language plays in the development of understanding. These processes can be messy and ambiguous (Bruner, 1996). **Scaffolding** is a term closely associated with Bruner. With Wood and Ross he conducted research (Wood et al., 1976) which investigated whether it was possible for teaching/instruction to be sensitive to Vygotsky's ZPD. Could it enable learners to move beyond their current level of competence towards achieving their potential or, conversely, might it underestimate the learner's potential? To explore this question, researchers observed how mothers taught their pre-school children to put together a pyramid of wooden blocks, pegs and holes. They used the metaphor of 'scaffolding' (Wood, 1998: 99) to represent structures (involving child–adult interaction and communication) which are perceived to surround and support a young learner in order to help shape their development to its fullest extent. Wood described the level of support as 'contingent' (1998: 100) in that it is only provided when necessary: the child is never left to struggle alone or, alternatively, given too much help which could stifle their developing independence.

Scaffolding can be seen in use in various classroom strategies where staged and structured support will enable completion of complex tasks. As a child becomes more confident with a specific task, and secure in their learning, the scaffolding can gradually be dismantled and support withdrawn. **Writing frames** are perhaps the most frequently occurring examples of scaffolding. These originated in the work of the Exeter Extending Literacy project (EXEL) (see Wray and Lewis, 1997) and are, in the twenty-first century, widely used across the curriculum in the UK. The frames usually consist of paragraph openings or sentence stems (sometimes with supporting questions) which the students complete with their own words. This structure can help them to shape their ideas or arguments in a particular form such as a news report, a piece of argued writing or a response to a literary text. In science they could be used to develop pupils' procedural understanding (see Warwick et al., 2003). Researchers are critical of the potential rigidity of a frame-based approach (Fones, 2001; Myhill, 2001). Writing frames need to be used flexibly and with care if students are to be given the chance to develop original responses and teachers are not to find themselves faced with sets of identical pieces of writing to assess. For further information about writing frames refer to Chapter 3.

Alongside scaffolding, other classroom methods closely allied to constructivist theory include self-directed tasks such as problem-solving and simulations together with those involving **inductive thinking**, **Directed Activities Related to Texts (DARTs)**, and other small group activities which help students engage with texts and other classroom materials we want them to understand. DARTs, first developed by Lunzer and Gardner (1984), are activities for engaging with all kinds of texts (literary and non-literary and including visual texts) in ways which take the readers beyond straightforward comprehension and involve reflection. When used effectively, DARTs can enable learners (often working in small groups or pairs) to explore their developing interpretations of texts in creative, open-ended ways in order to make meanings for themselves. For further information about specific DARTs refer to Chapter 3.

Brain, neuroscience and learning

The brain is divided into two hemispheres – right and left. Although the hemispheres are said to have different specialist functions they are both used when a person is involved in complex tasks such as learning to speak an additional language or using metaphorical language, drawing a **mind map**, learning the music and lyrics of a song.

The right and left hemispheres of the brain are said to communicate with each other via bundles of nerve fibres which cross from one side of the body to the other. This means that the left side of the brain can control the right side of the body and vice versa (see Figure 2.1). With right-handed people, the logical left brain hemisphere tends to

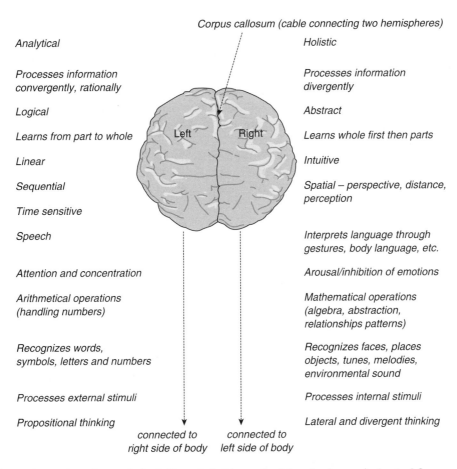

Corpus callosum (cable connecting two hemispheres)

Left	Right
Analytical	*Holistic*
Processes information convergently, rationally	*Processes information divergently*
Logical	*Abstract*
Learns from part to whole	*Learns whole first then parts*
Linear	*Intuitive*
Sequential	*Spatial – perspective, distance, perception*
Time sensitive	
Speech	*Interprets language through gestures, body language, etc.*
Attention and concentration	*Arousal/inhibition of emotions*
Arithmetical operations (handling numbers)	*Mathematical operations (algebra, abstraction, relationships patterns)*
Recognizes words, symbols, letters and numbers	*Recognizes faces, places objects, tunes, melodies, environmental sound*
Processes external stimuli	*Processes internal stimuli*
Propositional thinking	*Lateral and divergent thinking*
connected to right side of body	*connected to left side of body*

Figure 2.1   Functions of the left and right cerebral hemispheres (adapted from Smith, 1996 and Sousa, 2006)

dominate the intuitive, creative right. This is known as left-sided dominance. However, it has also been argued that girls have right-sided dominance whereas boys tend to be left-sided. There is no evidence to support the idea that one type of dominance makes one individual more intelligent than another. However, there are some suggestions, which need to be viewed with considerable caution, that males and females perform better at different types of tasks which could reflect the differences in hemisphere dominance. For example, as a group, females are said to be more verbally fluent, able to read character and social cues better, manage multi-tasking, sequence objects and talk while they solve mathematical calculations. In contrast, males as a group are said to be better at seeing shapes embedded within complex patterns and at solving mathematical problems (Moir and Jessell, 1993). Some researchers perceive that school-based learning favours right-hemisphere dominant learners. They argue that the whole brain (that is, both hemispheres) supports learning through the selection of a balanced and varied set of classroom activities and implementation of assessments designed to provide equality of opportunity (Sousa, 2006). Furthermore, it is said that students should be encouraged to try activities which occasionally challenge their preferred hemispheres and take them out of their comfort zones. In selecting these activities, you will also need to be very aware of your own personal preferences/ways of learning, since these personal choices, which may be revealed in your teaching plans, are unlikely to challenge everyone in your class.

Within the body of research on how the brain functions, the issue of retention of learning is another important aspect for you to consider. The level of retention can vary quite significantly during the course of a lesson. Sousa shows that potentially there are two *prime-times* for retention during a lesson. These occur during *prime-time 1* (the first 10–20 minutes, which has been shown to be the period of greatest retention) and *prime-time 2* (the final 5–10 minutes) (Sousa, 2006: 90). He argues that students will be able to recall almost any information relayed during this first period. This should then be followed up by a period of review or practice, while in *prime-time 2* students can consolidate or make sense of what they have learned. Consequently, for Sousa, the first 10–20 minutes of a lesson are not a time to engage students in speculating about what is to follow. In his view, this period should only deal with presentation of 'correct information' (Sousa, 2006: 90). In addition, he argues that teachers can tend to waste this first prime-time learning opportunity by filling it with administrative tasks such as announcements, registration and homework collection. You will learn more about lesson structures in Chapter 4. However, for the moment, think through the implications of what you have just read by completing Activity 2.2.

Activity 2.2   Using your brain to learn

This activity requires you to work in pairs, or with a small group of peers.

(a) Remind yourself of the right–left brain hemisphere functions in Figure 2.1. With another beginning teacher, preferably of the opposite sex, discuss which brain hemisphere appears to dominate for each of you. Is there any evidence about the way each of you learns that appears to contradict researchers' suggestions about gender and hemisphere dominance?

(b) In the same pair or a small group, discuss the opening 10–15 minutes of several lessons you have observed so far. Explore what you have noticed about how experienced teachers use this period of the lesson to begin students' learning. What did the observed teachers do in this prime-time and when did they tend to fit in administrative tasks? In your view, what impact did the introduction of these sorts of tasks have on the learners and the learning process?

(c) Now focus on the closing ten minutes of the lesson. How were the students enabled to make sense of what they had previously learned?

(d) If you would like to read more about how the brain works follow the link on the companion website to sample chapters from *How the Brain Learns* by David A. Sousa.

Kolb's four learning styles

As you have read in Chapter 1, Kolb's theory of *Experiential Learning* (1984) has had a considerable influence on perceptions about how people learn. He perceives learning as a cyclical, continuous process which involves: actively experiencing a new situation; reflecting on what has occurred; theorizing about what has been experienced; and, finally, preparing for the next stage. In focusing on developmental learning, Kolb reinterpreted Piaget's four sequential phases of learning as four distinctly different learning styles with no hierarchical structure. He named these:

- accommodative – active learners who like to take risks, carry out plans and involve themselves in new experiences
- divergent – imaginative learners who are interested in people, values and feelings and like to view situations from many perspectives
- convergent – problem-solvers and decision-makers who prefer technical tasks to **interpersonal** issues
- assimilative – learners concerned with abstract concepts and ideas, who will create theoretical models and use inductive reasoning

Although learners might use a mixture of learning styles, Kolb believed that essentially they would all be drawn to one of these four. Yet again, this acknowledgement of differences in the ways individuals learn suggests that a variety of teaching and learning strategies are essential in all classrooms if *all* students are to be included in the learning. Kolb's descriptions of learning styles are derived from his work with individual university students and are perhaps more relevant to an exploration of adult learners. Nevertheless, his model can be used to help us understand group and individual learning needs in secondary school classroom situations. Beresford (2001) provides an accessible summary of the characteristics of Kolb's four styles by exploring each type's ability to learn to use a computer:

- Accommodative learners will try out different methods in a 'hit and miss' approach, listening to other people's advice but trusting their own judgement.
- Divergent learners will initially watch others using the computer, speak to them and then try out varied approaches.

- Assimilative learners will watch, listen, make notes then try out their own approach.
- Convergent learners will refer to manuals and work on their own using a logical approach.

The existence of these different learning styles has implications on a macro level in school (in terms of curriculum structures, students' entitlements and class groupings) and, on a micro level (in terms of your own **lesson planning**, teaching and your expectations for individual learners' achievements). For example, Martin (2010: 1) explores how teachers are 'torn between research and accountability' in his investigation of learning style instruments in UK secondary schools. However, as educational systems move to address issues of personalized learning (see Chapter 3), the extent to which each individual student's preferred learning style can and should be catered for within curriculum planning remains an important subject for debate.

Intelligence quotient (IQ)

Intelligence quotient is a measurement of general intelligence arrived at through completion of a set of standardized tests of **deductive**/mathematical reasoning. For many years it has been assumed that one's IQ is a stable entity which is established in childhood. However, recent research suggests that IQ scores could increase or decrease during adolescence. Ramsden and her colleagues state that their results could serve to encourage those teenagers whose intellectual potential may improve but would also 'be a warning that early achievers may not maintain their potential' (Ramsden et al., 2011: 1). Although this is a finding which requires further investigation, in the long term it could have significant implications for secondary teachers.

Multiple intelligences

In *Frames of Mind*, Howard Gardner (1983) argues that learners could be said to have strengths in particular types of intelligences rather than a level of intelligence based on their IQ. Gardner's intelligences were originally arranged in seven groups of skills and abilities:

- linguistic intelligence
- logical-mathematical intelligence
- visual-spatial intelligence
- bodily kinaesthetic intelligence
- musical intelligence
- interpersonal intelligence
- **intrapersonal** intelligence

This list of intelligences is not finite. In the late 1990s Gardner suggested that naturalistic and (more tentatively) spiritual or existential intelligences could also be added to the above (1999). In his view, the balance of these intelligences within an individual will affect their preferred way of learning. Gardner also became bolder in his claims about how these seven or nine **multiple intelligences (MI)** could lead to new definitions of human nature. The work of Gardner and his *Project Zero* team has been influential in school improvement worldwide, particularly in terms of:

- understanding about students' aptitudes
- development of differentiated approaches to learning and teaching
- curriculum content

In some schools, decisions about students' *intelligences* are arrived at through completion of questionnaires (for examples, see Activity 2.3). In others, learners appear to have been made very aware of their *intelligences* and preferred learning styles to the extent that they may even carry labels identifying them from class to class. In addition, Gardner's terminology has triggered identification of other *intelligences* within some specific school contexts. In her paper 'Leading the intelligent school', MacGilchrist asserts that 'successful schools appear to be using at least nine intelligences in the process of addressing simultaneously the core business of learning, teaching, effectiveness and improvement' (MacGilchrist, 2006: 1).

Although it has been acknowledged by Davies that use of methods based on MI can lead to a rise in students' self-esteem and a potentially more liberal approach to curriculum planning (2006), the concept of MI is not without its critics. One of the most vocal is John White (see particularly White 2005 and 2008) who questions how the artistic/subjective and non-empirical nature of Gardner's research has generated the 'myth of multiple intelligences' (2005: 1). In his view, intelligence has always been linked with the notion that humans need to be flexible to achieve their desired goals and he argues that, in this respect, Gardner offers nothing new to the debate. White suggests Gardner's theory confuses the development of social intellectual activity with a system predicated on a set of biologically based characteristics (drawn from Piagetian developmentalist theory). He also questions whether the adoption of an MI 'shrink wrapped' (2005: 2) approach by educators could lead students to develop potentially damaging (or even limiting) false perceptions about their own capabilities.

Gardner's theory of multiple intelligences underpins the principles of *accelerated learning* developed by Alistair Smith. Smith suggests that by encouraging the development of a full range of intelligences a teacher can promote lifelong learning. He argues for a supportive classroom environment which enables learners to be receptive to new ideas and to set themselves high personal targets. Teachers need to be alert to the physical state of their students to ensure that their basic needs are met and they are alert and ready to learn. He suggests music might be played to help students achieve a state of 'relaxed alertness' (1996: 10). Students might be able to drink water during the lesson as dehydration is thought to be bad for the brain. They will occasionally participate in five-minute *brain gym* activities designed to stimulate thinking by connecting left and right brain functions. Learners are also encouraged to regularly review and reflect on their learning methods.

The accelerated learning methods of Smith centre on a range of visual, auditory and kinaesthetic (often referred to by teachers as *VAK*) strategies which are designed to support the three types of learner identified by **Neuro-Linguistic Programming (NLP)**. NLP models of communication indicate that people have specific sensory preferences for how individuals make sense of the information which their brains receive from their five senses. The three types are defined as follows.

The visual learner

This is the person who learns most effectively through visual means, preferring to receive information through charts, diagrams, visual images or demonstrations and (in some cases) written texts. Such people prefer to demonstrate their learning through visual representations such as: turning a short story into a digital **storyboard**; drawing a cartoon which shows their interpretation of a historical event; making a collage of a poem they have studied; describing a chemical process as a flow chart.

The auditory learner

This person learns most effectively through listening and prefers to listen to recorded interviews, lectures, discussions or teacher explanations than to other methods of delivery. They demonstrate their learning best by, for example, giving an oral presentation, performing a rap or contributing to discussion.

The kinaesthetic learner

This is the person who learns most effectively if they participate physically in their learning and demonstrate this learning through *doing*, for example, role-plays, activities in the field and other types of visits, practical investigations, perfecting free kicks on the football pitch, or making models or other objects. (It is important to be aware that active learning of a practical nature does need to be supported by discussion and opportunities for reflection on what has been learned if the activity is to have a lasting impact.) Some strategies used to support learners include the following.

Giving the 'big picture'

The teacher provides an overview (or **'big picture'**) of what students will learn (and participate in) during the lesson at the beginning of a session and indicates how this will connect with prior learning and intended future learning.

'Chunking down' a topic

This involves breaking down a topic into a manageable number of items – ideally between five and nine items (Smith, 1996). It can be used once the teacher has introduced the 'big picture'.

Use of mind maps and visual note-making

Mind-mapping is a graphic technique which enables both teachers (in their planning) and students (in their learning) to explore, revise and summarize ideas about a topic in a very visual and creative way that reflects how information is encoded in the brain. A modern version of the mind map was devised by Tony Buzan (2002), and the form is now used widely in education and in business. Mind maps can be hand-drawn or compiled using a variety of mind-mapping software programs such as Mind Manager and Inspiration. They have a number of key elements: different categories of information are arranged in different sections of the page or screen; different categories are colour coded; key words, symbols and highlighting are used to label the categories; flowing branches, stems, arrows and links (of different thicknesses) are made between the categories to show relationships or potential connections between them.

If you have not tried mind-mapping before you might want to refer to Buzan (2002) and visit www.mind-mapping.co.uk/make-mind-map.htm to learn how to get started.

Visual note-making includes many of the features of mind-mapping such as symbols, arrows, flow charts, sketches, circled words, colour-coding and other features which enable the note-maker to record their notes in a way which will be memorable to them.

Use of concept mapping

Concept mapping involves creating diagrams that contain a limited number of concepts (ideas) with the propositional relationships which join them written on the linking arrows (see Osbourne, 1993). Group concept mapping provides many opportunities for students to have enhanced dialogues on a range of topics – that is, to question each other's ideas and interpret their meaning to one another. (For an example in science teaching see Sizmur, 1994.) They can also be used to support learners' summary skills and their developing understanding of texts (see, for example, Conlon, 2009). Other teaching ideas might be to present a concept map which deliberately contains some true and some false propositions. The students are asked to locate all the errors on the concept map. They then go on to construct it correctly.

Displays of key words

Displays can be made in the teaching room on posters, word walls or hanging mobiles – these will only be effective if they are removed after use rather than becoming a permanent feature of the classroom landscape. A simple teaching strategy might involve providing a selection of the key words (to do with a given topic) and asking the students to make up five true sentences by choosing an entry from each column. The same word can be used several times to reinforce understanding and the sentences can then be displayed. Table 2.1 provides an example.

Use of jingles, rhymes and mnemonics

Mnemonics are short phrases used to jog the memory. For example, *Richard Of York Gave Battle In Vain* spells out the colours of the spectrum, as seen in a rainbow: Red,

Table 2.1   Making true sentences

microbes		all	green plants	to get rid of	oxygen
animals	depend	some	microbes	to make	nitrogen
decomposers	use	on	animals	to provide	water
green plants				to recycle	carbon dioxide

Note: The key words are shown in italics.

Orange, Yellow, Green, Blue, Indigo, Violet; *Friend to the end* helps you to remember how to spell the word friend correctly and to place the 'i' and the 'e' in the correct order.

Taking part in brain gym or break states

These group activities are used *for a brief period of time only* either at the beginning or end of a lesson or at a transition point within it. The intention is to improve physical and mental alertness and co-ordination. They can provide a break at a key moment in a lesson and enable students to move on, feeling re-energized and focused. Activities can include:

- rubbing hands in a circle on your stomach while patting your head (and vice versa)
- marching in time on the spot and touching a raised knee with the opposite hand
- reading letters of the alphabet in forward or backward sequence whilst following instructions about raising right or left or both arms
- breathing exercises
- use of different types of music for energizing, enhancing concentration, visualization or relaxation

Activity 2.3   What kind of a learner are you?

This is an activity which can be carried out individually.

(a) Refer back to the section on Kolb's four learning styles and reflect on your own preferred ways of learning. Which strategies have you found most helpful in the past when:

- making notes from your reading or from a lecture?
- revising for examinations?
- planning an essay or a presentation?

At what stage of your own education did you learn to use these strategies? What could they reveal about the way you use your brain? What could they tell you about your preferred learning style(s)?

(b) Use any search engine and you will discover many websites featuring question-naires on learning styles and multiple intelligences. For example go to: Walter McKenzie's Multiple Intelligences Survey at http://surfaquarium.com/MI/inventory.htm.

Try out one of the questionnaires. Did it help you to identify your own differ-ent strengths as a learner? Look again at the particular questionnaire with a critical eye. What do you notice about how the questions are constructed? What view of 'intelligence' is being presented and assessed?

Activity 2.4   Learning styles

This activity can be completed individually.

(a) Review two lessons you have observed so far. Which learning theories may have influenced the teaching and learning strategies chosen and used by the teach-ers? Were the students able to learn in different ways? If so, what strategies were used and with what effect?

(b) Refer to White (2005 and 2008) and reflect on your own classroom observa-tions. What do you think might be the advantages for the teacher and the students of a *learning styles* focus in the planning and teaching of a lesson? What potential difficulties could arise from this approach?

Thinking skills

This term has become an umbrella term for a range of activities including logic, enquiry, problem-solving and critical thinking. The influential psychologist Jerome Bruner believes we use different sorts of thinking strategies depending on our knowledge, the context in which we are working and the subject matter. He argues that the school context engenders distinctly new forms of learning and consequently new ways of think-ing (Bruner, 1966). The development of thinking skills in school-based education has been influenced by the work of several individuals with contrasting approaches. These include Reuven Feuerstein, Matthew Lipman, Edward De Bono and Benjamin Bloom.

Feuerstein et al.'s instrumental enrichment (IE) programme (1980) was developed after the Second World War for use with traumatized and seemingly ineducable Israeli young people. This is a programme based on 'mediated learning experience', a dynamic process through which adults interact with young learners to support their cognitive development. Objects and events in their worlds are crucial aspects of the mediational encounter and are used to bring about change (Falik, n.d.). For further information and research papers on Feuerstein's work refer to www.icelp.org/asp/Aspects_of_Mediated_Learning_Experience.shtm.

Matthew Lipman et al.'s pioneering *Philosophy for Children* (or P4C) programme in the USA (1980) is underpinned by the belief that children have a natural curiosity about the world and they want to ask questions about it. The programme uses a creative, enquiry-based approach that draws on the processes of Socratic dialogue. It stimulates children to learn about the nature of learning. The scheme uses novels that are read in class and have been deliberately written to guide their readers to raise questions, argue and explore ideas. This approach has been further refined and adapted for use in UK classrooms by Robert Fisher (1995) among others and P4C approaches can be found in both primary and secondary schools. For more information go to www.sapere.org.uk/.

Edward De Bono's work on cognition emphasizes creative approaches to thinking which include his six 'thinking hats' strategy (1991). This is widely used both in primary and secondary schools (particularly in English teaching and personal and social education programmes) for encouraging consideration of a range of perspectives. Wearers (either individuals or small groups) of the six differently coloured hats each have to explore the same situation, argument or text from a certain perspective (depending on the colour* of hat they are wearing) and to present their ideas to the rest of the class:

- * White = neutral and factual
- * Yellow = optimistic, positive and offers praise
- * Red = emotional, opinionated and intuitive
- * Black = offers critical judgements
- * Green = alternative, speculative or creative thinking
- * Blue = provides overview or summary, acts as a control

Activity 2.5   Using De Bono's hats

This activity can be completed in conjunction with your mentor.
Refer to De Bono's six thinking hats (described in this section).
Think about how you might use this approach to teach one aspect of your subject with one of your current classes.
Discuss your choices of topic and approach with your teacher–mentor. If they are appropriate, develop them into a plan, try them out and evaluate their success.

In focusing on how they learn as well as what they learn, students need to develop their **meta-cognition** – their ability to reflect on their own thinking processes. Some psychologists argue that meta-cognition is 'the one factor unique to human thinking' (Fisher,

1995: 11) and Fisher stresses the importance of meta-cognition as 'a key element in the transfer of learning' (1998: 1) if learners are to fully understand how they learn.

In the twenty-first century, thinking skills have become a more prominent feature of UK school curricula. In some schools, students' thinking skills are explicitly taught and numerous publications have been produced to support this teaching (for example, see Bowkett, 2006). However, the development of students' thinking skills can (and should) be embedded within their learning in all subject areas through selection of activities which stimulate and challenge all learners in a variety of ways. Thinking skills have been promoted within the **Personal learning and thinking skills (PLTS)** framework of the National Curriculum http://curriculum.qcda.gov.uk/key-stages-3-and-4/skills/personal-learning-and-thinking-skills/index.aspx. The PLTS framework itself comprises six groups of skills:

- independent enquirers
- creative thinkers
- reflective learners
- team workers
- self-managers
- effective participants

The significance of the framework, particularly for planning and assessment, is explored further in Chapters 3, 4 and 5.

The National Curriculum previously identified thinking skills more specifically as:

- information-processing skills – locating and collecting relevant information, sorting, classifying, sequencing, comparing and contrasting, analysing part/whole relationships
- reasoning skills – giving reasons to support actions or opinions, drawing inferences, making deductions, making judgements and decisions informed by reasons or evidence, using precise language to explain
- enquiry skills – asking relevant questions, posing and defining problems, planning and researching, predicting outcomes and anticipating consequences, testing conclusions and improving ideas
- creative thinking skills – generating and extending ideas, applying imagination, suggesting hypotheses, searching for alternative innovative ideas
- evaluation skills – evaluating information, making value judgements, developing criteria for judging their own and other people's work and having confidence in their own judgements (DfES, 2002 www.nc.uk.net/ learn_think.html)

This list is closely allied to the hierarchy of higher-order thinking skills developed by Bloom (see next section). The 1999 National Curriculum for science (DfEE, 1999: 9) acknowledges the important role of science education in developing thinking skills: 'science provides opportunities to promote thinking skills, through pupils engaging in the process of scientific enquiry'. Subject-specific programmes, such as cognitive acceleration through science education (CASE) or through mathematics education (CAME), were developed with the aim of improving general cognitive functions. CASE in particular had a focus on developing scientific thinking in Years 7 and 8. It was promoted in many secondary schools with in-service training and support materials and thoroughly evaluated (see Shayer and Adey, 2002; Baumfield et al., 2005).

Bloom's taxonomy

Benjamin Bloom and his colleagues devised a hierarchical 'taxonomy of educational objectives' (Bloom et al., 1956). This classified educational objectives into groups in relation to their cognitive complexity and the different levels of thinking that would be required to meet these objectives. The levels extended from simple recall towards increasingly complex, higher-order thinking (Figure 2.2). The taxonomy was constructed on the understanding that higher-order skills embrace all those levels lower down the order. In other words, knowledge has to be acquired before it can be fully understood and evaluated. Its potential in providing an educational framework became widely known and it was eventually translated into 22 languages (Krathwohl, 2002).

Objectives that describe intended learning outcomes as a result of teaching are usually arranged in terms of subject matter (content) and a description of what is to be done with that content. The former would be written as nouns for example and the associated cognitive processes would be written as verbs. An example of this is: 'the student will be able to recount (*verb*) Newton's second law of motion (*noun phrase*)'. In a revised version of the taxonomy these two aspects of the learning outcome are presented as

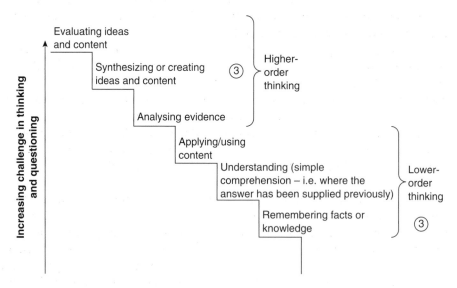

Figure 2.2   Bloom's taxonomy

separate dimensions. It allows for a knowledge dimension (noun) and a cognitive process dimension (verb) (Anderson and Krathwohl, 2001). For a more detailed discussion of how to classify educational goals, objectives and standards, see Krathwohl (2002).

One of the challenges you will face as a beginning teacher is learning to ask questions of your students which will stimulate their higher-order thinking. You will find that Bloom's taxonomy can help you to devise **learning objectives** and to plan questions which offer increasing levels of challenge to all your students and should help to build their confidence. Ultimately all students should be given opportunities to work at all levels of thinking but remember that not everyone has the capacity within their working memory to sift essential and non-essential knowledge efficiently or to grasp complex ideas at the same speed. Table 2.2 provides examples of tasks and question stems from a range of different subject areas to help you think through the challenges which each level will offer. You will explore the subject of questioning further in Chapter 4.

Table 2.2   Putting Bloom's taxonomy into practice

Thinking skill	What the students need to do	Examples of questions and question stems	Task examples
Remembering	Define Recall List Match Label Name Identify Collect Describe	Describe the scene in … What do we call a …? What are the types of …? Where would you find …? What did we find out last lesson about …?	Identify the main figures in the battle List all the characters in the novel Match the written descriptions to the mapped locations Pick out the prime numbers
Understanding	Explain Interpret Outline Illustrate Summarize Discuss Distinguish	Why do you think …? What happens when …? Explain why we should…? What are the most important points? How did you …?	Explain how the nurse felt in this scene Draw a mind map® – to show what you have learned about volcanoes
Applying	Apply to new context Transfer Modify Use Predict Demonstrate Solve	What do you think she will do next? How can you use a quadratic equation to …? What does this reaction suggest to you?	Predict the ending of the story Imagine you were alive in 1940s Britain Show your partner how to hold the racket

(Continued)

Table 2.2   (Continued)

Thinking skill	What the students need to do	Examples of questions and question stems	Task examples
Analysing	Deduce Infer Explore Investigate Relate Classify Categorize Compare	How have you arrived at that evidence? Which is fact and which is opinion? What do you think this really means? What purpose does it serve?	Compare the use of colour in the two paintings Sort the statements into agree and disagree piles Analyse the impact of longshore drift on the beach
Synthesizing or creating	Design Invent Create Reorganize Compose Rewrite	What else would you add or change? What alternatives are there? How are these two different?	Write an alternative speech for the last scene Devise an advertising campaign to promote a healthy snack
Evaluating	Assess Evaluate Judge Appraise Justify Conclude	How successful ...? Why is that valid? What do you recommend? Which is more acceptable?	Put the character or historical figure on trial Decide which photograph is most effective

Source: adapted from DfES, 2003 and Dobson, 2006

Within each level of the taxonomy there is also the potential for an increasing degree of difficulty of task which may be needed before learners are ready to progress towards a greater level of complexity in their thinking. Sometimes teachers can confuse complexity with difficulty but they are different. Complexity is concerned with the level of thought required whereas difficulty determines how much effort needs to be expended within each level (Sousa, 2006).

The following examples illustrate the differences: 'Tell me five facts you have learned about global warming and three points about global footprints' is *not* a more complex task than 'Recall five facts you have learned about global warming' but it is more difficult in that it relies on the recall of a greater body of knowledge. Alternatively, 'Explain what happens in the narrative poem *The Rime of the Ancient Mariner*' involves a lower-order thinking skill which requires the learner to demonstrate their understanding of the events of the text whereas 'Create an additional section in the poem written from the point of view of another character' demands more complex higher-order thinking skills to complete the task effectively. This will involve students in drawing on their knowledge and understanding of the events of the poem and their analysis of how it has been written in order to synthesize this knowledge in the creation of new verses with appropriate content and written in the same style.

Teaching and learning strategies such as odd one out, card sorting, cloze, sequencing, finding key words, concept mapping and hot-seating can be very effective in supporting the development of thinking skills. Australian writer and learning consultant Tony Ryan devised a series of 'Thinker's Keys' which could be used to develop students' creative thinking and help them to respond flexibly in different situations. They are extremely useful for teaching in many different subject areas and have undergone many refinements since they were first introduced in the 1990s. They can be downloaded from www.tonyryan.com.au/blog/wpcontent/uploads/Thinkers_Keys_Version1.pdf.

If you want to learn more about thinking skills frameworks, Moseley et al. (2005) undertook a review and evaluation of frameworks for understanding thinking in education and training, and how they might pertain to work with Post-16 students. Appendix 1 of their article provides a very useful taxonomy in which they present the frameworks in four different groupings:

- Group 1: all-embracing frameworks, covering personality, thought and learning
- Group 2: instructional design frameworks
- Group 3: frameworks for understanding critical and 'productive' thinking
- Group 4: explanatory models of cognitive structure and/or cognitive development (Moseley et al., 2005: 384–390)

Activity 2.6 Developing thinking skills

The activity is best completed as a paired activity.

(a) Discuss with another teacher the examples you have seen of *thinking skills* planning and teaching in departmental **schemes of work** and lesson observations. In your view, which of these showed that thinking skills could be embedded within the subject teaching (rather than being in addition to the topic or concepts taught)?

(b) Look again at the section in this chapter on Bloom's taxonomy. Choose a specific topic which you will be teaching. How will you ensure that your teaching promotes the development of thinking skills at all levels in this topic? Think about ways in which you can keep a check on this in your lesson planning and recording.

(c) You might want to plot your ideas in brief on to a hierarchical chart. Now review the chart. Are there places where you may need to add increasing levels of difficulty to reinforce learning before moving on to the next level? Discuss your ideas with your mentor.

(d) Can thinking skills be taught? Refer to Valerie Wilson's paper 'Can thinking skills be taught?' (2000) at www.pre-online.co.uk/feature_pdfs/spotlight79.pdf. Think about what you have learned so far through your reading, lesson observations, practical experience and reflections. Draw a mind map in which you explore your response to this question. Share it with your mentor or another teacher.

Creativity and risk taking

Much of the above focus on thinking also encompasses the need to engage creatively with a problem and to be prepared to take risks in resolving it. The word creativity, which originated in the nineteenth century as a 'creative power or faculty; ability to create' (Brown 1993: 544), has increasingly come to the fore in discussions about learning. Anna Craft, one of the leading researchers in this field, defines 'little c creativity' or 'LCC' (Craft 2001: 45) as the aspect that we can all participate in and learn from. LCC is different from the highly creative acts demonstrated by composers, scientists or people with exceptional creative skill in that it is not concerned with choreographing a new symphony or discovering the patterns of DNA. Instead, it pertains to how we live our lives, how we identify and actively initiate or respond to the challenges and contexts in which we find ourselves, how we innovate, make choices or effect changes in order to move on. In placing emphasis on the personal, Craft also presents a challenge to teachers to think beyond rigid subject definitions and barriers in order to consider the place of creativity and the creative processes involved in all areas of knowledge and skills development, not just those traditionally labelled as 'arts' or 'creative subjects'.

In educational policy terms, the publication of *All Our Futures: Creativity, Culture and Education* (NACCCE, 1999) focused attention in the UK on the need to support and encourage the creative potential of individual learners. It stated that, given the right opportunities, we are all creative, or have the potential to be creative, to varying degrees. Following in its wake, government-funded programmes and initiatives, such as the National College for School Leadership's (NCSL) creative leadership seminars and the now defunct Creative Partnerships, came into being and a plethora of projects developed in individual schools. You can gain a flavour of this work by looking at some of the Creativity in Action projects archived at www.webarchive.org.uk/wayback/archive/20070327120000/http://www.ncaction.org.uk/creativity/new_examples.htm.

The creative emphasis also permeated the 2007 iteration of the National Curriculum. Its creativity and critical thinking section indicates how creative activity is not only achievable in everyday life but is also 'essential for the future well-being of society and the economy' (QCDA, 2010). In spite of this economic imperative, there are still many tensions in locating creativity within educational contexts. For example, consider the following questions with reference to your own subject area and the curriculum frameworks which underpin it.

- What opportunities do you think there are for students to demonstrate creative approaches within your subject?
- What could constitute a creative risk taking in your subject area?
- To what extent is it possible to assess students' creative responses in your subject area within existing curricular or examination assessment frameworks?
- How are such responses assessed and what issues/problems might arise in their assessment?

You might want to talk to your mentor, or another teacher from your subject discipline, about your ideas.

Critical reading at Master's level

(a) Select one of the areas listed below that you are interested in exploring further. Locate and read the article or summary associated with it.

1 *Learning Styles*: Martin, S. (2010) 'Teachers using learning styles: Torn between research and accountability?' *Teaching and Teacher Education*, 26, 1583–1591.

2 *Thinking Skills*: Higgins, S. et al (2004) 'Thinking skills approaches to effective teaching and learning: what is the evidence for impact on learners? Summary', *Research Evidence in Education Library*. London: EPPI-Centre, Social Science Research Unit, Institute of Education, University of London. http://eppi.ioe.ac.uk/cms/Default.aspx?tabid=336.

3 *Creativity*: Craft, A. (2006) 'Fostering creativity with wisdom', *Cambridge Journal of Education*. 36 (3): 337–350.

(b) What were the main reasons that the author(s) wrote your chosen article?

(c) What are the main findings or arguments that your chosen article conveys? Try to summarize both (b) and (c) in 200 words each.

(d) Now identify *two or three* key articles referred to in the text you have chosen. How do these references appear to have influenced or shaped the author's argument or discussion? (For example, the references could have influenced the research questions that the author wanted to investigate or the way the research was carried out – its methodology.)

(e) If you wish to develop your research skills and your understanding of your chosen topic further: use a research database or library catalogue to locate these new references, read them and begin to explore more fully how they contribute to research in the particular field. In doing so, you are beginning to compile your own reference list which might inform further reflection or Master's-level assignment writing on the topic.

Conclusion

In this chapter you have been introduced to different theories of learning and the ways in which these can shape and inform classroom practice. You have also had the opportunity to reflect on yourself as a learner, to explore your own views about theoretical aspects of learning and begin to apply your new understandings to aspects of your subject teaching. In Chapter 3 we move on to consider the contexts in which teaching and learning take place.

References

Anderson, L. and Krathwohl, D. (eds) (2001) *A Taxonomy for Learning and Assessing: A Revision of Bloom's Taxonomy of Educational Objectives*. New York: Longman.

Barnes, D., Britton, J. and Rosen, H. (1972) *Language, the Learner and the School*. London: Penguin.

Baumfield, V., Edwards, G., Butterworth, M. and Thacker, D. (2005) *The Impact of the Implementation of Thinking Skills Programmes and Approaches on Teachers*. London: University of London, EPPI-Centre.

Beresford, J. (2001) 'Matching teaching to learning', in F. Banks and A. Shelton Mayes (eds) *Early Professional Development for Teachers*. London: David Fulton. pp. 226–246.

Bloom, B., Engelhart, M., Furst, E., Hill, W. and Krathwohl, D. (1956) *Taxonomy of Educational Objectives: The Classification of Educational Goals. Handbook 1: Cognitive Domain*. London: Longman.

Bowkett, S. (2006) *100 Ideas for Teaching Thinking Skills*. London: Continuum.

Britton, J. (1974) *Language and Learning*. London: Penguin.

Brown, L. (ed.) (1993) *The New Shorter Oxford English Dictionary*. Oxford: Clarendon Press.

Bruner, J. (1966) *Toward a Theory of Instruction*. New York: W.W. Norton.

Bruner, J. (1996) *The Culture of Education*. Cambridge, MA: Harvard University Press.

Buzan, T. (2002) *How to Mind Map*. London: HarperCollins.

Conlon, T. (2009) 'Towards sustainable Text Concept Mapping', *Literacy*, 43(1): 20–28.

Craft, A. (2001) 'Little c Creativity' in A. Craft, B. Jeffrey and M. Leibling (eds) *Creativity in Education*. London: Continuum. pp. 45–61.

Davies, R. (2006) *Multiple Intelligences (MI) in the Classroom: An Evaluation of the Effectiveness of an 'MI Approach' through the Teaching and Learning of History*. National Teacher Research Panel for the Teacher Research Conference. http://webarchive.nation alarchives.gov.uk/20101119131802/www.standards.dcsf.gov.uk/ntrp/publications/ (accessed 21 May 2012).

De Bono, E. (1991) *Teaching Thinking*. London: Penguin.

Department for Education and Employment (DfEE) (1999) *The National Curriculum for England: Science*. London: DfEE.

Department for Education and Skills (DfES) (2002) *Key Stage 3 National Strategies: Teaching and Learning in the Foundation Subjects: Unit 12: Thinking Together*. London: DfES.

Department for Education and Skills (DfES) (2003) *Unit 4: Questioning, Teaching and Learning in Secondary Schools: Pilot*. London: DfES.

Dobson, H. (2006) 'Thinking and reading', *Secondary English Magazine*, 10(2): 29–32.

Falik, L. (n.d.) *Using Mediated Learning Experience Parameters to Change Children's Behavior: Techniques for Parents and Childcare Providers*. www.icelp.org/asp/ Aspects_of_Mediated_ Learning_Experience.shtm (accessed 10 November 2011).

Feuerstein, R., Rand, Y., Hoffman, M.B. and Miller, R. (1980) *Instrumental Enrichment: An Intervention for Cognitive Modifiability*. Baltimore, MD: University Press.

Fisher, R. (1995) *Teaching Children to Think*. 2nd edition. Oxford: Blackwell.

Fisher, R. (1998) 'Thinking about thinking: developing metacognition in children', *Early Child Development and Care*, 141: 1–15.

Fones, D. (2001), 'Blocking them in to free them to act: using writing frames to shape boys' responses to literature in the secondary school', *English in Education*, 35(3): 21–31.

Gardner, H. (1983) *Frames of Mind*. London: Heinemann..

Gardner, H. (1999) *Intelligence Reframed: Multiple Intelligences for the 21st Century*. New York: Basic Books.

Gillen, J. (2000) 'Versions of Vygotsky', *British Journal of Educational Studies*, 78(2): 183–198.

Higgins, S., Baumfield, V., Lin, M., Moseley, D., Butterworth, M., Downey, G., Gregson, M., Oberski, I., Rockett, M. and Thacker, D. (2004) 'Thinking skills approaches to effective teaching and learning: what is the evidence for impact on learners' in *Research Evidence in Education Library*. London: EPPI-Centre, Social Science Research Unit, Institute of Education, University of London. http://eppi.ioe.ac.uk/cms/Default.aspx?tabid=336 (accessed 10 November 2011).

Ileris, K. (2009) 'A comprehensive understanding of human learning' in K. Illeris (ed.) *Contemporary Theories of Learning*. Abingdon: Routledge. pp. 7– 20.

Kolb, D.A. (1984) *Experiential Learning: Experience as the Source of Learning and Development*. Englewood Cliffs, NJ: Prentice-Hall.

Krathwohl, D. (2002) 'A revision of Bloom's taxonomy: an overview', *Theory into Practice*, 41(4): 212–218.

Levykh, M. (2008) 'The affective establishment and maintenance of Vygotsky's zone of proximal development', *Educational Theory*, 58 (1): 83–101.

Lipman, M., Sharp, A. and Oscanyan, F. (1980) *Philosophy in the Classroom*. Princeton, NJ: Temple University Press.

Lunzer, E. and Gardner, K. (1984) *Learning from the Written Word*. Edinburgh: Oliver & Boyd.

MacGilchrist, B. (2006) 'Leading the intelligent school'. National College for School Leadership. www.nationalcollege.org.uk/download? ... leading-the-intelligent-school.pdf (accessed 1 November 2011).

Martin, S. (2010) 'Teachers using learning styles: Torn between research and accountability?' *Teaching and Teacher Education*, 26: 1583–1591.

Moir, A. and Jessell, D. (1993) *Brain Sex: The Real Difference between Men and Women*. London: Penguin.

Moseley, D., Elliott, J., Gregson, M. and Higgins, S. (2005) 'Thinking skills frameworks for use in education and training', *British Educational Research Journal*, 31(3): 367–390.

Myhill, D. (2001) *Better Writers*. Westley: Courseware Publications.

National Advisory Committee on Creative and Cultural Education (NACCCE) (1999) *All Our Futures: Creativity, Culture and Education*. Report to the Secretary of State for Education and Employment and the Secretary of State for Culture, Media and Sport. www.cypni.org.uk/downloads/alloutfutures.pdf (accessed 10 November 2011).

Osbourne, J.F. (1993) 'Alternatives to practical work', *School Science Review*, 75(271): 117–123.

QCDA (2010) http://curriculum.qcda.gov.uk/key-stages-3-and-4/cross-curriculum-dimensions/creativitycriticalthinking/index.aspx (accessed 8 March 2010).

Ramsden, S., Richardson, F., Josse, G., Thomas, M., Ellis, C., Shakeshaft, C., Seghier, M. and Price, C. (2011) 'Verbal and non-verbal intelligence changes in the teenage brain', *Nature*, doi:10.1038/nature10514. www.nature.com.ezproxy.lib.le.ac.uk/nature/journal/vaop/ncurrent/full/nature10514.html#auth-1 (accessed 1 November 2011).

Shayer, M. and Adey, P. (2002) *Learning Intelligence*. Buckingham: Open University Press.

Sizmur, S. (1994) 'Concept mapping, language and learning in the classroom', *School Science Review*, 76(274): 120–125.

Skinner, F.B. (1968) *The Technology of Teaching*. New York: Appleton-Century-Crofts.

Smith, A. (1996) *Accelerated Learning in the Classroom*. Stafford: Network Educational Press.

Sousa, D.A. (2006) *How the Brain Learns*. 3rd edition. Thousand Oaks, CA: Corwin/Sage.

Vygotsky, L.S. (1978) *Mind and Society: The Development of Higher Psychological Processes*. Cambridge, MA: Harvard University Press.

Warwick, P., Stephenson, P., Webster, J. and Bourne, J. (2003) 'Developing pupils' written expression of procedural understanding through the use of writing frames in science: Findings from a case study approach', *International Journal of Science Education*, 25(2): 173–192.

White, J. (2005) 'Howard Gardner: the myth of multiple intelligences', lecture at the Institute of Education, University of London, 17 November 2004 http://eprints.ioe.ac.uk/1263/1/WhiteJ2005HowardGardner1.pdf. (accessed 10 November 2011).

White, J. (2008) 'Illusory Intelligences?', *Journal of Philosophy of Education*, 42 (3–4): 611–630.

Wilson, V. (2000) 'Can thinking skills be taught? A paper for discussion', Scottish Council for Research in Education. www.pre-online.co.uk/feature_pdfs/spotlight79.pdf (accessed 1 November 2011).

Wood, D. (1998) *How Children Think and Learn*. 2nd edition. London: Blackwell. (1st edition, 1988.)

Wood, D.J., Bruner, J.S. and Ross, G. (1976) 'Collaborative learning between peers: an overview', *Educational Psychology in Practice*, 11(4): 4–9.

Wray, D. and Lewis, M. (1997) *Extending Literacy: Children Reading and Writing Non-Fiction*. London: Routledge.

CHAPTER 3

LEARNING AND TEACHING CONTEXTS

Ingrid Spencer and Sue Dymoke

By the end of this chapter you will have:

- gained greater understanding of the way learning is structured in schools and how learners are grouped and supported within inclusive environments
- explored how policy shapes teaching, curriculum content and the qualifications frameworks
- considered some of the impacts of e-learning

Introduction

This chapter reviews the contexts within which learning and teaching take place, namely the overarching structures which determine how learners are grouped and how learning and teaching are organized within schools. It considers the ways in which policy translates into practice and will encourage you to reflect on the impact of significant recent education polices as well as the notion of a 'national' standardized curriculum. Although at the time of writing, many aspects of the curriculum and qualification frameworks are under review, teachers in UK state schools are still teaching to the 2007 National Curriculum (DCSF and QCA, 2007) and working in the spirit of *Every Child Matters*. This state of flux is far from unusual in British education which is a hotly contested site for different political and social agendas. Over the course of your career, there will inevitably be changes in how teaching and learning are perceived by both the public and policy makers, and as an educator you will be expected to adapt to policy changes very quickly. One way to develop resilience in the face of near-constant change is by developing your own critical perspectives on what education is for and what it should deliver to students, parents and the wider community. Therefore it is important for you to develop critical responses to the policies that have shaped the system you are now entering, in particular the National Curriculum, the now defunct National Secondary Strategy (including literacy, numeracy and information and communication technology [ICT] across the curriculum) and the 14–19 qualifications framework. The chapter also provides an introduction to **special educational needs (SEN)** and provision for those with learning difficulties. **English as an Additional Language (EAL),** working with **gifted and talented** students, and other aspects of inclusion are explored. Furthermore, you will begin to consider the impact of e-learning and other topics which are revisited in more depth in subsequent chapters. Throughout Chapter 3 you are given opportunities to ask questions of those professionals you are working with and to reflect on aspects of your own developing practice and educational philosophy.

What are the contexts within which learning occurs?

Types of schools

The majority of children aged 11–18 in the UK attend mainstream state secondary schools or colleges while others are educated privately in the independent sector or receive home tuition. The nature and type of these state schools are increasingly varied. There are three types of maintained state secondary schools: community, foundation and voluntary schools. Any maintained school can also be a specialist school which teaches the full National Curriculum but has a special focus on the teaching of several other curriculum areas such as sports, technology or performing arts. Specific government funding for specialist schools was withdrawn from October 2010, and so some schools may not continue with all specialisms. The key organization which provides support and guidance to both Specialist and non-Specialist schools is the Schools and Academies Trust (SSAT). You will also find information about a growing school type, the **academy**, on their website (www.ssat.org.uk). Academies, like city technology colleges, are technically independent schools. They are no longer **local authority (LA)** maintained once they gain academy status, instead drawing funds directly from the government and sponsors. There has been a rapid rise in both new and old schools becoming academies since the coalition government took power in May 2010. Another initiative they have championed are **free schools**, described on the Department for Education website as 'all-ability state-funded schools set up in response to what local people say they want and need in order to improve education for children in their community' (DfE, 2011a). The first free schools opened in September 2011. Other new types of school proposed include Technical Academies, University Technical Colleges and Studio Schools, which will offer a more vocational route for 14–19-year-olds. The Studio Schools will be particularly innovative in that they will be small – typically with around 300 pupils – delivering mainstream qualifications through project-based learning. Studio School students will work with local employers and a personal coach to gain skills and qualifications to enter employment or further education and training. As this scheme is only at the planning stage it is unclear whether these Studio Schools are intended to take over from pupil referral units (PRUs) and secure training units (STUs) or whether they will be a specialist employment-related alternative to mainstream education. In some parts of the country, grammar schools, which select the majority of their students according to their high academic ability, are still prevalent. There are also faith schools and trust schools which have a variety of funding and application models.

An initiative pioneered by the Labour government of 1997–2010 is the extended school, which enables local providers and other agencies to provide access to services such as childcare (in primaries); parenting and family support; study support; sport and music clubs; ICT facilities and referral to other services including health and social care. As of September 2010 more than 99 per cent of UK schools were providing some extended services, so perhaps this should now be thought of as a core part of a school's role within the community, rather than an addition. You can find out more about extended school services and read case studies by visiting www.education.gov.uk/popularquestions/schools/typesofschools/extendedservices/a005585/what-are-extended-services.

Depending on which routes they choose to follow at post-16 level, students continue their studies entirely within their own 11–18 school, or attend courses within a consortium arrangement offered by neighbouring 11–18 schools, or move on to a sixth form college or a college of further education. Following a review of the school leaving age (DCSF, 2007a) the Labour government had proposed that from 2015 secondary education (or an equivalent training programme) would be compulsory to the age of 18. The coalition government has undertaken to support this change which will have wide reaching impacts on school budgets and provision.

National initiatives: how do they shape the learning experience?

It is clear that education in Britain is in the throes of great debate and potentially greater change. However, any history of British education is likely to demonstrate the old adage that the only thing that is certain is change. A very significant change that has affected all state schooling since 1990 is the National Curriculum, and, for those of you who are recent university graduates, this is likely to have had a powerful shaping experience on your own education. Those of you beginning to teach within the English state educational system today will find you are located within a heavily prescriptive and centralized system, dominated by a set of curriculum initiatives and a 'high stakes' testing agenda which undoubtedly exert an influence on your emerging classroom practice. Clearly it is important that you learn about what is required and expected of you within any classroom context and, indeed, national initiatives will inform aspects of your initial teacher education. However, to become a critically reflective practitioner, it is also vitally important that you take the opportunity to develop independent, critical judgements about initiatives and overarching curriculum structures within whichever system you are working. In this way you will be able to serve the interests of the specific learners you are teaching and be better placed to both challenge and contribute to debates about the future shape and content of teaching and learning. Having an understanding that the National Curriculum is a historically and culturally specific response to organizing learning is a useful starting point.

The National Curriculum

The National Curriculum underpins teaching and learning from five to 16 in England and Wales in all core (English, Maths, Science and ICT) and foundation subjects. Its programmes of study (PoS) are statutory. Since its inception in 1990, it has gone through a number of revisions. The latest version, launched in schools in September 2007 following a period of review and public consultation, became statutory in September 2008. This version is itself under full review as the book is being written. The National Curriculum is based on a statement of values which include valuing ourselves, our relationships with others, and the society and environment in which we live. Its aims, which have been shaped by the ***Every Child Matters* (ECM)** agenda, and are included in the programmes of study for every National Curriculum subject, are:

> The curriculum should enable all young people to become:
> - successful learners who enjoy learning, make progress and achieve;
> - confident individuals who are able to live safe, healthy and fulfilling lives;
> - responsible citizens who make a positive contribution to society. (DCSF and QCA, 2007: 5)

The 2008 National Curriculum includes a series of dimensions: global, enterprise, creativity, cultural understanding and diversity. These are intended to provide a context and focus for work within and between subjects and across the whole curriculum. They give students opportunities for engaging with ideas and issues that affect their lives and the world beyond school (QCA, 2007b). You will need to explore how each term is interpreted and exemplified within your own subject area online and across the curriculum as a whole. For developments and new curriculum documentation refer to www.education .gov.uk/schools/teachingandlearning.

In the past ten years, approaches to teaching and learning in England and Wales have been heavily influenced by the introduction of the non-statutory, but widely implemented National Primary and Secondary Strategies. These first arrived in all schools in 1998 and 2001 respectively and were developed significantly over time. Although funding to support teachers in delivering these programmes has now ended, they are still highly influential in how teaching and learning are structured in many schools. Certainly in the core subjects of English, Mathematics and Science, at least, it would appear that Key Stage 3 Strategy documents have superseded National Curriculum documentation. Together with **GCSE** and A level **specifications**, these are the most regularly referred to by departments to inform their schemes of work and day-to-day planning. As a revised National Curriculum is still being formed, it is too early to be certain of how previous strategies will be integrated into new programmes of study (PoS).

14–19 curriculum

A Labour government White Paper in 2005 (DfES, 2005) set out proposals for reforming 14–19 education in England and Wales, with the aim of equipping young people with the skills and knowledge they will need for adult life. The proposals give vocational qualifications (such as levels 2 and 3 diploma courses as shown in Figure 3.1) parity in terms of esteem with academic GCSE and A level courses and provide alternative pathways into higher or further education. Students in the 14–16 age range would also have greater opportunities to participate in work-based learning and courses in further education colleges than previously. It stated that provision of the increasingly popular **International Baccalaureate (IB)** post-16 multidisciplinary diploma course would double by 2010 (for further information on the IB refer to the website at the end of this section). Reaction to the proposals in the 2005 White Paper was mixed. Some expressed disappointment that the radical proposals for change previously made by the Tomlinson Working Group on 14–19-year-olds in their final report (DfES, 2004) had been sidelined while opportunities had also been missed to close the divide between GCSE and post-16 qualification routes which remained very separate within the new proposals. Some critics questioned a perceived lack of challenge for the most able students at A level standard (Mansell and Lee, 2005). One outcome of this is that the Cambridge Information Examination Board worked with some independent schools to develop a Pre-U diploma for candidates applying for undergraduate courses. This entrance examination currently exists outside of the national framework described here. However, from September 2008, each A level specification has contained four modules of assessment (two in AS and two in A2). The A2 units were designed to offer a greater degree of *stretch and challenge* than those on offer previously through use of a range of assessment strategies. Overall, the curriculum choices (available from 2008) to the overwhelming majority of students have a different shape than that which you were examined under. Further change is likely with the new coalition governmental reviews. Figure 3.1 provides an outline of the structure as it stood in September 2010.

It must be noted that an early act of the coalition government was to cancel the intro-duction of several diploma courses planned for September 2010, leaving 14 subjects on offer, none of which are traditionally seen as academic. This has led some critics to com-plain that the divide between academic and vocational subjects has been widened rather than bridged by these qualifications. Another focus of coalition government attention has been to distinguish between subjects in terms of their perceived difficulty and value.

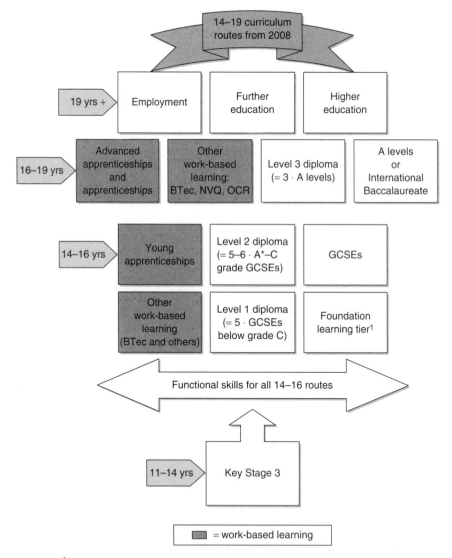

Figure 3.1   Curriculum routes for 14–19-year-olds (adapted from Jewell, 2007)

This has resulted in very heated debate within education and the national press. One result of this is the 'English Baccalaureate' (or E-Bacc) which is described on the DfE website thus: 'The measure recognizes where pupils have secured a C grade or better across a core of academic subjects – English, mathematics, history or geography, the sciences and a language' (DfE 2011b). It is the exclusion of subjects such as Art & Design from the list that has led some critics of the policy to describe the plans as 'perpetuating a two-tier education system' (Financial Services Skills Council, 2008). How any new National Curriculum and qualification frameworks will address these concerns is unclear at the time of writing. However some indications may be found in the Wolf Report (2011). This report commissioned by Education Secretary Michael Gove proposes some radical changes to 14–19 education including 'access to a common general core as a basis for progression' (Wolf, 2011: 13). It also criticizes league tables for encouraging schools to put pupils into as many exam subjects as possible rather than guiding them to consider what future career they might want to pursue. Wolf advocates greater flexibility within the curriculum for 14–19-year-olds so they are able to move between vocational and academic pathways more easily than at present.

For further information on the different routes available currently and subject specific details you should also refer to the DfE and examination board websites at:

Department for Education site www.education.gov.uk
Assessment and Qualification Alliance examination board www.aqa.org.uk
Edexcel examination board www.edexcel.org.uk
'Independent advice and support' for Pre-U. www.pre-u.co.uk/
International Baccalaureate Organization www.ibo.org
OCR examination board www.ocr.org.uk
Welsh Joint Examination Council www.wjec.co.uk

Activity 3.1   Curriculum routes for 14–19-year-olds

A small group activity (working in a small group with other beginning teachers who are all in different placement schools or colleges with 14–19-year-olds).

Those of you in the group who have suitable access should try to interview the curriculum co-ordinator in your placement school or college about the 14–19 curriculum routes. Find out:

- how the institution implements the different routes within its curriculum structures
- the curriculum co-ordinator's views on the national qualifications framework (and also, if relevant, the Pre-U diploma)

(Continued)

(Continued)

Then summarize what kind of guidance is being offered to students at 14, 16 and 18 about which route(s) they should consider taking.

Share your individual findings with the rest of the group. What conclusions can you arrive at (as a group) about the choices and the guidance on offer in these different institutions? Write up these conclusions. Ensure you consider:

- How are vocational qualifications perceived generally, and how are they perceived within particular curriculum areas?
- What are the common features of provision and what are the areas of contrast?
- What particular concerns have these co-ordinators expressed?

Functional skills

Functional skills are currently embedded within all curriculum areas at KS and KS4 at three levels with the intention of bringing together key ICT skills, adult literacy and numeracy (see Figure 3.1). The DCFS (2007b) describes functional skills as 'core elements of English, Maths and ICT that provide an individual with the essential knowledge, skills and understanding that will enable them to operate confidently, effectively and independently in life and at work'. Their introduction came during a period when employers and the Confederation of British Industry (CBI) repeatedly argued that poor basic skills cause lost productivity (Edexcel, 2007). The implementation of functional skills testing in English, Mathematics and ICT at GCSE level began in 2009 (for English and ICT) and 2010 for Mathematics. They are compulsory parts of a Diploma qualification but non-compulsory for other 11–16 routes. Concerns have been raised about the nature of the functional skills tests and their relationship to the subjects within they will be assessed. For example the National Association for the Teaching of English (NATE) expressed fears that functionality will be taught and tested in a de-contextualized way (NATE, 2006). Functional skills' work also needs to acknowledge that education is a lifelong experience and that employers have a responsibility to support employees through work-based training. The tests are not compulsory in most cases, and anecdotal evidence indicates that their take-up has been patchy in schools which are already over-burdened with increased examination schedules due to modularization. You are advised to keep up-to-date with developments in this area by consulting the examination board websites (listed earlier in this section) for details and referring to www.education.gov.uk/16to19/qualificationsandlearning/functionalskills/a0064058/functional-skill.

Activity 3.2   Finding out more about functional skills

You can complete part (a) individually and the remaining parts in conjunction with beginning teachers, teachers and students in different areas of the curriculum in one school.

(a) What are your personal views about the teaching and the testing of functional skills? How do your views compare with those of a beginning teacher in another subject area? If you are training to be an English, ICT or Mathematics teacher you may find that you have very different thoughts on this from a teacher in another curriculum area.

(b) Now investigate the views of some experienced teachers in different curriculum areas and students learning about functional skills. Do their various perspectives change or confirm your own earlier impressions?

(c) Find out how your school has embedded the teaching of functional skills within the whole curriculum. You could focus on one specific skills area and investigate its implementation and teaching together with the way this is being monitored at a whole-school level.

Literacy

You will need to develop your understanding of literacy within your own subject area, as well as across the curriculum. Use of the term *literacy* is widespread in primary schools and has even begun to be seen as a discrete element of the timetable in some secondary schools. But what does *literacy* mean and why should it be of concern to beginning teachers from *all* subject areas? Prior to the late twentieth century, literacy was deemed to be concerned largely with *reading* and *writing*. In the twenty-first century, *speaking* and *listening* are more readily accepted as being key elements of literacy. The importance of early development of strong oral skills as foundations for other learning has been highlighted by two important reports. In 2006 children's charity I Can published *The Cost to the Nation of Children's Poor Communication* (Hartshorne, 2006) report, which suggested that up to 50 per cent of children have difficulties with speaking and listening when they start school. This prompted a governmental review chaired by Lord Bercow which gathered evidence about young people's communication skills' development from 0 to 19. The findings published in 2008 as *A Review of Services for Children and Young People (0–19) with Speech, Language and Communication Needs (SLCN)* was damning of previous efforts to address pre-school language development issues. It also offered statistics that show the life chances of young people with SLCN are significantly worse than their peers without them:

> At the end of primary school, although nearly 80% of all children achieve the expected level in English, just 25% of children with SLCN reach that level – a gap of almost 55%. The gap in Maths is 46% and in science it is 41%. At the end of Key Stage 4, the gaps are similar: just 15% achieve 5 GCSE A*–C or equivalent compared to 57% of all young people. (Bercow, 2008: 7)

That poor communication skills impact on learning across the curriculum may surprise some of you who are new to working in the classroom. However, it must be remembered that English is the vehicular language for all learning in British schools and so all teachers of whatever subject are also teachers of literacy. The links between early language and reading skills development and later academic attainment has been highlighted even more recently in the 2011 **Ofsted** report *Removing Barriers to Literacy*. This report identifies what it considers to be best practice in raising literacy levels across the entire state sector from three to 19. Drawing on 190 different education institutions including a prison and a young offenders' centre, it lists as one of its eight recommendations: 'a rigorous, sequential approach to developing speaking and listening and teaching reading, writing and spelling through systematic phonics' (Ofsted, 2011: 5). **Systematic Synthetic Phonics (SSP)** has been extremely widespread in primary schools since the *Independent Review of the Teaching of Early Reading* in 2006, usually referred to as the Rose Review. Significantly for new teachers, the 2011 Ofsted report advises its use in secondary schools for pupils with lower attainment in literacy, SLCN or English as an additional language (EAL), asserting the 'fact that for learners without a grasp of the link between sounds and letters, this knowledge is necessary to develop their literacy' (2011: 8). Given the strength of both of these statements, it is highly likely that a revised National Curriculum will require all teachers to have some phonics understanding, regardless of age phase or subject. Certainly the revised standards for teaching make explicit reference to knowledge of SSP being essential for anyone teaching early reading, which will include secondary teachers working with pupils in the early stages of learning English, for example.

Furthermore, in recent years terms such as *media literacy*, *visual literacy*, *emotional literacy* and *scientific literacy* have also become familiar, as has the term *multiliteracies* to reflect this new understanding of the complex nature of literacy. In Australia and New Zealand some of these terms have been more fully acknowledged within these nations' curriculum structures. If it is carefully integrated within the curriculum, literacy should be about learning to apply reading, writing and speaking skills and strategies in a range of different situations and should be about far more than form-filling, writing job applications and using functional English.

In England and Wales, the National Literacy Strategy was introduced by a government intent on pushing up standards and developing a more literate young workforce that would be equipped for entering 'a fulfilling adult life' (DfEE, 1998: 1). The Strategy's *Framework for Teaching English in Years 7, 8 and 9* (DfEE, 2001) was introduced to all schools, midway through a pilot project and before its evaluation was complete (Furlong et al., 2001). Although a non-statutory document, the 'policing of Key Stage Three teaching' (Fleming and Stevens, 2004: 19) through Ofsted and Strategy team consultants ensured its widespread adoption in schools. Undoubtedly, it had the most impact on English teaching. However, the Strategy also had a strong cross-curricular focus. Ensuring students become literate members of society is not just the remit of the English department: all teaching staff from every subject area have a responsibility to teach students to use language accurately and effectively to express themselves, as the rationale for the *Framework for Teaching English* states:

> Teachers have a genuine stake in strong language skills because language enables thought. Language goes beyond just 'writing up' what is learnt and 'looking up' information in a text; it is in acts of reading and writing that meanings are forged, refined and fixed. Finding the right words, giving shape to an idea, articulating what is meant: this is where language is synonymous with learning. (DfEE, 2001: 15)

A member of staff will have responsibility for co-ordinating literacy policy and practice across the school. In terms of your responsibilities, it will be important to ensure that:

1   you model accurate and appropriate use of written and spoken Standard English in your instructions, questioning, management of discussion, writing on the whiteboard, assessment feedback, teaching resources, displays, planning documents, reporting to parents and carers and so on
2   your students are taught to use reading strategies to help them locate information, follow arguments and synthesize or summarize ideas
3   your students are taught to organize their writing coherently and to use correct spelling and punctuation and follow grammatical conventions
4   you give students opportunities to share and try out their initial ideas orally and to experiment with different forms of presentation which require little or no writing (such as drama activities involving role-plays, tableaux and still pictures or storyboards, posters, diagrams, collages, debates and PowerPoint presentations)
5   you enable students to learn to use and spell correctly the technical and specialist vocabulary, expressions and other language structures associated with your particular subject(s)

Point 4 is particularly important as teachers can tend to ascertain their students' understanding via written responses. This emphasis on writing can not only devalue skills development in other methods of communication but also make it difficult for those English as an additional language learners (who have newly arrived in the country or have little English) to participate or demonstrate their understanding. The need to use more 'talk for learning' is also supported by the findings of Bercow (2008) and I Can (Hartshorne, 2006) mentioned above.

The following sections on reading, writing and spelling provide further specific details about these key processes.

Reading

Whatever your subject area, you will need to enable your students to read and engage with written and visual material when not all of those in your classes will be confident readers. It is important that you develop an understanding of the challenges students face when they read different types of texts such as reports, calculations, graphs, surveys, poems, instructions, scripts, historical artefacts and *multi-modal texts* (that is, texts that use more than one mode of communication such as films, gaming texts and web pages). You also need to be aware of the variety of strategies which readers can use so that you can support your own students' reading and learning.

The main types of reading are:

- continuous reading
- close reading (with attention to details and/or aspects of style)
- skimming
- scanning
- reading backwards and forwards (for example, to check for clues or evidence)

Through the work of Wray and Lewis (1997) on the *Nuffield Extending Literacy Project* (EXEL) the EXIT Extending Interactions with Texts model was developed (Lewis and Wray, 2000). This model is said to have had a major influence on aspects of the *Framework for English in Years 7, 8 and 9*, especially that concerned with writing non-fiction and *Literacy across the Curriculum* (Harrison, 2002). Lewis and Wray (2000: 17) identified ten elements of the complex process that occurs during the reading of information texts:

elicitation of previous knowledge
establishing purposes
locating information
adopting an appropriate strategy
interacting with text
monitoring understanding
making a record
evaluating information
assisting memory
communicating information

A number of strategies for reading, writing or 'interacting with texts' (ibid.) link closely with the above ten reading processes. The most well-known and widely used of these are DARTs (Directed Activities Related to Texts) (see also Chapter 2). Lunzer and Gardner's development of DARTs stemmed from research which uncovered the limited interactions that took place during reading in school either between a reader and a text or between groups of readers in the classroom (Lunzer and Gardner, 1984). Consequently, DARTs are activities that create opportunities for shared exploration of texts, thus providing feedback which is especially needed by weaker readers if they are to develop their textual comprehension. Ultimately, the interaction and discussion which DARTs stimulate about a text or an issue should be of primary importance rather than the dogged pursuit of correct answers. DARTs include the following:

Reconstructive activities

Examples include:

- prediction (of next lines, chapters, events, endings)
- cloze (a type of prediction where words, phrases, line endings or rhymes are blanked out and readers use contextual clues to 'make' the text)
- sequencing (of lines, sentences, paragraphs, stanzas, images, and so on)

Processing activities

Examples are:

- highlighting, underlining or text marking
- labelling
- card sorting and statement games
- drawing **spider diagrams**, mind maps or graphs
- generating questions about a text

Re-creative activities

These include:

- storyboarding
- rewriting the text in a different genre or from a different point of view

DARTs are very prevalent in the teaching of English, humanities and science subjects and are also used to promote the development of thinking skills across the curriculum. Like any activity they need to be used as and where appropriate. Over-use of any one teaching strategy will limit its effectiveness.

Activity 3.3   Embedding and supporting reading activities in your planning and teaching

This activity involves paired work with another teacher.

(a) Take stock of the range of reading material which students will be required to engage with in your subject area and the purposes of this reading (refer to the list of text types in the first paragraph of this section). What particular challenges do you think each text type could present them with? In consultation with another beginning teacher or your mentor try to decide on what might be the most suitable activities you could use to make each of these different text types accessible to your students.

(b) Take three short pieces of a text type on a related theme which are commonly used in your subject area with a particular year group. Submit them to a readability test such as SMOG (simplified measure of gobbledegook) available at www.niace.org.uk/current-work/readability.

What issues does this test raise for you about the suitability of the texts you have chosen and of the readability test itself?

(c) In your lesson observations look carefully at the different reading activities (such as DARTs) used with each teaching group. Which appear to be the most effective in engaging students and developing their understanding? Are any activities over-used or under-used? Make sure you follow up your reflections with your mentor and aim to try out some of the activities with your own classes.

Writing

As a beginning teacher you may well be someone who has previously been successful at writing. Therefore, you might find it hard to understand that some students will find writing to be a laborious and stressful activity. It is essential that you do not underestimate the skills needed for what might seem to be simple tasks such as jotting down homework information or making notes when watching a film clip or summarizing key points heard in a talk you have listened to. If students are to make progress with their writing you will need to ensure you build their confidence by:

- modelling and demonstrating the forms and styles of writing you wish them to create
- ensuring students understand the intended audience and purpose(s) for their writing

- providing opportunities to rehearse ideas orally and/or make rough drafts where appropriate
- allowing alternative forms of presentation (for example, storyboard, poster, diagram, PowerPoint, role-play) which may have a limited writing requirement
- giving clear instructions about your expectations (in terms of length, structure, layout, headings, spelling, and so on) and the criteria you will use to assess the written work
- thinking carefully and seeking advice about how you will assess the writing (for example, what type of corrections, whether you will grade the work, how you will provide feedback to inform future written work)
- not using writing tasks as a means of control in your classroom

One strategy which you might use to *scaffold* their writing is the *writing frame* (see Chapter 2). Originally advocated for use by primary school children as a way to initiate the writing of whole texts or to enable students to make links between sections of a text, writing frames are now widely used across many subject areas across all ages. Forests of worksheets have sprung up as a result. The frames are intended to support learners' interactions with texts and provide an integrated approach to their development of reading, writing, speaking and listening, and social skills. Writing frames can be invaluable for less confident communicators in that they give them a structure for their ideas which can be withdrawn as the writer becomes more confident. The structure might include:

- sentence stems for completion (that is, 'I agree that …', 'In my view …', 'In contrast, you could say …')
- sentence shells with blanked out phrases (that is, 'The verbs … and … used in the line show the writer's …' or 'When the … mixes with … solution, a … reaction occurs')
- paragraph openings
- paragraph endings
- word banks (that is, words connected with fire to support descriptive writing: flame, alight, fiery, burst, smoulder, smoke, tinder, rage, billow, crackle, flicker, spark, blaze, scorch, incinerate, sweltering, ignite, molten, flare, draw, burn, kindle, fume, incandescent, conflagration, wildfire)

However, unless writing frames are used with care, they can become straitjackets which reduce both the level of challenge offered by a text and the opportunities for high-level individual responses to it. Furthermore, students could spend whole days using one writing frame after another in different subject areas. It will therefore be important for you to investigate the different writing strategies used in your placement school to ensure that you use a variety of approaches to engage learners.

Activity 3.4   Literacy

An individual activity.

(a) Look again at points 1–5 on page 83 concerning your responsibilities for literacy within your own teaching. What challenges do they present for you as a beginning teacher? Think honestly about your own spoken communication skills and the accuracy of your written expression. Can you identify aspects of your literacy skills that might need attention before you model them with a class? Make a list and share these with your mentor or an English teacher or your course tutor. Identify the strategies or resources you might need to adopt to build your own confidence.

(b) Carry out a personal check on your own spelling and investigate strategies for learning words which you find difficult to spell. These include look–cover–say–write–check, rhymes, words within words and mnemonics (see Chapter 2). You could ask a beginning English teacher to help you get started with these strategies.

(c) Develop a glossary of words and phrases you would want students aged 11–19 to use confidently in your subject.

(d) Find out about the cross-curricular policy and strategies used in your placement schools to support spelling and vocabulary building by talking with your school's literacy co-ordinator.

Numeracy and mathematics

Numeracy skills are essential for adult life. Those learners who leave school without them have been shown to place themselves at a serious disadvantage:

> Research shows that problems with basic skills have a continuing adverse effect on people's lives and that problems with numeracy lead to the greatest disadvantages for the individual in the labour market and in terms of general social exclusion. Individuals with limited basic mathematical skills are less likely to be employed, and if they are employed are less likely to have been promoted or to have received further training. (Smith, 2004: 12)

As with literacy and ICT, there is an expectation that teachers are numerate and able to use their skills effectively in the classroom. The term *numeracy* is sometimes used interchangeably with mathematics. It is concerned primarily with number and the way numbers operate. A numerate person is someone who is able to solve numerical problems such as those involving money or measurement. They will also be familiar with how numerical information can be stored, counted and presented. However, numeracy is but one element of the much broader subject of Mathematics, as is demonstrated below in the Key Stage 3 **programme of study**:

> Mathematical thinking is important for all members of a modern society as a habit of mind, for its use in the workplace, business and finance, and for both personal and public decision-making. Mathematics is fundamental to national prosperity in providing tools, for understanding of science, engineering and technology, and for participation in the knowledge economy. The language of mathematics is international. The subject transcends cultural boundaries and its importance is universally recognized.
>
> Mathematics equips pupils with uniquely powerful ways to describe, analyse and change the world. Pupils who are functional in mathematics and financially capable are able to think independently in applied and abstract ways, to reason, solve problems and assess risk.
>
> Mathematics is a creative discipline. It can stimulate moments of pleasure and wonder for all pupils when they solve a problem for the first time, discover amore elegant solution, or notice hidden connections. (QCA, 2007a)

The Mathematics curriculum therefore aims to develop learners who are not only numerate but who are creative, have enquiring minds and are able to solve problems.

National policy in England and Wales has enforced the place of numeracy as a key skill within the curriculum across the 5–19 age range both within the Primary Framework for Mathematics (revised 2006 version) and the Key Stage 3 Strategy for Mathematics. Some critics have previously questioned whether the Strategy has a research basis (Brown et al., 1998; Costello, 2000) and the extent to which daily mathematics lessons have had an impact on learners' confidence and competence (Kyriacou and Goulding, 2004). Associated developments in assessment and examinations are intended to support the development of aspects of numeracy for all learners through, for example, functional skills testing at Key Stage 3 and assessment of **key skills**.

Many teachers have questions concerning the place and provision for numeracy within the curriculum. The following activities should help you to explore some of these.

Activity 3.5 Numeracy and mathematics

An individual activity.

(a) What are the personal pleasures and challenges for you of numeracy and, more broadly, of mathematics? Reflect on your own mathematics education as well as your current numeracy skills. Build up a list of your strengths and areas for development. What do you need to do in order to contribute fully to numeracy within your taught programmes in school?

(Continued)

(Continued)

(b) Select one of the following topics and investigate it either on your own or with another trainee from your subject area.

    (i) What is the range of mathematical skills and mathematical language required in your subject area? Does there appear to be progression in these mathematical demands? To what extent do these demands correlate with programmes of study in Mathematics?

    (ii) In your placement school is there a whole-school policy for developing numeracy? If so, does the policy involve a numeracy co-ordinator? What is this person's remit? Does the policy refer to use of calculators across the curriculum? How, and how effectively, in your view is the policy being implemented in practice? To what extent is the potential for developing the use and application of mathematical skills in other subjects recognized, realized and actively supported by the Mathematics department

    (iii) What support does the special needs department in your placement school provide for students in coping with numeracy across the curriculum? How are mathematical weaknesses – knowledge gaps, errors or misunderstandings – managed across the curriculum as they arise in different subjects?

Information communications technology and e-learning

All beginning teachers are required to have a working knowledge of information and communications technology (ICT) terminology, practical skills and a range of applications suitable to their subjects, as well as to take opportunities to use ICT with their own students when and where appropriate in different learning situations.

Kirschner and Paas define e-learning as: 'learning (and thus the creation of learning and learning arrangements) where the Internet plays an important role in the delivery, support, administration and assessment of learning' (2001: 350). This type of learning can take a number of forms, including the use of the Internet for research purposes or to find usable data. In whatever way it is used, the teacher needs to consider how the learning of the students will be structured. Will students be allowed to find websites by themselves (which could possibly lead to expenditure of a large amount of time to locate and utilize only small amounts of data)? Or will students be given a list of websites to visit? In addition, as the Internet has no medium for checking the truth of 'facts', how will the information retrieved be assessed for its validity? An obvious example is that of **Wikipedia**, where anyone can add information, possibly resulting in incorrect materials. (For more about **wikis** refer to Chapter 4.)

Opportunities for use of ICT and e-learning are increasingly embedded within subject schemes of work and whole-school policies. Indeed, all classrooms can be viewed as multi-modal information and communication spaces: you might want to explore the best use of interactive displays, working wall, and other 2D media for your own classroom, and then consider the digital and computer-mediated resources available in many classrooms, such as interactive whiteboards and visualizers. When used with care, ICT resources of all kinds can aid the development of students' speaking and listening and personal skills and enable them to work in pairs or small groups with considerable independence. Wireless devices such as wireless keyboards and mice can release teachers from the front of the classroom and facilitate greater student participation (Dymoke, 2005). Videoconferencing can give students access to a wider world, not only geographically but also to a world of experts and experiences that would be difficult to replicate in the classroom (Lawson and Comber, 2010; Lawson et al., 2010). Interactive whiteboards (IWBs), which are now a common feature in many classrooms, can also aid engagement in learning (if all students in a group are encouraged to use the IWBs' tools) and enable greater access to web-based resources. However researchers are still divided on their impact on learning (for example Glover and Miller, 2001). For case studies and teachers' views on IWBs refer to www.virtuallearning.org. uk/?s=iwb. Caution is needed to ensure that IWBs do not simply become an expensive twenty-first-century version of the blackboard and chalk. As a beginning teacher, you will need to observe the use of IWBs to gauge how they can be most effectively employed. Any plans that you devise for using an IWB in your own teaching should ensure that the IWB use is fully integrated into the teaching and learning, rather than being an add-on. You should always have a back-up plan too – in case you experience technical problems.

New technologies also offer the potential to develop virtual learning environments (VLEs) and communities. Discussion boards within VLEs or carefully monitored chat rooms can be very powerful tools for enabling previously separate groups (either within or across different types of **learning communities**) to think collaboratively and creatively and to experiment with new directions for teaching and learning (Leach, 2001). Lewis and Allan (2004) identify a number of reasons for the establishment of virtual learning communities within an organizational structure. They translate to a classroom environment as including:

- a response to an identified need for student development
- encouraging integrated responses to complex issues/questions
- enabling students to overcome geographical boundaries in time and space
- supporting continuous development
- bringing students together to share good practice
- providing new approaches to learning
- supporting learning programmes
- achieving project outputs

As a result of these different aims, they identify three types of community: simple, managed and complex.

Simple virtual learning communities

These often come together spontaneously due to a shared interest. There might be a small core active group with a closed or open nature with respect to membership. Alternatively, a large initial membership may exist dependent on the dynamic of the situation. These communities can be exemplified by discussion boards on VLEs such as Blackboard.

Managed virtual learning communities

In a managed virtual learning community, there is more *formal* support from an organization than in a simple VLE (through a moderator or facilitator) and there is a flow of knowledge and skills between the community and the wider organization. For example, in a classroom context this might include a teacher involving other colleagues in responding to specific questions from students, or shared provision of resources/ support from staff members.

Complex virtual learning communities

These are communities which exist across a region, or across a complex organization. In the case of a school, this might be the community extending between schools, or a community within a school and across the whole curriculum. Hence, this might include such opportunities as collaborative projects, or student participation with students from other places.

Within a school context, the complexity of any virtual learning community will be determined, and perhaps limited, by the nature of the need(s), available technology and technical abilities of the staff involved. However, the development of free VLEs such as Mamba and Moodle (which work in similar ways to Blackboard) make such developments more realizable for school-based frameworks. Where such VLEs are not available, common software packages such as presentational, word processing, spreadsheet and desktop publishing packages still offer a huge degree of flexibility and much potential in developing the ICT strand of learning.

Wherever they are trained, all beginning teachers need to develop both confidence and competence in ICT in order to know when its use will enhance or contribute in a distinctive way to the learning experience being planned. Think about the learning objectives and outcomes you will want to achieve and how the '**affordances**' (Laurillard et al., 1998: 1) or potential benefits of the software or device(s) you are using will help you to achieve those objectives within the context in which you are working. It is also important to remember that affordances are not open (Somekh, 2004) since they can be constrained by other factors such as school timetables, rooms, resource allocations and previous ICT experiences of students or the other staff you are working with. Therefore, if the ICT use is simply an add-on rather than integral element of your lesson plan, then think again. Information and communications technology developments need to add value to what can already be achieved through use of previously established approaches (Hennessey et al., 2003). Allow yourself plenty of time for careful planning to ensure judicious and effective use of the available ICT resources. You can develop your thinking further about planning for ICT use in Chapter 4.

You will also find that many schools use ICT systems for administrative and data collection purposes such as registration, record-keeping, report-writing, student assessment and progress profiling. You should gain hands-on experience of some of these during your placements. You will learn more about using ICT for assessment purposes in Chapter 5.

The range and quality of software applications, learning platforms, handheld devices and other hardware continues to grow. The main computer hardware and software applications of ICT that you should aim to be familiar with are listed below but the level of competency required will depend on the needs of your specific subject:

- word processing and desktop publishing
- communications (Internet, email, VLEs, web authoring, social software like Facebook, Flickr, Twitter and YouTube)
- mind-mapping programs
- graphics and animation packages
- information systems (databases, CD-Rom, DVD)
- spreadsheets for processing numerical data
- data-logging for scientific measurement
- control technology (computers controlling machines)
- presentation software and hardware (such as PowerPoint and digital projectors)
- videoconferencing and web cams
- digital photography and film editing packages
- handheld and wireless devices including interactive voting systems, wireless mice, iPads and other tablets, personal digital assistants (PDAs), iPods and MP3 players
- interactive whiteboards
- sharing and collaborating on documents through open access sources such as Google docs

The variety of applications and software can seem challenging. To get started in the classroom it is best to concentrate on a small number of uses at first and gain confidence in them. Above all, you need to know how well the ICT serves the needs of students and enables them to engage and make progress with their learning. You may well find that many students are much more computer literate and confident than you are. Try not to be daunted by this but use it to your advantage and enable them to take the initiative as well as to support others in the classroom. There are many exciting examples of ICT using students' own ICT equipment such as mobile phones on the JISC (Joint Information Systems Committee) website but you will need to ensure you work within your school's ICT policies at all times, or request special permission from the head if you want to try something outside its remit (www.elearning.ac.uk/innoprac/learner/index.html).

You should be able to develop your ICT skills further in at least some of the following ways:

1 by the research, preparation and presentation of your assignments, class resources, lesson plans and other teaching materials
2 by exploring potential applications in your classroom teaching and developing awareness of appropriate use
3 by using your training institution's virtual learning environment and/or your school's intranet to communicate with other student teachers, your tutor and/or your school mentor, to share resources and to explore issues related to your own developing practice

Activity 3.6   ICT Skills

An individual/group activity (parts (a) and (c)); individual (part (b) and part (d) – individual with mentor support).

(a) Identifying and refining your ICT skills

(i) Refer to the list of ICT hardware and software applications listed on page 93. What are your current levels of familiarity and competence with each of these?

(ii) Check what ICT resources (including human resources) are available in your training institution and in your placement schools.

(iii) Find out from your tutor what level of competence you will be expected to have attained in order to achieve QTS or to improve your skills further (if you are already at QTS level) in both use of ICT in your classroom teaching and in other professional aspects of your work. Set yourself clearly defined and realistic half-termly or termly targets and log your progress with these.

(iv) Refer to points 1–3 of the guidance on ICT skills development above. Discuss with other beginning teachers in your own subject area how you can support each other in developing your skills. Agree a programme and put it in place.

(b) Identifying your students' ICT skills. Find out about the existing and required skills of the students you will be teaching. What is their existing level of competence? How does it compare with yours? What are the minimum ICT requirements in your main teaching subject for students? How is ICT embedded within the curriculum? What are ICT policy and provision like in your placement school/college in terms of student access and teacher expertise/use?

(c) Arrange to observe and evaluate one or two lessons taught by other experienced teachers in your subject area where ICT is in use. These may involve whole classes but not necessarily so. There are several issues which you need to look out for: the skills needed by students, teacher and support staff; the management of the equipment and resources; the context in which tasks are set. In evaluating the lessons focus on the learning outcomes expected from the activities. Does the use of ICT offer affordances to the intended learning or could the outcomes have been achieved more effectively through simpler, more conventional methods? What do the activities contribute to the development of students' ICT capability?

(d) Teaching a lesson with ICT. Using ICT in the classroom may seem a daunting prospect at first but you should aim to become confident in using ICT wherever it is appropriate in your teaching. Ensure you prepare and teach at least one lesson (and preferably a sequence of lessons) in which teacher and student use of ICT is fully integrated into the learning.

With your mentor's support:

- Draw on your observation experiences and ensure that you have planned the lesson(s) carefully. Make sure you have a clear idea about what you want your students to achieve and how ICT will help them to learn.
- Book equipment/room access well in advance and give yourself plenty of time to practise using equipment and software while planning.
- Ask your mentor to observe your lesson and make sure you reflect on this observation and your own lesson evaluation with this person so that you can identify further developments needed.

Inclusive education

The final sections of the chapter will consider what is meant by inclusive education and pedagogy, and introduce some aspects of special education needs and disability (SEND) issues. How different groups of students are managed will be considered, including pupils designated as 'gifted and talented' and having EAL. It is salutary to remember that any student can be placed in a number of categories, and that all children may have a special educational need at some point in their academic lives. Therefore this section will also consider personalized learning. The key overarching policy that aims to ensure all children are able to achieve success in schooling is the *Every Child Matters* initiative launched by the Children Act 2004. Whilst certain fine detail of this is currently under review, schools across the UK are still operating in the spirit of this legislation.

Every Child Matters

The *Every Child Matters* (*ECM*) policy initiative came into force in England with the passing of the Children Act 2004 and, following subsequent related legislation, was fully implemented by 2010. It stipulates an integrated multi-agency approach to supporting the well-being of children and young people from birth to age 19. This involves all those organizations which are responsible for providing services for children (including health, education, police and voluntary groups) in working together to protect, nurture and enable young people to achieve their full potential. It was perceived that this collaborative approach represents a challenge to all concerned, including teachers who now need to look beyond their narrower or more traditional roles and learn to work together for the good of the community (Brindle, 2006). However, we have seen that more than 99 per cent of UK schools now have some form of extended services so perhaps this fear has been misplaced. The intention of *ECM* is that children and young people will also have a greater voice in commenting on issues which will affect them both individually and collectively. Every child, whatever their background or personal circumstances, should have the support they need to:

- be healthy
- stay safe
- enjoy and achieve
- make a positive contribution
- achieve economic well-being

These five *outcomes*, as they have been called, permeate all aspects of current education policy, including curriculum developments. For discussion of the implications of the ECM agenda, and video clips which show how it has been implemented in two different schools, you can refer to www.teachersmedia.co.uk/search?q=every+child+matters.

In other countries in the UK similar legislation to *ECM* exists to support an integrated approach. For example, in Scotland, *Getting It Right for Every Child* (*GIRFEC*), which came into force in 2005 has paved the way for implementation of new Children's Services legislation. For further information go to www.scotland.gov.uk/Topics/People/Young-People/childrensservices/girfec.

Social exclusion to integration to inclusion

Prior to the Children Act 2004, much attention was given to avoiding social exclusion; however, with ECM this has been reframed and widened to a discourse about *inclusion*, which encompasses children from 0–19 and all the stakeholders involved in their care. During the 1990s and into the twenty-first century how and where young people with SEN or disabilities were educated became increasingly politicized and there were strong moves towards full integration into mainstream education for all. However, this did not always mean that the mainstream school was adapted to suit the needs of the SEND pupils, and in some cases led to special units that just happened to be housed within mainstream schools where the pupils rarely mixed. So the debate has moved on to inclusion, which means that SEND pupils must be fully accepted into mainstream settings and their needs provided for so that they can access anything on offer within the school. Again provision for young people with SEND is under review, but inclusion is still likely to be the preferred route. So what does this mean in practice?

Inclusion

Inclusion of children with special educational needs and disabilities (SEND) is the priority for twenty-first-century schooling and is underpinned by the ECM legislation outlined above. The policies and practices of an inclusive school involve everyone and ensure that all are involved and valued. The emphasis on an inclusive approach to learning has replaced a previous focus on integration and is about *acceptance* and *supporting all learners* to achieve their maximum potential within a context where they are equally valued and their individual rights and freedoms are respected. The term *learners* includes those learners:

- at all levels of attainment
- of all ages
- of whichever gender, culture or social group
- from ethnic minority groups
- with disabilities, sensory impairments or ill health
- with Speech, Language and Communication Needs (SLCN) or literacy difficulties

Schools have a responsibility to provide a broad and balanced curriculum for all learners which caters for the specific needs of individuals and groups of students. They are also encouraged to provide other curricular opportunities outside the National Curriculum to meet individual needs. These might include speech, language or physical therapy. Teachers are able to modify, as necessary, the National Curriculum programmes of study to ensure that all students are engaged in relevant and appropriately challenging work.

The Qualifications and Curriculum Development Authority (QCDA) sets out three essential principles for developing a more inclusive curriculum:

1 setting suitable learning challenges
2 responding to students' diverse learning needs
3 overcoming potential barriers to learning and assessment for individuals and groups of students

If these principles are applied then the need for **dis-application** of aspects of the National Curriculum should theoretically be minimized.

To gain a better understanding of how to develop inclusive practice download Inclusive teaching and learning for pupils with special educational needs (SEN) and/or disabilities training toolkit available from the TDA (Teacher Development Agency – now called Teaching Agency (TA)) website (www.tda.gov.uk/teacher/developing-career/sen-and-disability/sen-training-resources/nqt-itt-resources/~/media/resources/teacher/sen/itt/e5_itt_pillars.pdf). It was created as a result of work by researchers at the Institute of Education who have developed an 'Eight Pillars of Inclusion' approach:

- *inclusive learning environment* – sound and light issues, seating, resources, displays, low arousal areas, health and safety
- *multi-sensory approaches*, including ICT – when teaching, for pupil recording and to promote security and organization
- *working with additional adults* – consulting pupils about support, planning support, evaluating support
- *managing peer relationships* – grouping pupils, managing group work and discussion, developing responsibility
- *adult /pupil communication and language* – teachers' and pupils' communication, pupil–teacher interaction
- *formative assessment/assessment for learning* – understanding the aims of the lesson, focusing on how pupils learn, giving feedback, understanding assessment criteria, reviewing progress and helping pupils to improve, gathering assessment evidence
- *motivation* – understanding the structure of the lesson, relevant and motivating tasks, reward systems
- *memory/consolidation* – recapping, reducing reliance on memory, consolidating learning, independent study/homework

(For further information, read Florian and Black-Hawkins (2011) or look at the Exeter University site http://education.exeter.ac.uk/projects.php?id=485.)

Learning difficulties and the special educational needs code of practice

Whilst provision for pupils with SEND is currently being considered by the Select Committee, the *Special Educational Needs Code of Practice* (DfES, 2001), which came into effect in January 2002, is still the guidance document followed by schools. It provides guidance on policies and procedures enabling learners with special educational needs and disabilities (SEND) to reach their full potential, be included fully in their school communities and make a successful transition into adult life. It stipulates that all mainstream secondary schools will admit students who have already been identified as having SEND while at primary school as well as those in Year 7 who may have as yet unidentified special educational needs. In addition, they should recognize that children's needs span a continuum and may also change over time. The result of this is that the transition to a new school might present particular challenges for students with SEND. The provision for students with SEND is the responsibility of the whole school. The Department for Education and Skills (DfES) code clearly states: 'All teachers are teachers of pupils with special educational needs' (2001: 59). If you would like to refer to the code, it can be downloaded at www.education.gov.uk/publications/standard/publicationDetail/Page1/DfES%200581%202001. It is lengthy so you could refer to Chapters 1 and 6 in that document to begin with. These pages will provide you with further background about principles and processes.

Children are deemed to have special educational needs if they have a *learning difficulty* which requires *special educational provision* to be made for them. The DfES code defines children as having *a learning difficulty* if they:

(a) have a significantly greater difficulty in learning than the majority of children of the same age
(b) have a disability which prevents or hinders them from making use of educational facilities of a kind generally provided for children of the same age in schools within the area of the local education authority
(c) are under compulsory school age and fall within the definition at (a) or (b) above or would so do if special educational provision was not made for them

Children must not be regarded as having a learning difficulty solely because the language or form of language of their home is different from the language in which they will be taught.

Special educational provision means:

(a) for children of two or over, educational provision which is additional to, or otherwise different from, the educational provision made generally for children of their age in schools maintained by the LA (local authority), other than special schools, in the area
(b) for children under two, educational provision of any kind (DfES 2001: 6, 1.3)

The **Special Educational Needs Co-ordinator (SENCO)** in each school or college, together with the head teacher and other staff, have particular responsibilities for the way the code is operated in the school. For information about the key responsibilities of the SENCO refer to page 65, section 6.5, in the DfES code. Most schools have a small special educational needs or learning support department whose staff support students both in withdrawal groups or in situ alongside the subject teacher in their classroom. Also, as a result of work force remodelling many schools offer additional types of support both in the classroom and beyond.

You will observe and work with some students with special educational needs who have been **statemented**. This means that an assessment of their learning difficulties will have been carried out by the local authority and a statement of their learning difficulty will have been produced. Not all students who are assessed will be given statements; some are referred to as *School Action* or *School Action Plus,* which will mean they have some additional in-class and other support. The code requires that those students with statements, School Action or Action Plus should have short-term targets set. The targets and strategies for achieving these targets are usually arrived at after discussions with the student concerned, parents/carers and teaching/support staff. The agreed strategies are then set out in an **Individual Education Plan (IEP).** The IEP only records provision which is additional to or different from the school's normal differentiated curriculum provision. Each student's IEP is reviewed annually and new targets set. There are also special arrangements for review at key transition stages such at the end of Year 6 and Year 9. If you are given any IEPs to read or are asked to participate in review processes, you should be aware that IEPs are confidential documents and you must handle them with great professional care. The Green Paper *Support and Aspiration: A New Approach to Special Educational Needs and Disability* (DfE, 2011c) proposes significant changes to provision for SEND pupils from 2014, including a new single assessment process and the creation of 'Education, Health and Care Plans' for all SEND-identified children from birth to 19. It also proposes utilizing a single SEND category rather than the three existing categories to streamline assessment practice. At the time of writing these plans were under consultation.

Activity 3.7   Finding out more about whole-school approaches to Special Educational Needs students

Parts (a) and (d) require you to work closely with a more experienced teacher. For parts (b) and (c) you should work with a small group of beginning teachers in the same school.

(a) Read through Chapters 1 and 6 of the SEN Code of Practice (DfES, 2001). Then ask your mentor or special educational needs co-ordinator (SENCO) to allow you to read the school or college's own guidelines relating to children with special educational needs. Discuss with this person how the school implements and monitors these guidelines. Ask for examples of how this is done.

(b) Working in a small group of beginning teachers, consider a selection of IEPs used in your school or college. Discuss the range of special needs which have been identified and explore how as subject teachers each of you might start to develop some practical strategies to teach these students.

(c) For each IEP select one target from the box headed IEP TARGETS and write down some practical strategies you could use to enable the student to reach their target. For example:

IEP Target: 'Increase self-esteem'

Strategy 1: give appropriate praise when student behaves as agreed

Strategy 2: select student to carry out responsible task

Discuss your ideas with the SENCO or other suitably experienced teacher, reflect on their advice and refine your ideas further as necessary.

(d) Ask your mentor or the SENCO to explain the roles and responsibilities of *others* who support students' learning and to suggest ways in which teachers can effectively manage 'other adults' to improve their students' learning. Make a list of key suggestions to help you to liaise and work effectively with others in this learning team.

Managing learners' different abilities

This section will consider issue relating to how teaching can impact on learners with different learners' ability. Whilst some form of *ability grouping* is common in UK schools, every class is to a degree 'mixed ability' so after considering grouping strategies, we will look at **differentiation**. Then we will consider provision for 'gifted and talented' pupils, EAL pupils and, finally, personalized learning.

Ability grouping

Within every school, learners and learning processes will be organized in slightly different ways. Traditionally these could be determined by: whole-school policy; the specific nature of the school population; student–teacher staffing ratios or even the buildings themselves. In Chapter 4 you will be able to explore the different ways in which teaching spaces and specific groups/ individual learners can be managed, but first we need to consider the different types of ability groupings which are commonly found in schools:

- **Streaming:** the students' assignment to a class is based on an assessment of their overall ability, arrived at through consideration of their prior attainment and/or cognitive test results. Students stay in their **streamed** classes for most of their lessons. In some schools streaming is taken even further in that students wear different uniforms and are taught in completely separate buildings (see the report on Crown Woods College at www.guardian.co.uk/education/2011/jul/25/secondary-school-streaming?INTCMP=SRCH).
- **Banding:** this has similarities with streaming in that students are assigned to broad bands across a year group on the basis of an overall assessment of their ability. They stay in their band for most of their lessons.
- **Setting:** this is when students are grouped according to their ability in a particular subject. They might be in different higher or lower sets for each subject.
- **Mixed-ability grouping:** this occurs when students are placed in groups which reflect the full ability range of that specific year group within the school.
- **Vertical grouping:** becoming more common in pastoral areas of education such as tutor groups. It is not necessarily linked to ability but can enable *More Knowledgeable Others* (Vygotsky, 1978) to engage in **peer teaching** and **coaching**. (For more on vertical grouping refer to Chapter 6.)

Kutnick et al.'s 2006 report *Student Grouping Strategies and Practices at Key Stage 2 and 3* and the journal article 'Secondary school students' preferences for different types of structured grouping practices' by Hallam and Ireson (2006) will both help you to explore the issue of ability grouping further. Kutnick et al.'s research focused on 24 case studies. It underlines how difficult it is to prove whether use of mixed ability or setting leads to higher attainment. The report also raises issues about progression from primary to secondary level. In Hallam and Ireson's paper, 62 per cent of the students they questioned expressed a preference for setting over mixed-ability teaching. The reasons for student preference are interesting to consider.

Activity 3.8   Grouping by ability

Part (a) of this activity can be completed on your own. Part (b) requires paired work, for example, with another beginning teacher.

(a) Think about your own education. Which of the types of groupings outlined in this section have you experienced? How aware were you of the ability range within each of your classes? How did you feel about being assigned to a particular group? What impact do you think the nature of the groups you were in had on your learning?

(b) Read the following statements about grouping and think about them from a teacher's perspective. Discuss your responses with another beginning teacher.

Which do you agree or disagree with? Which are not so clear cut? Why?

1 In streamed classes all students are working at the same level which makes the teaching easier.

2 Mixed-ability classes prepare students better for the real world beyond the classroom.

3 **Setted** groups enable teachers to support students in a more carefully targeted way.

4 Mixed-ability classes enable lower-ability students to make faster progress than if they were in a low-ability group.

5 Streaming means labelling students at an early age which can stigmatize them for life.

6 Banded grouping has no educational value: it is just a device to make school timetabling easier.

7 Setted groups are motivating for learners.

8 Mixed-ability classes are more enjoyable to teach than the other types.

9 Most able students are not stretched sufficiently in mixed-ability groups.

10 Streaming allows for better whole school sharing of information about student progress.

11 Mixed-ability groupings develop students' social skills rather than raise their attainment.

12 Late developers will have the best chance of succeeding if they are placed in a mixed-ability group.

13 Mixed-ability teaching requires considerably more preparation than the other types.

14 Setted groups ensure that a student's capabilities in each subject area can be recognized and encouraged.

15 Very able students can learn to work independently in mixed-ability groupings.

16 Single-sexed groupings are beneficial to both genders.

17 At primary school, students are used to being grouped by ability for literacy, numeracy and some other subjects. If they are to continue to make progress in secondary school then a system of setting must be adopted.

(Continued)

(Continued)

18 Mixed-ability classes are less disruptive than other types.

19 Streaming enforces a competitive streak to learning.

20 Most students' learning occurs autonomously without the direct teacher intervention so it should not matter how students are grouped.

21 All classes are mixed ability.

22 Mixed-ability classes provide teachers with more opportunities to work with
lower-ability students.

23 The choice of grouping arrangements should depend on the subject being
taught as setting is more appropriate for some subject areas and mixed ability
for others.

Critical reading at Master's level

1 We would like you to read:

(a) the executive summary (or the full report if you have time) by Kutnick et al.
(2006) *Pupil Grouping Strategies and Practices at Key Stage 2 and 3*

(b) the journal article 'Secondary school pupils' preferences for different types
of structured grouping practices' (Hallam and Ireson, 2006).

2 Summarize (either as a list of statements or a mind map) what the implications
of the findings presented in the report and the article might be for your own
developing practice.

3 Now read Abraham (2008) 'Pupils' perceptions of setting and beyond – a
response to Hallam and Ireson'.

What issues does Abraham raise about Hallam and Ireson's research? Highlight the
key points.

What can you learn from reading Abraham's critique and his own use of the
data which might inform your own development as a reader and researcher at
Master's level?

Differentiation

The materials you use with all groups of learners will need to be differentiated to suit the learning needs and prior learning of your students and to ensure that all are engaged in activities which challenge them appropriately. Differentiation can be planned for in many different ways, for example as follows:

- By task: different tasks or versions of the same task are provided for different students – some versions/tasks may be *scaffolded* using *a writing frame* whereas other versions may rely on the student to start the task without support.
- By resource: the same task is provided but with a range of easier or more demanding resources.
- By support: some students in the group may work with a support teacher or learning assistant to complete the activity according to need.
- By outcome: the same task is provided but it is open-ended so that different responses can be made by different students.
- By grading: a task is provided with many parts. Some parts are more demanding and not all students will cover these.

You will need to choose the methods which are most appropriate for the individuals in your class. Learning how to *plan* for differentiation and how to introduce differentiated materials or tasks sensitively to students *without drawing undue attention to their differences* are both challenging aspects of your developing practice. As you become increasingly familiar with the students in your classes you will begin to develop your skills in this area. The reflective cycle of lesson planning and evaluation together with lesson observations and conversations with your mentor will all help you to identify specific support needs and appropriate strategies to use. Further guidance on differentiation can be found in Chapter 4.

There are several archived websites which you might want to refer to when exploring the different learning needs of your students and effective strategies to support them.

Multiverse

This website included a comprehensive range of resources that focus on the educational achievement of students from diverse backgrounds. It is archived at: http://webarchive.nationalarchives.gov.uk/20101021152907/http://www.Multiverse.ac.uk/.

Behaviour 4 Learning

This website provided high-quality and relevant resources that focus on the principles of behaviour for learning to improve the management of classroom behaviour, enable achievement and foster the emotional well-being of learners. It is archived at: http://webarchive.nationalarchives.gov.uk/20101021152907/http://www.behaviour4learning.ac.uk.

Gifted and talented learners

There are many definitions of the diverse group of 'gifted and talented' learners you will teach. The term was first used in the **Excellence in Cities (EiC)** initiative with the aim of identifying the 5 to 10 per cent of students within each school who were eligible for a particular teaching programme which would meet their educational needs (QCA, 2007b). This QCA guidance on how to define these students identifies:

- gifted learners as those who have abilities in one or more subjects in the statutory school curriculum other than art and design, music and PE
- talented learners as those who have abilities in art and design, music, PE, or performing arts such as dance and drama

Being gifted and talented is not only about attaining high test scores. It can also include those who might demonstrate leadership qualities, high-level practical skills or creative thinking. Furthermore, the skills of some of the gifted and talented students you teach might not be apparent to you. Some learners are underachievers with learning difficulties, while some may lack motivation or have low self-esteem. Other students could be suffering as a result of low teacher or parental expectations which means they might not be sufficiently challenged or stimulated by their learning. Boredom and frustration in high-ability children can be expressed in disruptive behaviour, with the result that they may be treated as if of low ability. These are just some of the reasons why adopting an inclusive approach to planning for learning is so important. Such reasoning is based on an understanding that the terms *achievement* and *attainment* are not interchangeable, and that care and attention is needed in the way in which teachers attach labels such as *low attainer* or *low ability* to particular students in their care.

There have been many attempts to define the characteristics of gifted and talented learners. The following list extends some earlier lists which were developed as a means of identifying those students of exceptional ability (see, for example, George, 1992). Gifted and talented students are a highly diverse group, but more able learners will show some of the following characteristics. They:

- can think quickly and accurately
- work systematically
- generate creative working solutions
- work flexibly, processing unfamiliar information and applying knowledge, experience and insight to unfamiliar situations
- communicate their thoughts and ideas well
- are determined, diligent and interested in uncovering patterns
- achieve, or show potential, in a wide range of contexts
- might be particularly creative

- show great sensitivity or empathy
- demonstrate particular physical dexterity or skill
- make sound judgements
- could be outstanding leaders or team members
- are fascinated by, or passionate about, a particular subject or aspect of the curriculum
- demonstrate high levels of attainment across a range of subjects within a particular subject, or aspects of work

You need to treat lists like this with caution as they cannot fully describe the nature of individual learners, each of whom may exhibit different characteristics from each other. However, they do provide a starting point for further reflection. There are a number of websites which contain a wealth of information, guidance and resources in relation to working with gifted and talented students, including:

- National Association for Able Children in Education (NACE) website at www.nace.co.uk
- National Association for Gifted Children at www.nagcbritain.org.uk

Activity 3.9   Gifted and talented learners

The first two parts are paired activities, part (a) involving another beginning teacher and part (b) your mentor. Part (c) can be built into your planning, teaching and evaluation processes during school practice.

(a) After reading the section above on gifted and talented students and referring to the suggested website links, discuss the following with another beginning teacher:

  (i) Clarify your views on the use of the term 'gifted and talented' and the definitions provided in the list of characteristics.

  (ii) Indicate whether you have encountered (either in your own education, in your classroom observations or teaching so far) students who may be considered 'gifted and talented'. How were their gifts or talents evident? How were these qualities accommodated and or encouraged within the systems provided by that school or college?

Examples might include: the Fast Thinkers' club; a residential course for Year 9 to consider the demands of Key Stage 4 and courses/choices beyond that stage;

(Continued)

(Continued)

quizzes and competitions such as entering the BA CREST (CREativity in Science and Technology) awards.

(b) Ask your mentor about how the youngest gifted and talented students might be identified and supported early on within your own subject area and across the curriculum. Make a list of the implications that these processes might have for your own approaches to planning and monitoring students' progress.

(c) Plan a lesson that involves you in using one or more differentiated learning strategies for the more able students in your class. Review your lesson using the following questions:

 (i) How did you make judgements about these students' abilities?

 (ii) How did you make judgements about the level of difficulty or challenge of the work?

 (iii) Did you choose to give the more able students more work to do (in terms of quantity) or more difficult work?

 (iv) Did these students appear to enjoy their given work/tasks? How well did they get on? What kinds of interest (or questions) did they reveal to you?

Finally, consider the advantages and disadvantages of each differentiated strategy that is available. Discuss these with your mentor.

English as an additional language (EAL)

It is estimated that approximately 240 languages are now spoken by children in British schools and 11.6 per cent (378,200) of all state-funded secondary school children have a first language known to or believed to be a language other than English (CILT, 2010). The number for whom English is an additional language (EAL) has risen by 50 per cent since 1997 (NALDIC, 2007). Students for whom English is an additional language are those for whom English is not the language usually spoken in their home (their mother tongue). They have diverse needs in terms of support they require to develop their English language learning. Some students may arrive in your classroom already being able to speak two or more languages other than English. They may be refugees or asylum seekers still recovering from the trauma of what they have left behind. They may have moved with their parents to the UK for employment reason or may already be fluent in English and without need of language support. Cummins (1981) makes the important point that EAL students can become conversationally fluent within approximately two years of their initial exposure to English, but they will require five to seven years to catch up with native English speakers in terms of their academic language proficiency. The planning of appropriate and inclusive support strategies for these students must take into account factors such as: their age; the length of time they have been in the UK; their previous educational experiences; and their skills in other languages (DfEE and QCA, 1999).

Some schools make additional provision for EAL learners and, until May 2011, used Ethnic Minority Achievement Grant (EMAG) funding to finance additional specialist teachers and support staff. These might include EAL and EMA teachers or co-ordinators, bilingual teaching assistants (BTAs) and **Higher-Level Teaching Assistants (HLTAs)**. However specialist staffing is usually limited to schools/colleges with significant numbers of bilingual or ethnic minority learners. This ring-fenced funding is now included within school budgets which may lead to fewer specialist staff being available to support teachers and EAL pupils in future. In mainly monolingual areas, specialist staff are likely to be employed by the local authority (LA) rather than a school. They may undertake only advisory visits, short-term placements or offer peripatetic support to schools (Rankine and Thompson, 2007).

In planning and teaching your own lessons, you will need to think carefully about the subject terminology you are using and your own idiomatic use of language. When giving instructions, explaining concepts or asking questions ensure that you express yourself clearly and unambiguously. When students first arrive in your classroom and begin to try to make sense of their new linguistic context, they may appear to be very quiet but this does not mean they are not listening. Their confidence can be boosted at an early stage if they are given opportunities to use their mother tongue and to be involved in some way in speaking and listening activities. Here are some further suggestions for good practice which are just as useful for all other learners too. Think about why each of them might be helpful:

- using pictures, photographs and other visual aids to support written text
- distinguishing between reading and talking
- organizing tasks into groups where collaboration must take place
- using alternative ways of recording information other than writing
- giving students opportunities to talk ideas through before discussing them in front of class
- using mind maps to organize ways of thinking before writing
- allowing students to work in a language other than English
- using bilingual skills as part of the learning process
- organizing reading tasks in pairs where one stronger reader supports a weaker reader
- offering lots of opportunities for students to talk about what they are learning

Refer to the separate subject support booklets entitled *Access and Engagement in …* (followed by the name of the National Curriculum subject name) which are available at www.naldic.org.uk/docs/resources/documents/ks3_en_eal_access_engagement.pdf. These will provide you with a range of practical strategies to support your students' EAL learning. You should also visit the ITT pages of the National Association for Language Development in the Curriculum (NALDIC) website (www.naldic.org.uk/ITTSEAL2/teaching/ealncsubjects.cfm), which includes a bank of portraits of EAL students, annotated reading lists and a wide variety of other materials designed for teachers in the initial stage of their training.

Bilingualism is an asset and research has shown that children who are bilingual can draw on their linguistic abilities in other learning processes. It is every teacher's responsibility to utilize and celebrate the diversity of language and culture within their own classrooms in order to ensure that all students are fully involved in their learning.

Activity 3.10   EAL fact finding

In your placement school or college try to find some answers to the following questions:

- How many different languages are spoken by students in the school?
- Are students given the chance to speak languages other than English at the school? If they are, where does this occur?
- Is written language (other than English) used around the school and, if so, where and why?
- What provision is made for specialist EAL support?
- How many students are there with EAL needs and what is known about their ethnicity?
- How are their English language learning needs identified, monitored and supported?
- How are their levels of literacy in their home languages assessed?
- What sort of cognitive testing is available to assess non-language-based skills (for example, memory, sequencing, and so on) and who does this?
- If your school does not have any EAL students, try to find out what would happen if a new EAL student were to start today. What support or provision is made available for this possibility?

Compare your findings with those of a beginning teacher working in a different location.

Personalized learning

In the twenty-first century there is an increasing emphasis on personalized learning in which curriculum and teaching methods are tailored to meet every individual's needs, interests and aptitudes to ensure they receive equality of opportunity (in terms of support) as they strive to achieve the highest standards possible in their subject-based learning (wherever they are placed on the ability spectrum) and to develop their *personal learning and thinking skills* (PLTS). Within the various ability grouping arrangements already explored, the particular needs of the individual learner must be a priority. It is an admirable aim but is also one which can present significant challenges for teachers. The implications of personalized learning and how this is embedded in assessment for learning are explored in Chapter 3.

A group that is considered to have particular need of personalized learning programmes is the one of 16–19-year-olds described as NEET (Not in Employment, Education or Training). For more information see www.education.gov.uk/16to19/participation/neet/a0064101/16-to-18-year-olds-not-in-education-employment-or-training-neet. This group is thought to be disproportionately involved in criminal and anti-social activities, and also disproportionately to have underachieved in literacy and numeracy or to have SLCN difficulties. One response to avoid vulnerable individuals becoming NEET is Foundation Learning; a basic 'platform' of qualifications to ensure access to employment or further training. More information on this is available by visiting www.education.gov.uk/16to19/qualificationsandlearning/foundationlearning/a0064167/foundation-learning.

Learning in out-of-school contexts

Learning does not just take place within a school building, nor does it end when students leave compulsory schooling behind. E-learning can facilitate learning (including feedback dialogue) in the home and elsewhere. The National Curriculum emphasizes the importance of learning in out-of-school contexts such as fieldwork, theatre and museum visits and employment-related settings, and in taking opportunities for cross-curricular work in these situations (QCA, 2007b). The amount of time devoted to learning outside the classroom could vary significantly, depending on the schools and teacher training institutions in which you are working and their own priorities (Kendall et al., 2006). There is evidence of a decline in education outside the classroom in recent years which could be due to teachers' concerns about health, safety and litigation, issues of subject knowledge, their lack of confidence in teaching outdoors, and curriculum requirements which limit opportunities for learning in out of school contexts (Ofsted, 2004; Rickinson et al., 2004). Although it is not currently compulsory for beginning teachers to teach in out-of-school contexts, you should be able (with support from experienced staff) to plan opportunities for purposeful learning outside of the classroom in a safe environment. You will be able to reflect further on how to plan for such learning in Chapter 4.

Conclusion

In this chapter you have learned about the different ways in which learners can be managed, grouped and supported within inclusive education environments. You have gained insights into the impact of national policies which determine (to a greater or a lesser extent) lesson content, delivery and assessment of learning. You have begun to consider the implications of these contexts and policies for your own developing practice. In the next chapter, our lens zooms in from this wide angle to a much tighter focus on the teaching rooms themselves in order to explore how learning and teaching are managed within these often small but always vital spaces.

Useful websites

Education Outside the Classroom (the Labour government manifesto of 2005) can currently be accessed at www.education.ed.ac.uk/outdoored/research/education_outside_classroom.pdf .

For outdoor classroom resources see also www.field-studies-council.org/resources/.

References

Abraham, J. (2008) 'Pupils' perceptions of setting and beyond – a response to Hallam and Ireson', *British Educational Research Journal*, 34(6): 855–863.

Bercow (2008) *A Review of Services for Children and Young People (0–19) with Speech, Language and Communication Needs (SLCN)*. London: DCSF-00632-2008.

Brindle, D. (2006) 'It's all about results: interview with Mark Friedman', *Society Guardian*. http://society.guardian.co.uk/children/story/0,,1935963,00.html (accessed 2 June 2007).

Brown, M., Askew, M., Baker, D., Denvir, H. and Millett, A. (1998) 'Is the National Numeracy Strategy research based?', *British Journal of Educational Studies*, 46(4): 362–385.

Children Act 2004 (c.31). London: HMSO.

CILT (National Centre for Languages) (2010) *Annual School Census: Language Data Collection*. www.cilt.org.uk/home/research_and_statistics/statistics/languages_in_the_population/annual_school_census.aspx (accessed 15 November 2011).

Costello, J. (2000) 'The National Numeracy Strategy: evidence from the research base of mathematics education', *Mathematics in School*, 29(2): 2–5.

Cummins, J. (1981) 'Age on arrival and immigrant second language learning in Canada: a reassessment', *Applied Linguistics*, 2: 132–149.

Department for Children, Schools and Families (DCFS) (2007a) *Raising the Participation Age in Education and Training to 18: Review of Existing Evidence of the Benefits and Challenges* (November 2007) DCSF-RR012. London: The Stationery Office.

Department for Children, Schools and Families (DCFS) (2007b) *Generic Definition of Functional Skills.* London: The Stationery Office.

Department for Children, Schools and Families and the Qualifications and Curriculum Authority (DCSF and QCA) (2007) *The National Curriculum for England.* London: The Stationery Office.

Department for Education (DfE) (2011a) www.education.gov.uk/schools/leadership/typesofschools/freeschools

Department for Education (DfE) (2011b) www.education.gov.uk/schools/teachingand learning/qualifications/englishbac/a0075975/theenglishbaccalaureate

Department for Education (DfE) (2011c) *Support and Aspiration: A New Approach to Special Educational Needs and Disability – A Consultation* (March 2011) CM 8027. London: The Stationery Office.

Department for Education and Employment (DfEE) (1998) *The National Literacy Strategy: Framework for Teaching.* London: DfEE Publications.

Department for Education and Employment (DfEE) (2001) *Framework for Teaching English in Years 7, 8 and 9.* London: DfEE.

Department for Education and Employment and the Qualifications and Curriculum Authority (DfEE and QCA) (1999) *The National Curriculum for England: English.* London: DfEE and QCA.

Department for Education and Skills (DfES) (2001) *Special Educational Needs Code of Practice.* London: DfES.

Department for Education and Skills (DfES) (2004) *14–19 Curriculum and Qualifications Reform: Final Report of the Working Group on 14–19 Reform.* London: DfES Crown Publication.

Department for Education and Skills (DfES) (2005) *The Schools White Paper: Higher Standards, Better Schools For All* (October 2005) HC 633-1. London: The Stationery Office.

Dymoke, S. (2005) 'Wireless keyboards and mice: could they enhance teaching and learning in the secondary English classroom?', *English in Education*, 39(3): 62–77.

Edexcel (2007) *Functional Skills: Edexcel Thinks.* www.edexcel.org.uk/VirtualContent/103617/2007_5_8_March_Functional_Skills.pdf (accessed 15 March 2007 but no longer available).

Financial Services Skills Council (2008) *Skills Matters* newsletter, 4. www.fssc.org.uk/skillsmatters_issue_4.pdf (accessed 23 June 2011).

Fleming, M. and Stevens, D. (2004) *English Teaching in the Secondary School.* 2nd edition. London: David Fulton. (1st edition 1998.)

Florian, L. and Black-Hawkins, K. (2011) 'Exploring Inclusive Pedagogy', *British Educational Research Journal,* 37(5): 813–828

Furlong, T., Venkatakrishnan, H. and Brown, M. (2001) *Key Stage 3 National Strategy: An Evaluation of the Strategies for Literacy and Mathematics Interim Report.* London: ATL.

George, D. (1992) *The Challenge of the Able Child.* London: David Fulton.

Glover, D. and Miller, D. (2001) 'Running with technology: the pedagogic impact of the large-scale introduction of interactive whiteboards in one secondary school', *Journal of Information Technology for Teacher Education*, 10(3): 257–276.

Hallam, S. and Ireson, J. (2006) 'Secondary school pupils' preferences for different types of structured grouping practices', *British Educational Research Journal*, 32(4): 583–601.

Harrison, C. (2002) *Key Stage 3 English: Roots and Research.* London: DfES.

Hartshorne, M (2006) *The Cost to the Nation of Children's Poor Communication.* London: I Can charity report I CAN TALK 2. www.ican.org.uk/~/media/Ican2/Whats%20the%20Issue/Evidence/2%20The%20Cost%20to%20the%20Nation%20of%20Children%20s%20Poor%20Communication%20pdf.ashx (accessed 15 November 2011).

Hennessey, S., Ruthven, K. and Brindley, S. (2003) 'Teacher perspectives on integrating ICT into subject teaching: commitment, constraints, caution and change', *Journal of Curriculum Studies*, 37(2): 155–192.

Jewell, S. (2007) 'Plan your route to work', *Guardian, 14–19 Reforms*, supplement, 6 March: 2.

Kendall, S., Murfield, J., Dillon, J. and Wilkin, A. (2006) *Education Outside the Classroom: Research to Identify What Training is Offered by Initial Teacher Training Institutions*, National Foundation for Educational Research, Research Report RR802. London: DfES.

Kirschner, P. and Paas, F. (2001) 'Web enhanced higher education: "a tower of Babel"', *Computers in Human Behavior*, 17(4): 347–353.

Kutnick, P., Hodgkinson, S., Sebba, J., Humphreys, S., Galton, M., Steward, S., Blatchford, P. and Baines, E. (2006) *Pupil Grouping Strategies and Practices at Key Stage 2 and 3,* DfES Research Report 796. Brighton: University of Brighton.

Kyriacou, C. and Goulding, M. (2004) 'Have daily mathematics lessons enhanced student confidence and competence?', *Proceedings of the British Society for Research into Learning Mathematics*, 24(2): 57–62.

Laurillard, D., Stratfold, M., Lucklin, R., Plowman, L. and Taylor, J. (1998) 'Affordances for learning in a non-linear narrative medium', OU Knowledge network. http://kn.open.ac.uk/public/document.cfm?docid=942 (accessed 27 July 2011).

Lawson, T., Comber, C., Gage, J. and Cullum-Hanshaw, A. (2010) 'Images of the future for education? Videoconferencing: a literature review', *Technology, Pedagogy and Education*, 19(3): 295–313.

Lawson, T. and Comber, C. (2010) 'Videoconferencing in English schools: one technology, many pedagogies?', *Technology, Pedagogy and Education*, 19(3): 315–326.

Leach, J. (2001) 'Teaching's long revolution: from ivory towers to networked communities of practice', in F. Banks and A. Shelton Mayes (eds) *Early Professional Development for Teachers*. London: David Fulton/Open University. pp. 379–394.

Lewis, D. and Allan, B. (2004) *Virtual Learning Communities*. Maidenhead: Open University Press.

Lewis, M. and Wray, D. (2000) *Literacy in the Secondary School*. London: David Fulton.

Lunzer, E. and Gardner, K. (1984) *Learning from the Written Word*. Edinburgh: Oliver & Boyd.

Mansell, W. and Lee, J. (2005) 'Stillborn A level shake-up mourned', *Times Educational Supplement*, 25 February, p. 1.

National Association for Language Development in the Curriculum (NALDIC) ITT resources. www.naldic.org.uk/ITTSEAL2/teaching/ealncsubjects.cfm (accessed 15 November 2011).

National Association for Language Development in the Curriculum (NALDIC) (2007) *Teaching and Learning*. www.naldic.org.uk/ITTSEAL2/teaching/working.cfm (accessed 27 July 2011).

National Association for the Teaching of English (NATE) (2006) *Statement on Functional English*, 14 April, www.nate.org.uk (accessed 15 March 2007 but no longer available).

Office for Standards in Education (Ofsted) (2004) *Outdoor Education: Aspects of Good Practice*. Document reference number: HMI 2151. London: Ofsted.

Office for Standards in Education (Ofsted) (2011) *Removing Barriers to Literacy*. Document reference number: HMI 090237. London: Ofsted.

Qualifications and Curriculum Authority (QCA) (2007a) *Programme of Study: Mathematics Key Stage 3*. http://webarchive.nationalarchives.gov.uk/20100823130703/http://curriculum.qcda.gov.uk/key-stages-3-and-4/subjects/key-stage-3/mathematics/index.aspx (accessed 27 July 2011).

Qualifications and Curriculum Authority (QCA) (2007b) *Guidance on Teaching the Gifted and Talented*. http://webarchive.nationalarchives.gov.uk/20040105000032/qca.org.uk/qca_2346.aspx (accessed 15 November 2011).

Qualifications and Curriculum Authority (QCA) (2007c) *The New Secondary Curriculum: What Has Changed and Why?* www.tgsonline.co.uk/assets/files/why%20the%20curriculum%20has%20changed.pdf (accessed 15 November 2011).

Rankine, J. and Thompson, A. (2007) *Working with EAL Specialists and Other Support Staff*. Naldic website: www.naldic.org.uk/ITTSEAL2/teaching/working.cfm (accessed 7 July 2011).

Rickinson, M., Dillon, J., Teamey, K., Morris, M., Choi, M., Sanders, D. and Benefield, P. (2004) *A Review of Research on Outdoor Learning*. Shrewsbury: Field Studies Council.

Rose, J (2006) *Independent Review of the Teaching of Early Reading*. DFES-0201-2006 London: The Stationery Office.

Smith, A. (2004) *Making Mathematics Count: The Report of Professor Adrian Smith's Inquiry into Post-14 Mathematics Education*. London: The Stationery Office.

Somekh, B. (2004) 'New technologies in education symposium', *British Educational Research Association Conference,* University of Manchester Institute of Science and Technology, September.

Vygotsky, L.S. (1978) *Mind and Society: The Development of Higher Mental Processes.* Cambridge, MA: Harvard University Press.

Wolf, A. (2011) *Review of Vocational Education – The Wolf Report.* Department for Education. www.education.gov.uk/publications/eOrderingDownload/The%20Wolf%20 Report.pdf (accessed 10 November 2011).

Wray, D. and Lewis, M. (1997) *Extending Literacy: Children Reading and Writing Non-Fiction.* London: Routledge.

CHAPTER 4

CLASSROOM MANAGEMENT

Phil Wood

By the end of this chapter you will have:

- been introduced to the importance of classroom management in developing as a reflective practitioner
- considered the need for both planning and evaluation of classroom practice
- been introduced to the dynamic nature of the classroom environment

Introduction

Classroom management is a central concern of beginning teachers, as they need to ensure that the classroom is a secure and positive place within which learning can take place. Classroom management itself covers many aspects of the day-to-day working of the learning environment. Here, classroom management is seen as a process which starts well before the students reach the classroom itself, involving careful preparation of both teaching and the room, alongside detailed planning. Once the lesson starts, it also involves behaviour management, the management of the physical space by the teacher, and the various pedagogical approaches the teacher intends to use. Perhaps the most central of these is the use of questioning and explanation, together with group work.

All teaching spaces are extremely complex environments requiring many different skills and approaches if they are to work efficiently and in a way which will allow for students to feel both secure and engaged. It should be highlighted here that classroom management is the most commonly cited concern of beginning teachers (McCormack, 1997), and therefore you should not feel that your own concerns in this area are anything but inevitable. It is how you prepare and develop from this starting point which counts.

Preparation

Careful preparation is essential to making early successes in the classroom. You need to anticipate what you believe the potential issues and problems are that you might face. The sooner you begin to confront any initial fears, the sooner you can start to plan in a way that minimizes these issues. One way in which you can begin to anticipate and plan for the classroom is by observing teachers and children. The more you can begin to identify and understand the various elements which make up a dynamic classroom environment, the more you can develop your own ideas and practices. Finally, being fully prepared for the classroom includes having a clear idea of what you yourself want to achieve once in the classroom. This requires the use of lesson planning so that you understand what it is each lesson will attempt to achieve and the medium through which this will be done.

Initial preparation

Before entering the classroom (or any other teaching space) to take a class, there is a need to understand the context of the classroom within the whole-school culture. Schools are complex places (Radford, 2006), and as a consequence they have different approaches and perspectives concerning issues such as expectations of uniform, behaviour, and so on. You need to understand these cultures and the policies which result from them as quickly as possible. Some schools may have a very rigid escalator of sanctions if students are badly behaved. In other schools these sanctions may be far less rigid and allow the individual teacher greater scope to develop their own behaviour strategies. Behaviour management is discussed in more depth later in the chapter, but it must be recognized that consistency is an important factor in behaviour management, and this often stems from the culture and policy of the school.

As well as understanding the 'formal' elements of the school culture and policy, you should begin to understand how classrooms operate as dynamic entities. The most effective way of doing this is through the use of observation (see Wragg, 1994). It is all too common for beginning teachers to feel as if they may be wasting their time when asked to observe lessons, but this is often because they have no focus for doing so. If we attempt to 'watch' a lesson with no particular purpose in mind, then there is too much happening for the experience to be meaningful. It is necessary to consider what elements of the classroom are of interest when carrying out a particular observation. Some ideas for particular foci are given in Table 4.1.

Table 4.1   Examples of observation foci for beginning teachers when observing a classroom

- How do students enter a room, and what are the 'rituals' they go through before starting to learn?
- What are the patterns of movement and body language of the teacher?
- How does the teacher communicate with students in different contexts?
- How does the physical layout of the room affect communication and learning, and how does it relate to the task undertaken by students?
- Where are the students seated and how does this impact on their learning?
- What are the strategies the teacher uses to ensure a positive climate within the classroom?
- How are resources introduced and used?
- What are the types of questions asked in the lesson and how does this impact on the quality of responses given?
- What is the last part of the lesson focused on?
- What rituals exist to ensure an orderly end to the lesson?

If different lessons are used to focus on different elements of the classroom and the people within it (perhaps focusing on one or two questions in each observation) a two-day period of observation becomes quite short and time well spent.

When observing, it is useful for you to have a clear method of recording what has been observed. This can be a series of simple bullet pointed notes, or, in the case of an analysis of the teacher's movements and the students who are asked questions, an annotated plan of the room might be more appropriate. This shows that not only preparation for teaching, but preparation for observation is important. Without a clear purpose for observation and a clear decision on how the information is to be recorded, the experience may not reap the same degree of understanding. As has been outlined in Chapter 1, a final element of observation is the inclusion of a reflective element. If at all possible, it is extremely useful to discuss the outcomes with the class teacher once the observation has been completed, as this may offer insights into the reasoning behind what has been seen, and will develop your understanding further. In your reflections on observations, become used to asking some basic reflective questions such as:

- What have you learnt?
- What observations did you make that were the same/different from those of the class teacher?
- What will you observe next?

Activity 4.1   Observation

Part (a) of this activity can be completed individually and part (b) with another beginning teacher or colleague.

(a) Draw an outline human figure in the middle of a sheet of paper. This is the teacher you are observing. As the lesson proceeds, annotate your diagram with anything that you notice which helps that teacher to teach effectively. You will probably find several things to note about eyes and voice, as well as some about hands, mouth, shoulders, legs and so on. Try to be aware of nonverbal communication or body language, and to look out for signals which convey confidence, self-assuredness, calmness, enthusiasm, and so on – all the things which you will want to emulate in your own physical presence. Be prepared to show the finished product to the teacher you have been observing and discuss your findings. Reflect on the important signals this gives you in considering your own practice in the classroom.

(b) Once you have completed this exercise ask someone to produce the same diagram based on their observation of you.

Lesson planning: a framework for preparing the classroom

The key to good teaching lies in careful preparation and planning of lessons. It is often the case that poor teaching, classroom management and behaviour stem from a lack of explicit planning. As you start to teach, there are a large number of elements which you need to take into account if a lesson is to work. These include the focus of the lesson, the management of the learning as identified in this chapter, alongside considerations of assessment and behaviour management. If such a complex situation as a lesson is to be successfully managed, there needs to be a clear framework for the learning and its management. This framework is most usefully characterized as a lesson plan.

It is tempting for the beginning teacher to see experienced practitioners apparently not making use of written lesson plans, and to assume that the creation of lesson plans is not a necessary task. This is to misjudge the often acute skill that experienced teachers have gained through experience of being in the classroom. These practitioners will carry in their minds patterns of lessons and a clear understanding of the learning they are aiming for, which have been assembled through hard won experience and development of curricula over a long period of time. At the same time, even these teachers will produce lesson plans, particularly for formal observations or for Ofsted inspectors. On these occasions the lesson plans are not merely for personal use, but are for a 'wider professional audience', a situation that you, as a beginning teacher, are in all of the time.

Lessons should not be seen in isolation and are usually grouped to allow students to develop understanding and skills within an area of knowledge. As Figure 4.1 shows, a number of lessons are used to cover the elements of a scheme of work, and a number of schemes of work cover a programme of study.

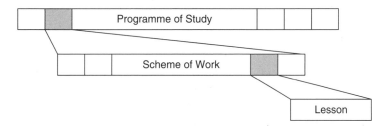

Figure 4.1   The links between lesson plans, schemes of work and a programme of study

A programme of study is an example of a long-term plan. A long-term plan outlines the learning to be covered over a lengthy period of time. In the case of a programme of study, it is a summary of all the work to be covered within a Key Stage. The format in which they are written can vary widely, from a very simple list of the topics to be covered, to a more detailed consideration of the content, skills and concepts to be developed and learned. Whatever the format, the development of long-term plans is central to the process of curriculum development. They determine the shape and nature of the learning which students will participate in.

There are a number of issues which need to be taken into account when developing programmes of study. First, there is the need to ensure that there are clear strands of progression. Students will find their learning more difficult if it does not follow a clear 'route'. The long-term plan will be broken down into a series of medium-term plans or schemes of work. These schemes, and the individual lessons within them, need to follow on from each other. If their focus constantly changes, and they do not relate to each other, the developing experiential basis of the learning embedded within them will be lost.

Second, there is the issue of resources. In some subject areas, there are not enough resources for all students to cover the same area of a programme of study at any one time. This is especially true of English, where there might not be enough books for all the students in a year group to read the same book at the same time. This leads to the need for the elements in a programme of study to still work well together, but at the same time allow for a great enough degree of flexibility for those elements to be completed in a variety of sequences.

There should be a consideration of the links between the elements, or schemes of work, which make up the programme of study. Students can begin to see each scheme of work as a hermetically sealed element of learning if you are not careful to show links between them. However, this is crucial for developing a wider sense of the content and nature of a subject, and in helping students to grapple with the inherent complexity which is contained within all subjects.

Finally, long-term planning should be considered as linked between Key Stages. This means that it is important not only to ensure that there are clear strands of progression within a single Key Stage, but that these strands link across Key Stages. When we begin to consider the types of skills, concepts and content we want students to demonstrate in the 14–19 curriculum, we need to give clear thought as to how we have laid the foundations for these over the course of Key Stage 3; we cannot expect students to use skills sets or have knowledge and understanding based purely on the fact they are of a certain age, these have to have been consciously nurtured at a younger age.

Figure 4.1 strongly suggests that lesson planning should include a conscious element which considers the scheme of work so that the work to be covered is considered in relation to both previous learning and future directions.

One of the first problems with successful planning is to recognize that the process is both difficult and time-consuming, at least at first. However, developing a good ability in lesson planning is essential as poor planning has been linked to poor classroom performance and lower achievement whilst training to be a teacher (Theoharis and Causton-Theoharis, 2011). Therefore you need to have a clear conceptualization of the process of planning. Butt (2006) suggests a series of questions that might be considered when starting to plan lessons:

- What is the scheme of work that the students are following?
- What has been taught and learnt in the previous lesson(s)?
- What do you want the students to learn in the lesson you are planning (and in future lessons)?
- How will your lesson plan facilitate learning?
- What resources will you need?
- What activities will the students undertake?

And post-lesson:

- How will you know what the students have learnt (assessment)?
- How will you know how effective the lesson has been from your perspective as the teacher and the students' perspective as learners (evaluation)?
- What action will you need to take in future lessons to ensure that effective learning is taking place? (Butt, 2006: 8)

These questions demonstrate that the process of lesson planning requires a number of ideas to be taken into account. One common problem with lesson planning at the start of an individual's training is that they see the lesson as an 'event'. This can lead to each lesson being planned in isolation from those which go both before and after it. As a consequence, this can lead to a lack of progressional thinking. It is important to first understand how a suite of lessons will fit together, either as a part of a scheme of work, or the scheme of work in its entirety (see Figure 4.1). This will then allow you to consider the different approaches you wish to take, the different assessment opportunities you want to embed within the learning, and the main concepts and principles you want the students to understand and develop over the period of the lessons. Once this initial consideration has been made, and the broader picture of the lessons to be planned has been understood, it is then possible to develop each lesson in more detail.

Any lesson is centred upon the learning activities which will take place within it. In turn, these are developed from consideration of the learning objectives which the teacher decides will be the focus for the lesson.

Learning objectives are a central element of the planning process as they give the lesson a focus. When shared with students, they give a very clear signal about the nature of the lesson and what you expect your students to know and understand by the end. Teachers should remember that they are developing learning objectives, and not *teaching* objectives. Hence the objectives need to be carefully constructed so as to make the students central to the process. This can be achieved by using some of the following stems:

- know that ... (knowledge and factual information)
- develop/be able to ... (skills: using knowledge, applying techniques, and so on)
- understand how/why ... (understanding: concepts, reasons, effects, principles, processes, and so on)
- develop/be aware of ... (attitudes and values: empathy, caring, sensitivity towards social issues, feelings, moral issues, and so on) (DfES/QCA, 2002: 72)

Weblink: visit the companion website at www.sagepub.co.uk/dymoke for further consideration and reading on learning objectives.

Having decided on the learning objectives, the next task is to develop the structure of the lesson. A simple structure, and that advocated by the DfES National Strategy (2002), is the three-part lesson:

Starter > Main learning activity > Plenary

This structure is intended to allow the teacher to introduce the lesson through some form of short activity which acts as a 'hook', that is, something which gains the interest of the students relating to what is to come. This should lead naturally on to the learning objectives for the lesson, which should clearly state to the students what the focus of the lesson is, what they should know, understand and be able to do by the end of the lesson, and how they will do this. This is then followed by the main activity/activities which should expand on the learning objectives and allow the students to develop their understanding and skills in the area of interest. The lesson finishes with a plenary which should enable the teacher to recap on the objectives and assess how much the students have learned and how well they have developed their understanding and skills. There should also be a clear link to the next lesson(s) in the sequence so that students can retain a clear understanding of their developing learning throughout a scheme of work.

Each of the planned activities should take account of the different needs of the learners in the group. Even where groups have been setted or streamed by ability, there will still be a range of abilities, strengths and weaknesses. Activity design must take account of this through the use of differentiation that focuses on students with special educational needs, those who are gifted and talented as well as all those in between. (See page 127 for further consideration of differentiation.)

The lesson structure described is a simplification, as it is often not the case that only one main activity will occur in a lesson. There might be a number of activities, some or all of which might be punctuated with a short plenary to gauge understanding. The number of activities used will depend on factors such as: the ability range of the group; the particular concepts or subject content being covered; the approaches being taken; the length of the lesson. To add to this complexity, it must also be remembered that, however they have been constituted, any group of students will have a mix of ability. Therefore, conscious use of differentiation (both in the process of planning and the final lesson plan document itself) must clearly indicate how the planned activities will take account of this.

Activity 4.2   Lesson plan formats (1)

Part (a) should be completed in discussion with other teachers and part (b) can be completed individually.

(a) The model of lesson format which is outlined in this section is that proposed by government agencies. However, what evidence is there that this format promotes learning in its most positive way? Discuss with teachers in your school the extent to which they use the three-part lesson, and what they believe the advantages and disadvantages of the format are. In their view, is it always the most appropriate format?

(b) Try to envisage some learning activities which might best fit into the three-part lesson. Why might this be the case, and what format would you substitute instead?

How these ideas are actually written down as a lesson plan are partly the result of subject conventions and personal preferences. A number of different possible templates are provided by the DfES/QCA (2002) as part of the Key Stage 3 National Strategy (*Training Materials for the Foundation Subjects: Module 3. Lesson Planning*) and are a useful starting point for considering useful formats for lesson plans. For an archived link to this site go to: www.secondarymathsite.co.uk/Assessment/ AssessmentforLearning/DfES%20Key%20stage%203%20training%20materials/ Module%203_%20Planning%20lessons.pdf.

In summary, the process of lesson planning can be seen (Figure 4.2) as a fusion of learning objectives, pedagogic approaches (approaches to teaching), learning and teaching strategies, and the contexts for learning.

You should see lesson plans not only as a framework for the lesson to be taught, but also as the starting point for evaluation and reflection. If practice is to improve, you need to give consideration to what has gone well and what has not within all lessons. This will require you to reflect on the experience of the lesson. One way in which this reflection can be structured is by using the lesson plan as a 'cognitive artefact' (that is, a physical record of the thought process and resultant learning sequence) of the lesson which has been taught. By doing this, the lesson plan can be directly utilized to help you understand how to improve your practice.

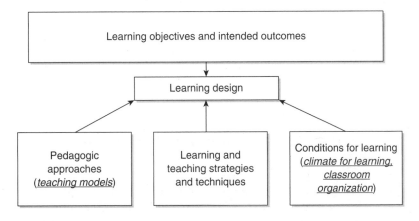

Figure 4.2   A framework for lesson planning (DfES, 2004)

Lesson evaluation

In developing your role as a reflective practitioner, the creation of a lesson plan and its subsequent execution within the classroom should naturally lead to the completion of a lesson evaluation. It is often the case that the immediate impression gained in a lesson is both subjective and inaccurate. More considered and developed reflection can begin to put emerging issues into perspective (refer to the advantages of reflective practice outlined in Chapter 1). A reflective approach ensures that successful aspects of the lesson and an objective consideration of those areas requiring improvement can both be highlighted in a critical but supportive environment.

Suggested areas for evaluation and reflection might include:

1   Summary – a brief overview of the lesson.
2   Were the learning outcomes achieved? How do you know?
3   Did the class respond to your lesson? If not, why not? Were any parts of the lesson particularly successful? If so, why?
4   What special difficulties did the students have with any practical, group or individual work? What were the causes of the difficulties? Consider ways in which you differentiated the learning and deployed other adults in the classroom.
5   How long did the activities take? Was the time allotted adequate?
6   Would you use a similar approach again when teaching this topic? How might you modify it?
7   In reflecting on this lesson, what issues have emerged about your developing classroom practice?

Ho (1995) offers an interesting approach to evaluation by making active use of lesson plans in the evaluative process. The lesson plan is the main artefact of the thinking behind the development of the lesson, and can therefore help in reflecting on how the lesson relates to the plan which had been created before. Ho (1995) suggests making a copy of a lesson plan on a larger piece of paper which can be folded in half. Once the lesson has finished, the blank half of the paper can then be used to annotate the lesson plan as a starting focus to relate the thinking which occurred before the lesson with the experience of the lesson itself.

Activity 4.3   Lesson plan formats (2)

This activity can be completed individually.

Use the Secondary Strategy materials (Module 3 – Lesson Planning) (DfES/QCA, 2002) to obtain several formats of lesson plans. Analyse the formats for what you perceive to be the advantages and disadvantages in their layout and content. Use this critique to help you to design your own format of lesson plan.

Differentiation

Differentiation is a complex concept which needs to be considered and built into the planning and execution processes of teaching and learning as each student is unique and has a unique set of needs and interests. Along with much of the process of classroom management, differentiation is part of the teacher's work which takes time to develop, and it might even be argued, will never be fully mastered. Differentiation is essentially the spectrum of interventions a teacher develops within a classroom to take account of the individual needs of learners, thereby maximizing their potential as learners. Moore (2000) classifies differentiation into four types:

1 *Differentiation by outcome.* All students complete the same task, and the teacher then assesses the level of competence reached by each individual. Some students will show a great degree of understanding, whilst others will show a poor level of competence.

2 *Differentiation by response.* Once students have completed an assignment, the teacher responds to the resultant work in a varied way dependant on the past performance of students. Where a student has done less well than expected, the response is different compared to a poor piece of work from a student who finds the subject difficult.

3 *Differentiation by task.* A number of tasks are created for a single activity, which may use a single set of common resources. Each task asks for a different level of competence and level of knowledge and understanding from students. The teacher uses their prior knowledge of each student to determine which level of task will be most appropriate for them to complete.

4 *Differentiation by stimulus.* This form of differentiation creates a spectrum of resources which take account of student ability, and/or learning preferences. This might include resources which have contrasting levels of challenge in the written language used, for example, in simple, short newspaper articles as opposed to longer, more challenging articles. Alternatively, different forms of resource might be offered, such as film, photos or audio files as well as written text.

Whilst classifications such as that above can be useful in identifying frameworks for help in planning and executing differentiation, it is important that they are not seen as operating in isolation from each other. Differentiation by task can be at its most positive when combined with differentiation by stimulus so that students have a spectrum of levels of challenge in the tasks they complete and the medium of the resources they use. However, this then leads to a number of questions which the teacher needs to consider in deciding the management of differentiation within the classroom:

- Who decides the task level at which the student will work?
- Who decides on the mix of materials and which each student will use?
- How will a mix of resources be developed over time to ensure that all students develop their learning in all media?

Teachers need to ensure that differentiation is carefully planned for and also need to decide on the level of autonomy students will have in deciding the level at which they will work. This is not as easy to manage in practice as it might seem in theory.

Differentiation can also be promoted through other activities within the classroom. As stated in Figure 4.2, lesson planning is in part based on a clear notion of the intended outcomes of a lesson. The outcomes might be different for different students, so that their prior levels of understanding as well as their ability can be taken into account. Such differentiated outcomes are often presented at the start of lessons as a 'must', 'should', 'could' menu. An example might be:

- All students *must* understand what farming is and how it works as a process.
- Most students *should* understand that different types of farming occur in different areas.
- Some students *could* understand the reason for the distribution of different farming types.

One common problem with this type of differentiation is that the statements are sometimes framed in a way which demonstrates more concern with the amount of work completed by students rather than the level of challenge. Therefore, the statements need to ensure that the level of challenge in the work required increases. The activities which are developed to ensure that the learning outcomes are reached must also clearly relate to the statements. This is where the link to differentiation by task and stimulus are important and need to be well considered and managed.

Differentiation should also be carefully developed through the more 'informal' elements of a lesson; questioning (see page 145) is an ideal opportunity to develop such informal differentiation during a lesson. Question challenge can be varied by using language carefully and subtly so that all students have an opportunity to be involved in discussion within a lesson. In the early stages of your development as a teacher you might want to write down questions which have central importance within a lesson on the lesson plan, with the question reframed at three different levels of challenge.

In broadening out the focus of planning for differentiation, associated documents should be consulted to help plan for differentiation. As is explained in Chapter 3, students with special educational needs will have an Individual Education Plan (IEP). This document will outline the particular issues which impact on the learning of the student, and will then list the specific help that should be included to access learning. At the opposite end of the spectrum, some students who are most able are identified as gifted and talented. There will normally not be specific documents for each individual at this end of the spectrum but many schools have a member of staff who is responsible for extending the curriculum for this cohort of children.

In all of the discussion above, the focus is on practical approaches to enriching resources, activities and outcomes for students to help their individual needs.

However, differentiation can begin to take on a merely 'technical' character, with lists and classifications used to offer a 'menu' of options for delivery within the classroom with little consideration of wider and deeper issues. Differentiation should be seen as much more complex than this, as it is essentially the central point around which many other important issues coalesce within the classroom. O'Brien and Guiney (2001) argue that for differentiation to have meaning and worth, it should focus on both students and teachers and how they learn and change, giving rise to a number of 'principles of differentiation' (pp. 11–13):

1 *All children have a right to high-quality education.* Expectations and support should never be affected by personal background, and high-quality education should therefore bring with it an expectation of differentiated practice.
2 *Every child can learn.* All children can learn and progress given the right support and encouragement and no child should ever be seen as incapable of learning.
3 *Every teacher can learn.* Teachers must see themselves as learners, as learning is impeded once the transaction is seen as one way.
4 *Learning is a process that involves mutual relationships.* Learning is a dynamic and social process, successful relationships are central to learning.
5 *Progress for all will be expected, recognized and rewarded.* When tasks are introduced, there should be an expectation of progress and achievement based on levels of prior learning. Progress should be praised by focusing on what has been achieved.
6 *People and learning systems can change for the better.* We need to believe in and foster positive learning environments so that all students can understand their potential through carefully differentiated provision.

These principles demonstrate that differentiation is a fundamental process which teachers must consider carefully and often, and which is linked to a number of areas of practice and expertise, including teaching and learning, inclusion, curriculum and the fostering of positive, working relationships. As such, differentiation needs to be seen as a constant iterative process, and part of what it means to be a reflective practitioner. At a more practical level, differentiation should be seen as a central link between the planning process and tangible outcomes within the classroom, including the messages we send out to students in the way we treat and manage the physical environment of the classroom.

The physical classroom environment

Part of successful classroom management concerns the way in which you manage the physical environment in which you will teach. This is very important as the pattern in which the furniture is arranged, the location of resources and the general physical appearance of the room in which you teach all have a potential impact on the way students will respond to you and the environment. As a consequence of this, there will be an impact on the level of learning and behaviour. The use of physical space is part of the need to develop and sustain a positive and conducive climate for learning.

Organizing the physical environment

All classrooms need space for learning, teaching and storage. Thought should be given to the needs of learners, and how the physical layout of a classroom will best serve the needs of the activities which will make up the learning experience. There are a number of different ways in which a classroom can be set out, and each way has both advantages and disadvantages.

Desks in rows
This is the traditional and most frequently seen layout of the classroom in many schools (Figure 4.3). Students are paired, and everyone faces the 'front' of the classroom, with the focal points being the teacher and the whiteboard.

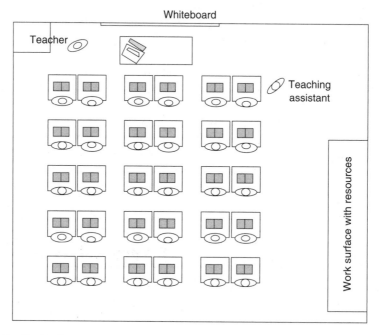

Figure 4.3   Desks in rows

Seminar layout

This type of layout is more often seen in post-16 teaching rooms (Figure 4.4). It is essentially a large horseshoe which allows for the students in the class to face each other and is especially good for whole-class discussion.

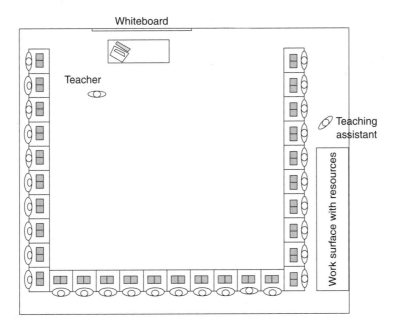

Figure 4.4 Seminar layout

Groups layout

Within the groups layout there could be less focus on the teacher at the front of the room for large parts of the lesson and more focus on working with other students in pairs or small groups (Figure 4.5).

Some classrooms are very different in nature to this typical layout. For example, science teachers will often work within laboratories or rooms where the pattern of desks, and the extent to which they can alter that pattern, are severely restricted. Here, there is a much greater emphasis on a safe environment, where management of students, their movement in the classroom, and the safe storage of their belongings are of primary concern (refer to Association for Science Education, 2004 and CLEAPSS, 2007). Similar issues will be important in design and technology classrooms where health and safety is again a central concern for the management of the physical space.

In some classrooms, such as drama studios and sports halls, there is little, or no, use of desks. In these cases there will be a greater emphasis on the management of students within a large space, and the need to ensure that students are able to interact positively

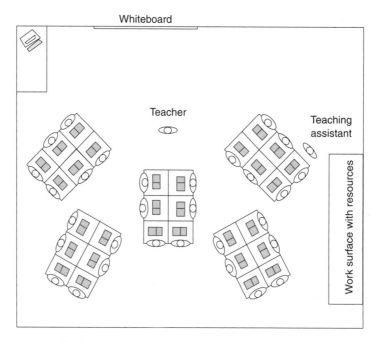

Figure 4.5   Groups layout

at particular points in a lesson. While the space itself may present far fewer physical issues and barriers, the management of students within that space may be more problematic and will need to be considered fully in the development of classroom-management skills.

Activity 4.4   Layout of teaching spaces

This activity can be completed individually and then shared with your mentor.

Using the diagrams in Figures 4.3–4.5, your own experiences in school and any observational experience you might have had to date, list what you think the advantages and disadvantages are concerning the types of layouts illustrated here. Also, make a point of observing in different spaces such as drama studios, science laboratories and sports halls. How does the management of these spaces differ? Share your developing perceptions with your mentor or another teacher.

Where possible, you should not consider classrooms as static spaces. In many classrooms, desks are rarely moved, and the activities which are used in the classroom are often the result of the layout which exists. Betoret and Artiga (2004) completed a questionnaire with over 130 beginning teachers, and found some simple patterns in their responses. Those who saw learning and teaching as a teacher-led exercise (with the outcomes of the activities being the reference for success) tended to prefer the 'desks in rows' style layout. Those who saw learning and teaching as being student-led, with the process as opposed to the outcome of the activities being the main criterion for success, preferred the 'groups layout'. Perhaps this indicates that the way in which the learning process is conceptualized by the teacher has a fundamental effect on the physical layout of the room and, as a consequence, perhaps even the types of activity the students will be involved in.

One interesting perspective to note is that many primary school classrooms are considerably more dynamic in terms of physical layout. Students are often capable of altering the layout of a classroom in one or two minutes in response to the medium and focus of the activity to be undertaken. There is little standing in the way of secondary teachers using their classrooms in dynamic ways, other than a perceived and accepted culture.

In planning for the physical environment, it is important for you to consider other aspects as well as layout. How will the layout relate to your use, and need, for resources? Are students to be given heavily managed, or very free, access to the resources that they will need for a lesson? These questions will have a significant impact on the way in which you locate resources within the room, and also the way in which students will be managed in their use.

It should be remembered that beginning teachers are often 'inhabiting' the space of another teacher, and you will need to take this into consideration when planning for the use of space. More experienced teachers often feel a sense of ownership of their classrooms, not only in terms of layout, but in how resources are stored and used, and how displays are managed. Tact and diplomacy in negotiating the use and alteration of space is therefore important.

Finally, over longer periods of time, there is also the need to manage the appearance of the classroom. This is particularly the case in terms of classroom displays. You should carefully consider the types of display produced and how they will relate to the learning which is taking place in the classroom; displays should not be static but should act as an active element in the learning environment itself. Haynes et al. (1992) believe that the learning environment is enhanced by displays and especially by exhibitions of student work. They argue that the use of creative displays stimulates the minds of students, whilst the individual display of student work inspires students to do better. However, if such displays are left on the walls of a classroom for a long period of time, their impact will lessen as the students

(Continued)

(Continued)

become used to them, and as the content of the displays becomes detached from the work being undertaken by the students themselves.

This section has shown that classroom management starts before the lesson itself, through careful consideration of the classroom environment. This encompasses what you choose to display on the walls and the layout which is felt to be the most appropriate for the activities to be undertaken. It must not be forgotten that the physical environment of the classroom is complex in its own right, and only through careful anticipation, planning, reflection and, ultimately, experience will this important element of classroom management be successful.

Managing the physical environment

Once organized, the physical environment then needs to be managed. You need to develop the confidence with which you use your teaching space. It can be tempting to stay in certain parts of the room, especially at the front of a class; behind the teacher's desk, or next to the whiteboard. However, experienced teachers move around the room to ensure that there are no 'no-go' areas. This is especially true for science teachers who need fast access to all parts of a classroom for health and safety reasons. Some students may gravitate towards certain areas of the room if they know that you will not go there. This can then lead to behavioural issues. There are some important ideas relating to the management of physical space:

- Use of proximity. If the teacher moves closer to students there is a natural tendency on their part to focus on the teacher. This can be useful where very low-level disruption or off-task behaviour is beginning to occur (Marlowe et al., 2004).
- Movement. When students are working, teachers should move around the room to check on progress and use their proximity to help keep students on task.
- Positioning when speaking to individual students. When speaking to individual students the teacher should try to get down to the same physical level of the student so that the communication can happen face-to-face. However, this can make it easy for 'blind spots' to develop and therefore the teacher should position themselves in such a way as to allow them to scan the room whilst talking to the individual.
- Using names. To manage students and the physical space effectively, the use of student names is essential. This makes it much easier to control a group as any comment can be effectively focused on a particular student.
- Developing rituals. Early in the life-cycle of a group, it is important to establish rituals that they can follow, especially on entering and exiting a classroom. This might

include expectations about taking off coats, sitting down or whether students must line up outside a classroom or come into it as they arrive. Again, the crucial factor of laboratory safety must be considered by those teaching in the sciences. As with the organization of the classroom furniture, you may need to accept that well-defined rituals, developed by experienced colleagues with their groups, might be in place already. These will need to be adhered to at least in the first instance.

- Seating plans. A crucial decision to be made in managing the physical environment is where individual students will sit. There are many different approaches to this but you should make a conscious decision taken as a group arrives for the first encounter with you, their teacher. More experienced teachers who have taught the students over a period of time are an excellent source of information when you make seating decisions: they know the students well and often have a clear idea of the permutations which will work and those that will not.

Activity 4.5   Managing physical space

This activity can be completed individually and then shared with a colleague.
    Using the categories for the management of physical space listed in this section, observe a colleague and note the techniques used to manage the physical space of the classroom. At the end of the lesson discuss your observations with the colleague. From this, note three foci you would like to focus on in developing your own practice in the classroom.

Behaviour management

The issue of behaviour management is possibly one of the most common concerns of beginning teachers, and will often be the element of the job which will continue to concern you well into your career. However, there are a number of perspectives which you can draw on to help you think about and develop your approaches to the behaviour of students. It is true, however, that behaviour can sometimes be less than positive through no initial fault of the teacher. Nevertheless, it is certainly their responsibility to take on the challenge and improve the behaviour of the students for whom they are responsible. As Paul Blum notes when considering experiences in difficult classrooms:

Contrary to increasing voiced school-improvement theory and Ofsted myth, good teachers and good teaching materials will not extinguish bad behaviour ... Bad behaviour is not simply a by-product of bad teaching which lacks pace and rigour. You must not allow these much-voiced doctrines to grind down your self-esteem as a teacher in a difficult school ... You will survive and succeed in a difficult school if you are steadfastly enthusiastic, plan carefully and communicate colourfully when you get the chance. You must stay calm in the face of constant provocation and confrontation. In lessons, you must pursue positive behaviour management strategies energetically ... (Blum, 1998: 15–16)

The student perspective

Perhaps one way in which behaviour can be considered is to start from the perceptions of the students themselves. Supaporn (2000) suggests that students are clearly able to identify both the appropriateness of certain types of behaviour within the classroom and the reasons for the appearance of misbehaviour. There is also evidence that the perceptions of classroom management differ between students and teacher (Zeidner, 1988) which can lead to a misinterpretation of actions in both directions.

A study by Cothran et al. (2003) gives us a very useful framework for student perspectives of classroom and behaviour management. This study was conducted through the use of interviews with 182 students in 14 US secondary schools across ethnic and socio-economic backgrounds and in a spectrum of rural to urban settings. Although such a widespread number of settings were used, there were consistent views concerning teacher behaviours which impeded or aided classroom management. The main elements which students picked out were:

- Early, clear expectations and consequences. Students identified clear expectations as important and believed they should be clear from the start. They also stated that if expectations were not clear, and rules were fitted in later, students would not pay attention to them. Additionally, students suggested that their teachers should expect to be tested as students explore the boundaries of what is permissible. They expressed a strong preference for teachers who were clear and consistent in their classroom management. When students test the boundaries they want a teacher who has clear and consistent consequences in place. Those teachers who only threaten consequences but do not carry them through are seen as far less effective.
- When asked why they thought some teachers were less effective, they gave two reasons, the first being that some teachers wanted to be liked and were therefore less willing to carry through consequences, and some had no confidence or knowledge concerning the control of a group. However, while being too 'nice' can be seen as a problem, the students also felt that overly strict teachers were just as poor. They often took the fun out of lessons and students therefore played to this to create their own fun. Strict teachers were perceived as good as long as they attended to building positive relationships with students.
- Relationships. Students saw the development of positive relationships as being of great importance, as this was the central way in which trust on both sides could be built. If the relationship with a teacher was negative, this led to a lack of trust, and the associated poor behaviour which followed.

- Care. Students wanted teachers who showed that they genuinely cared about the students as people and also with regards to their learning, both inside and outside of the classroom. Conversely, if the teacher demonstrates that there is no care involved, and as a consequence that they are not really concerned about the students, then the effort level on the part of the students declined. The ability of teachers to let the students know a little bit about themselves (but not too much) was deemed important so that they could see them as real people.
- Respect. Students highlighted the fact that they do not automatically respect teachers due to the sole fact that they are teachers. Students wanted to be treated like adults, and that meant that there had to be a building of respect in both directions. This meant that students' views should be heard and respected, and that decisions should sometimes involve the students, rather than the teacher merely stating how things would happen.

This study seems to give some very clear indications of the important factors to be considered when developing a positive learning environment and minimizing the chance of negative behaviour developing.

Considering models of behaviour management

There is a large body of literature which covers the issue of behaviour in classrooms. The issue can be framed in different ways with the result that there are a number of theories and frameworks for dealing with behaviours which are deemed to be unacceptable.

Rogers (1997, 1998) divides behavioural difficulties seen in classrooms into two types: *primary* and *secondary*. Primary behaviours are subdivided into three main types:

- *Excesses*: when a certain behaviour occurs more often than it should, or when it lasts beyond the normal expected development stage of the individual. An example of this might be overt aggression in a student. At a very young age, children might display aggression as they have not learned at that point to control their moods. However, if this was still seen in a 13-year-old, there would be an expectation that they had reached a development level where they would be able to control such behaviours.
- *Combinations*: when a number of small behaviours begin to accumulate to become an obvious disruption. Each by themselves is not an issue within the classroom, but when they accumulate, this causes explicit disruption to the class. One group of students which might demonstrate this type of behaviour might be those with **attention deficit hyperactivity disorder (ADHD)** where a number of small behaviours, such as pen-tapping, calling out and making funny noises, might, if isolated incidents, be easy to deal with, or even tactically to ignore. However, when

the behaviours come together, there is a potentially acute behaviour which has to be challenged.

- *Mistimed.* There are times when certain behaviours are not perceived as inappropriate, for example students talking in tutor time, or moving freely around a room during break-time. However, within the bounds of a lesson, these behaviours may be seen as wholly inappropriate and therefore mistimed if undertaken by a student.

Identified negative behaviours need to be challenged so that the learning environment is not disrupted, and it is the role of the teacher to ensure that they are dealt with positively, and in a way that neither disrupts the learning of others further, nor leads to further negative reactions from the student being challenged. This is of particular relevance in those settings, as already identified, where there are clear health and safety issues, such as in laboratories, or where students have a greater freedom in a large open space, such as in a sports hall or on a pitch outdoors.

The way in which a student reacts to being challenged about their behaviour is the *secondary* behaviour. This will range from being defensive and answering back to arguing with the teacher. It is important to consider how to respond to this type of behaviour. If a student merely responds in a negative tone, it may be judged best to *tactically ignore* their tone so as to dissipate the situation. However, if the response is very negative and public, it is necessary to ensure a positive and measured response. Again, your response as a teacher also needs to be set within the cultural context of the school. If there is a clear behavioural policy with regards to student communication, it needs to be followed. For example, if the secondary behaviour of the student includes swearing at the teacher, it may be the case that the school behaviour policy treats this as a serious breach of code and results in an automatic meeting with a senior member of staff. This should therefore be the basis of the response from the classroom teacher.

There are many approaches which teachers take in the classroom concerning student behaviour, and it is important that you realize that there is more than a single way to develop a positive culture within the classroom. Porter (2000) gives a detailed overview of the various behavioural theories which inform behaviour management within schools. Whilst there is not space here to detail all these theories, perhaps one of the main ways in which the theories can be illustrated is by positioning them on a graph, linked to the relative power given to students and teachers (see Figure 4.6).

At one end of the spectrum is the autocratic view of behavioural theories, where teachers are believed to need complete control over students. Dobson (1992) proposes that we must punish children to ensure that they develop a moral framework. However, this is based on biblical or philosophical beliefs and not on social theory. Equally extreme is the notion of laissez-faire behavioural approaches where students are given only minimal, or even no, behavioural guidance, and are therefore allowed to do whatever they choose. Neither of these extreme points is considered appropriate in modern school settings.

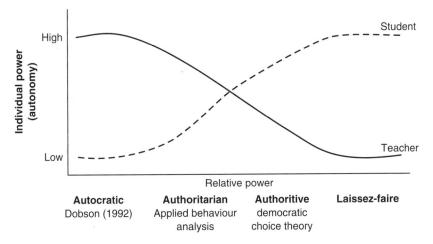

Figure 4.6   The balance of power between teacher and student in the classroom and its relation to different theories of behaviour (simplified from Porter, 2000: 11)

However, between these extremes are other theories which can act as the basis for behaviour management in classrooms. Two examples from different parts of the spectrum are:

- *Applied behaviour analysis*. This theory relies on the idea that behaviour is moderated by the response it receives. Hence, if the response to behaviour is positive, that behaviour will become more dominant, while if the reaction to a behaviour is negative, it will diminish. This theory therefore proposes that if we see behaviour in students which we want to encourage, we must follow its demonstration with a positive consequence. An example of this is the use of praise if a student has done something well, or the use of sweets with younger children if they have carried out a task or ritual which we are attempting to encourage. Conversely, if a student does something which we are aiming to discourage, their behaviour should be followed by a negative intervention, such as an appropriate punishment (see reference to behaviourism in Chapter 2).
- *Choice theory*. This theory focuses on the student as an active decision-maker. In other words, students act as they do out of choice. Therefore, the behaviours they demonstrate occur as they believe these will meet their needs. This then highlights the need for the teacher to act as a form of 'mentor' whose job is to help students make better choices, which still meet their needs but also do not impinge on the rights of others in the class. For example, if a student misbehaves, the teacher might give them a chance to defuse the situation by giving them a choice between two potential reactions; one which will lead to a worse result for the student if they wish to pursue it, or an alternative which will lead to the student perhaps apologizing or accepting they have done something wrong, but which leads to a conclusion of the situation. In this way the student has room to back down without losing self-esteem, and the teacher helps model good choice-making.

Activity 4.6   Behaviour management

This activity can be completed individually.

When you have the opportunity to observe lessons (perhaps at the start of a school placement) focus on the behaviour of students and the way in which the teacher manages their behaviour. Compare their management techniques with the theories described in this section. Which techniques seem to be most successful?

After observing some lessons also reflect on the link between the different theories and the views of students on behaviour and classroom management. Does a pattern begin to emerge from the theories, student perspectives, and your own experiences?

 Weblink: visit the companion website for further reading on behaviour management.

Transactional analysis: an alternative approach to behaviour management

Behaviour management can often be seen as a clear case of the teacher playing a neutral role in changing and enhancing student behaviour. However, transactional analysis changes the dynamic of behaviour management by highlighting the role that you as the teacher can have in causing behavioural problems in the classroom. Transactional analysis was developed as a psychological theory by Eric Berne (1966), who argued that all individuals have three ego-states (see Newell and Jeffery, 2002):

- *Parent*: behaviours copied from parents or parental figures.
- *Adult*: behaviours which are a direct response to the here and now, and tend to be wholly rational in character.
- *Child*: behaviours replayed from childhood.

Importantly, all individuals regardless of age are able to exhibit these behaviours, and can switch between them very quickly. For example, if two adults are arguing, it is often easy to hear one adult talking like a parent, trying to control the situation, while the other reverts to a child-like state and reacts very emotionally.

Berne (1966) further splits two of the ego-states into two subdivisions. Parents can be seen as either *controlling* parents, who try to control and discipline others (either positively in setting sensible rules, or negatively in constantly criticizing things), while *nurturing* parents attempt to look after others (either positively in watching over children empathetically, or negatively, by stifling children so that they have no opportunity to develop independence). The child ego-state can also be split into the *free* child who is spontaneous (either positively in being creative and having fun, or negatively in acting in energetic and inappropriate ways) and the *adapted* child who is constantly adapting their behaviour to gain approval from others (either positively by fitting into the dominant culture of the classroom, or negatively by following stronger characters unthinkingly).

These ego-states are the basis for the transactions which people carry out between each other, the most obvious being various forms of conversation. There are four basic transactional types (see also Burton and Dimbleby, 1995) which can occur between two people (Figure 4.7).

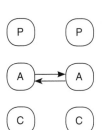

Complementary

A transaction where the ego-states complement each other, resulting in a positive change. This might include two teachers discussing some assessment data in order to solve a problem where they are both inhabiting the adult ego-state.

P = parent A = adult C = child

Angular

Here, the stimulation appear to be aimed at one ego-state, but covertly is actually aimed at another, such as the use of sarcasm. This may then lead to a different ego-state response from that which might be expected.

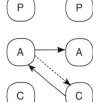

Duplex

This is a transaction that can appear simple, but entails two levels of communication, one often implicit. At a social level, the transaction might be adult to adult, but at a psychological level it might be child to child as a hidden competitive communication.

Crossed

Here, the parent acts as a controlling parent, but in aiming the stimulus at the child ego-state, a response from the adult ego-state, although perhaps perfectly reasonable but unexpected, bring conflict.

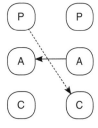

Figure 4.7 Complementary, angular, duplex and crossed models of transactional analysis

Using these four transactional types as a starting point, it becomes obvious that it is the crossed-transactions which can cause a problem within a classroom context. Within any classroom there is a constant, dynamic transaction going on between both teacher and students and between students. The management of this dynamic system can have important ramifications for both long-term and short-term relationships.

Some teachers assume that the transaction which they adopt with students should be a parent–child transaction. However, as teenagers begin to assert their independence and mature, they may well feel it appropriate to respond within a transaction in an adult-to-adult manner. If it is also accepted that teenagers have been identified as having problems with identifying emotions in others as a consequence of rapid growth of synapses in the neo-cortex (Morgan, 2005) the chance of a crossed-transaction is increased.

Activity 4.7   Behaviour and transactional analysis

This activity can be completed individually.

(a) Reflect on an early experience in the classroom where there was a particular issue concerning a student's behaviour, such as arriving to a lesson late, or not putting down a pen when instructed. Note down three different ways in which you could react to this scenario, and three ways in which the student might respond.

(b) Having completed (a), analyse your ideas using transactional analysis. What would the likely outcomes be and why? What does this add to your thinking with regard to behaviour management?

A simple example is the order to put down a pen. If you order the students to 'put your pens down now' (a parent to child transaction), and a student replies, 'I am just finishing off my sentence before I forget it' (adult-to-adult transaction) there is the potential for a negative conversation to occur, although the statement by the student seems wholly rational. Indeed if a colleague were to say this in a staffroom, we would not deem it out of place in any way. A more adult-initiated start to the transaction might be to say, 'I would like to bring you back to focus on the summary points of the work we have been doing. As you reach a convenient point at which to stop, please redirect your attention to me' (followed by a minute's take-up time).

Therefore, transactional analysis, as a behaviour-management framework, changes the emphasis from the teacher as manager, to teacher as part of the dynamic which has to be managed. It shows that we have a responsibility to the students to ensure that we model and encourage positive transactions/conversations in an attempt to develop positive climates within the classroom.

What the above discussion demonstrates is that behaviour management is a complex issue. It is only through careful planning, consideration through regular reflection and some understanding of the underpinning theory that you can begin to develop a behaviour management model that works with your various groups, and which allows you to help students learn in a safe and positive environment. However, this takes time and you should not expect that the practical skills which develop from a theoretical consideration will be mastered quickly.

Developing and managing different approaches to pedagogy through use of language

Questioning and explaining are two skills which are of central importance to the development of learning in the classroom. If you are unable to explain concepts and ideas, you will struggle to help students learn. In the same way, questioning is vital for developing students' enquiry skills and for helping you assess how much they actually understand as you progress through a scheme of work. It should be stressed at the outset that skilled questioning takes time to develop as it is a complex art form. Your ability to explain and assess will also have a major impact on the extent to which students listen and take part in the lesson – poor explanations can actually lead to behavioural issues.

Explaining

What does it mean to explain something to someone? At a very simple level the answer to this question must be that explanations are the medium through which we help another person understand something. Kerry (2002) sees explanations as being the response to one of three implicit questions:

- What?
- How?
- Why?

In considering these questions, the explanation itself needs to take account of a number of issues and factors. First, key terms and concepts need to be defined so that, as the explanation proceeds, the students can continue to understand what is being said. As a consequence, teachers must consider the form of language they are going to use in explaining something. For beginning teachers, this might be as part of the lesson planning process, but as experience and a widening repertoire develops it might occur during the lesson itself. Beginning teachers often misjudge the degree of understanding of students and can pitch an explanation at too high or too low a level until they have experience of the prior learning and conceptual level that the students are working at. If the concept or idea is a difficult one for students to grasp, the explanation may need to have built-in repetition so that there are a number of occasions on which the student can be aided in understanding. However, there is a thin line between useful repetition and becoming over-repetitive and boring.

Where concepts are abstract to the students (for example if students are working on atomic structure or the erosive processes beneath glaciers) they may well find it difficult to understand what is being said. To help their understanding, concrete analogies which are couched in their own experience can help, for example by using different coloured snooker balls in talking about atoms, or using the way sandpaper scratches and smoothes wood in explaining the work done beneath glaciers. By giving examples that the students can relate to, there is a better chance that they will understand the concepts and ideas underlying the explanation. Another way of helping students to understand what is being said is to connect the content to other areas the students have already covered and which they understand. This helps them to locate the ideas in a wider sense, and also demonstrates that the subject being studied is part of a larger whole.

Activity 4.8   Explanations

This activity can be completed individually and then shared with a teacher.

(a) Early in your first placement, observe an experienced teacher explaining a concept or skill to a group of students. What language is being used to help explain to the students clearly? Have everyday examples been used to help the student understand?

(b) At the end of the lesson, discuss your observations with the teacher.

It is also the case that the explanation needs to be carefully paced to ensure that it is neither too quick, losing a number of the students along the way, nor too slow, in which case many of the students might lose interest. Another way of keeping the interest of students is to inject some humour into the explanation. This can make an explanation more memorable and aid memory, but has to be used carefully so that the focus of the students is still on the subject matter and not on your performance as the teacher.

Questioning

Questions are the backbone of communication between students and teachers in classrooms. They are an important medium for learning, used to develop ideas, challenge students, assess levels of understanding and to steer and ignite interest and thinking. You will need to ensure that questions are used in a considered way and to their greatest effect.

So why use questions? There are a number of reasons including (see Kerry, 2002):

- so that students talk
- to show that we have an interest in students' thoughts and ideas
- to stimulate interest and curiosity
- to encourage a problem-solving approach to thinking
- to help students externalize and verbalize knowledge
- to help students learn from each other
- to improve deep thinking
- to promote independent learning
- to monitor levels of learning

Questions, when used well, can have a major impact on the level of learning of students, but to use them most effectively, it is important that the teacher understands the techniques and reasons for various approaches. Questioning can be simply classified in two ways which help us understand how we can better stretch students in their thinking: *closed* and *open* questions.

Closed questions are those for which the teacher has a particular 'correct' response in mind; a question such as 'What is the capital city of France?' or 'Who wrote *To Kill a Mockingbird*?' In each case, there is only one correct response. Open questions, on the other hand, are those which can develop a range of responses, and give a greater opportunity for thinking by students, such as 'Was the invasion of Iraq an ethically sound decision?' or 'How might we analyse the development of habitats over time in this newly cleared piece of forest?' In these cases, there is much greater room for discussion by students as they begin to grapple with complex ideas and concepts.

In deciding which of these techniques is employed, you need to have a clear understanding of why the questions are being asked and the intended outcome of their use. If a short plenary is focused on gauging the amount of knowledge and information the students have taken in, then a series of closed questions will allow for a short, fast paced review to occur. If the development of arguments and ideas is at the heart of the intention, then it is desirable to use more open questions which can lead to deeper, multifaceted ideas, concept development and opportunities for students to ask their own questions. This approach also allows you to facilitate greater development of reflection within the students.

In addition to closed and open questioning, it is also important that we challenge students in the level of thinking they engage in. One way of formalizing this is to use the levels of thinking suggested by Bloom (Bloom and Krathwohl, 1956; see Chapter 2, Table 2.2).

This demonstrates that the questions we ask have a direct impact on the level of thinking required by students. Unfortunately, it is sometimes the case that questions are in the lower order area of Bloom's taxonomy leading to a lack of challenge in learning. This shows that it is crucial to plan for questioning in the early stages of developing your classroom pedagogy.

When planning lessons early in the period of training, it can be helpful for you to consider some of the key questions which students need to answer before the lesson itself. These can be written down on the lesson plan so that they are not forgotten and can help shape discussion within the classroom, developing good habits of questioning. You should also consider how questions will be posed. There are a number of approaches to targeting questions:

- *'Hands up'* is where the question is asked and students raise their hands if they think they know the answer. This is the most frequently used method of 'choosing' a student to answer. However, it can lead to a small number of pupils dominating the session, and if only those who think they know the answer put their hands up, why do we choose them? Are we not equally interested in those who appear not to know the answer?

- *Enlisting* is a technique used by teachers where they choose those to answer and name them. This allows the teacher to focus on particular individuals to gauge understanding, and can be used very effectively in a number of ways. It can be used as a behaviour technique, to ensure that students stay on task as they may be chosen. It can also be used to praise students, especially those who might believe themselves to be weak in the subject. If the questions are chosen carefully so that the teacher knows the chosen student does know the answer, it then gives the opportunity for public praise. However, it is important that the teacher knows the students well to use this technique effectively.

- *Mini-whiteboards* can be used. These are small rectangular whiteboards. The teacher can ask a closed question and the students then write an answer on the board and hold it up. This can give a quick general idea of the level of understanding and means that individual students are not put under pressure. Whiteboards can also be used very effectively in plenary sessions to ensure everyone gives an indication of what they have learned during a lesson.

When you ask questions, students in all parts of the room need to be actively engaged. It is a natural reaction that teachers will tend to engage with students in their direct line of sight, and those in the teacher's peripheral vision will be lost. This can then be a useful place to 'hide' for those who wish to play little part in the lesson, or for those who are unsure of their understanding (just the group we should be helping to develop their understanding).

Careful consideration must also be given to the sequencing and challenge of questions. As has already been stated, differentiated questioning will play a major role in the structure of learning and help to develop understanding. In some cases, a question may be posed at a level too high for a student, or group of students to understand. Here, the notion of scaffolding (see Chapter 2) becomes important as the question might need to be broken down into simpler questions which build back towards the original more complex question.

As confidence in questioning develops, it is possible for the teacher to take an increasingly small part in the process of questioning itself. If we wish students to become increasingly independent learners, we need to help them become effective questioners in their own right. Wood and Patterson (2004) suggest that classrooms are at least in part artificial social and cognitive environments as students are asked the questions by the individuals who know the answers, as a test of their own, most likely incomplete knowledge. In the vast majority of other social situations, the novice will ask the questions as they want to further their knowledge and understanding, using the expert as a starting point for their development. This is supported by evidence highlighted by Tizard and Hughes (1984) who found that four-year-old children took part in 27 conversations per hour with their mothers on average, each having an average of 16 turns, with half the conversations being initiated by the children, asking an average of 26 questions per hour. As the children entered school, conversations fell to ten per hour, and the vast majority were started and controlled by adults. Identified consequences included a fall in the amount of speaking, questioning, the number of requests for information, restricted language, and less active reflection and planning.

By giving students the opportunity to question you can begin to give them a level of independence and a greater contribution to the learning process. This can take a number of forms, from allowing them a specified period of a lesson to ask questions, or the use of a 'post-box' where they can write down and leave questions which can be answered at a predetermined time, perhaps once a week or every three lessons, for example. The students might even be given the opportunity to work as a class to develop their own foci for a scheme of work. In this case the concepts to be studied can be decided by snowballing questions from the individual pupil to the whole class before deciding on a list to be covered in lessons (see Wood and Patterson, 2004).

Activity 4.9   Questioning

This activity can be completed individually and then shared with a teacher.

During a lesson observation, focus on the following issues and write some notes on what you see:

1   What is the ritual for asking questions? Are hands put up or are students conscripted? What effect does this have on the proportion of students who are involved in the answering of questions?

(Continued)

(Continued)

2 To what degree are students encouraged to ask their own questions, either of themselves and their peers, or the teacher?

3 If a question is asked which does not bring a quick answer, how does the teacher approach the situation?

4 To what extent do closed and open questions lead to further enquiry and learning?

5 If you get the opportunity, discuss some of these issues with the teacher you have observed.

Weblink: access the DfES module (at http://teachertools.londongt.org/en-GB/resources/Ks3_module_questioning.pdf) and reading on questioning via the companion website.

Group work

Questioning and explaining are both key skills for the beginning teacher to develop and refine. However, in both cases the focus of the learning is centred on the teacher. As your confidence grows, and basic classroom management is developed, it is a positive step to begin to help the students take a greater responsibility for their own learning. One way in which this can be done is through the introduction of group work.

Blatchford et al. (2003) define group work as any activity where students are working together as a team, which can obviously cover a number of different types of activity. However, there are some common features which group work should entail. First, as the theory underpinning the use of group work relates to social constructivism students should have ownership of the process and work together to create and extend their own understanding of a topic. The extent to which students are given ownership of this process will depend on their age and their level of exposure to the techniques used. If students have had little experience of group work, it is unrealistic to expect them to work well in a completely independent fashion; this can only come with experience. The students should act as co-workers, with no single individual taking a role as the 'quasi-teacher', as this then dilutes or even prohibits the true social nature of the exercise. Finally, the activity itself should be a structured opportunity for learning, not a casual chance to discuss. It can be quite easy to allow a large degree of independence, which then descends into an opportunity for students to talk about anything but the activity being undertaken.

Group work is actually quite complex, and needs careful consideration. It often does not work very well due to a lack of careful planning. This is due to a lack of focus on how students will be trained in group work skills, or the constitution of the groupings. Group work skills can only be developed over a long period of time. The interpersonal traits required are not well developed in many students, and it is necessary to help them develop these.

Blatchford et al. (2003) focus on some basic dynamics which need to be carefully considered:

1   *Preparation*: there are a number of issues which need to be addressed before the lesson even begins if group work activities are to succeed. The layout of the tables needs to be considered; it needs to be flexible and appropriate. This may require the movement of tables from normal positions, whilst ensuring that there is room for students to move about easily and safely if needed. The size of the groups is context specific; for example, the type and extent of resources may be important in deciding group size, and, whatever the size, careful consideration should be given with regard to ability and sex make-up of the groups. Group work is easier when the teacher knows the students well as they understand better the behaviour dynamics and abilities within the student group, and can therefore create groupings which they know have a better chance of being successful. Finally, group stability needs to be considered; will they need to work over a number of lessons or will the groups be flexible and changed on a lesson to lesson basis?

2   *Interaction*: group skills are naturally imbued, and also need to be developed. Teachers cannot expect students to be excellent communicators unless they are given the chance to use such skills and, as importantly, to discuss and debrief those skills once used. Hence a meta-level discourse needs to unfold, with time being given over to the discussion of the process itself, rather than the subject knowledge outcomes by themselves. Over the longer term, the focus of this reflection is on making the students ever more independent, and able to function as groups with little intervention from the teacher.

3   *Teacher's role*: teachers need to understand the underlying principles of social constructivism to ensure that they can support and develop the students' skills. The teacher is there to mentor and aid the work of students, and should attempt, as far as possible, not to become the focus of discussion. This is a role which should extend the zone of proximal development (see the section on Vygotsky in Chapter 2) by scaffolding student thinking, but not directing it. This can often be a difficult skill for teachers to develop as there is a degree to which they need to transfer some of their power as teacher to the students. This means that the teacher needs to have confidence in their own ability and the exercise they have developed to allow students the freedom to work without complete direction.

4   *Preparation of tasks*: as alluded to in point 3, group work is most positive when the task is well designed, not only taking account of the need to develop understanding

and skills, but also of the particular make-up and dynamics of the group with which the task will be used. This is often not considered enough, and may be one of the factors in group work not being fully successful on occasion. All group members need to be fully involved, and this will mean a consideration of differentiation of resources, and even the task itself. It may also require the assigning of roles if the teacher believes that individuals may dominate discussion, or where students find it difficult to focus if meaning the resources on their own terms. The task should also have a clear element of meta-analysis within it (as mentioned earlier) so that the students are required to reflect on the nature and process of the activity as well as the outcomes.

Activity 4.10   Linking group work and learning

This activity can be completed individually and then shared with a teacher.

Referring back to Chapter 2, and using the ideas presented here, make some notes on the elements of social constructivism you feel are crucial to develop through group work. Use these to make a list of the essential features you would need to include in setting any group-work activity.

As students develop their learning through the secondary curriculum, certain approaches will enable them to extend and deepen understanding and develop skills which will be helpful in either the jobs market or higher education. Such approaches include enquiry-based learning and independent learning.

Enquiry-based learning

Enquiry-based learning is an approach to learning which can be developed throughout the secondary phase (Roberts, 2003) but which should offer real opportunities to extend learning in the 14–19 curriculum. Enquiry-based learning is focused on students asking questions, or creating hypotheses which they then investigate and draw conclusions from (Figure 4.8).

Figure 4.8 gives a potential framework for enquiry-based learning based on the research of Roberts (2003) in Geography education. It begins with the development of questions or hypotheses which form the basis for an area of investigation. From this question, data is then selected and collected. Data needs to be taken in its widest sense and includes any form of information. This stage of enquiry learning focuses on developing students' capacity to handle and analyse information to answer questions. Having done this, the penultimate stage of the process involves synthesizing and extending understanding before reaching conclusions which are linked to the evidence developed

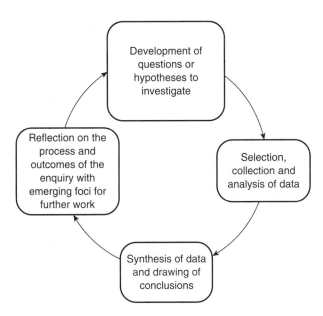

Figure 4.8   Outline of enquiry-based learning framework (based on the work of Roberts, 2003)

within the process. Finally, students need to reflect on how they reached their conclusions, and consider further questions that this enquiry might lead to. These questions then become the subject for subsequent cycles of enquiry.

Implicit in this approach to learning is a very different framework for teaching and classroom management. Students require a greater level of independence, whilst the teacher becomes more of a facilitator, creating a conducive environment in which students can carry out their enquiries. This may require the physical layout of the classroom to change, and may also lead to students needing to work outside the immediate classroom environment, such as using a library or computer room. Careful consideration needs to be given to how students and their learning are managed within this framework.

Independent learning

Allied to enquiry-based learning is the development of independence in learning. The autonomy of learners has been theorized by Ecclestone (2002), moving from procedural notions of autonomy (where students may be involved in pacing and evaluating their work) to personal and critical autonomies. In these latter forms of autonomy, students have become reflectors who are able to identify their level of understanding and can further develop through independent study, self-negotiated activities and self-evaluation (see Table 4.2 for an outline definition of each of these levels of autonomy). At this stage

Table 4.2   Levels of autonomy (based on Ecclestone, 2002)

Level of autonomy	Outline characteristics
Procedural	Some determination of pace, timing and evaluation of work, with the transmission of predetermined content and outcomes
Personal	Development based on a knowledge of one's own strengths and weaknesses. Becomes more student-centred with negotiated outcomes and processes for achieving them
Critical	Independent, critical thinkers who are able to self-evaluate. Formative assessment encourages critical reflection thereby questioning personal barriers to understanding

there is far less teacher-generated learning: their focus becomes more aligned to tutoring and mentoring as with enquiry approaches.

Both enquiry-based learning and independent learning should be carefully planned for. Planning may include some development of these skills in Key Stage 3, to ensure that the skills and learning approaches required have begun to be embedded. This exemplifies the point made earlier in this chapter that long-term planning should have progressional strands across Key Stages. By developing these core skills in the lower years of the secondary curriculum, they have the opportunity to become central approaches to learning in the 14–19 curriculum.

Working with other adults: the role of the teaching assistant

In developing good classroom management, the role of the teaching assistant (or learning support assistant) should be both recognized and developed, to create a more inclusive classroom not only for the students, but also for the staff involved. You will no doubt have teaching assistants in some of your lessons, and it is essential that you learn both how to integrate their skills into your teaching and how best to deploy them for the maximum impact on student learning.

Over the past five years the role of teaching assistants has become a major area for research. This has, in part, been the result of the increasing number of such professionals being employed within the English educational system (Cremin et al., 2005) but also has been due to major policy developments brought about by politicians. At the same time there has been a rapid change in the role of these professionals from the mundane 'housekeeping' role characterized by Duthie (1970) to higher-level teaching assistants of the twenty-first century who can take on some of the core responsibilities often reserved for teachers under a more traditional approach (Kerry, 2005). Kerry identifies 11 different titles from both the literature and practice which all relate to teaching assistant-style jobs, showing the difficulty in defining and even naming the role (Balshaw and Farrell, 2002). The resultant identified roles cover a spectrum. At one end, there is what is called the 'Dogsbody' where the tasks allocated are menial, such as filing, photocopying and so on, with little contact with students. Somewhere in the middle of the spectrum is the 'Behaviour manager' who works with students, but who provides support for an individual or for small groups. Here, there is obvious contact with students but it is limited to an emotional support role, the academic/content element of the lesson being of little concern. At the other end of the scale is the 'Mobile paraprofessional' often identified with high-level teaching assistants who takes on roles traditionally taken as being the preserve of the teacher, acting as an independent operator fulfilling a number of teaching and learning functions.

The role of the teaching assistant is variable, and is most likely determined, or negotiated, at individual school level. Moran and Abbott (2002) see the role of the teaching assistant as being multifaceted, with important characteristics including the need for a positive relationship with students, and as a consequence, often a motivator to students. Importantly, another central characteristic identified is the role of the teaching assistant in providing continuous feedback to the teacher as part of the on-going planning and reflection process. In their study of teaching assistants in Northern Ireland, both in mainstream and special schools, they see the teaching assistant as a central element in the development of an inclusive classroom. A crucial process in allowing this to happen, however, is that the teacher realizes that a crucial ingredient of team success is in the clear definition of roles, classroom tasks and activities (see also Thomas, 1992).

Mansaray (2006), working in a primary context, found that the situation of teaching assistants within an organization is often ambiguous. In some classrooms there was a 'core'/'periphery' model in operation where the teacher was the core element of the teaching dynamic with the teaching assistant very much on the periphery. However, while there was evidence that students, even at a young age, were able to distinguish between teaching assistants and teachers, they also identified their roles as clearly overlapping. Students also often stated that the teaching assistants were more approachable and, because of this, they played crucial roles as 'connectors' within the classroom, bridging the gap between student and teacher, and also as 'mediators'.

Cremin et al. (2005) considered models of teaching assistant deployment within the classroom. They offer three potential models, all based on previous models within the literature, which were then piloted in a number of schools and analysed for **learning gain**:

1 *Room management*: this is a model based on the identification of teacher tasks and responsibilities which are then divided with specific roles and activities being given to the people working in the classroom. Hence, where specific focused interventions might be involved, individuals have a clear framework to use to ensure that all such activities are undertaken, but as distributed actions across the team involved.
2 *Zoning*: this is a model for allocating roles of those working in the classroom according to the classroom 'geography' and the groups that exist therein. Here, particular groups who exist within particular locations in the room will be focused on by a particular individual, thereby 'localizing' the interaction between adult and students. This model was first described by LeLaurin and Risley (1972).

3 *Reflective teamwork*: this is a model whereby staff working together discuss thoroughly, develop and advance the ways in which they work together as a team. This approach reflects the importance of team planning and the vital role of the teaching assistant as the link between students and teacher.

Within the context of the study, the room-management model appeared to give the greatest increase in engagement but required substantial planning and management time. The zone also showed positive results, but there was a greater degree of variability between individuals. Finally, the reflective teamwork model showed the weakest evidence for quantitative increase (although the groups selected proved to be anomalous), but was deemed the most popular with both staff and students. What all the models showed was the need for training and the development of teaching assistant skills if the interventions were to be successful.

Activity 4.11   Deployment of teaching assistants

This activity can be completed individually and then shared with the teachers you have observed.

Using the model for teaching assistants outlined by Cremin et al. (2005), complete the following:

1 Observe two lessons which include the presence of teaching assistants. During the lesson, note down their activities and after the lesson, discuss with the teacher the extent to which they decide on the deployment of the teaching assistant, and their reasons for deploying them in that way.

2 Reflect on what you have experienced, and make some notes on what this has taught you about your deployment of teaching assistants which will inform your own future practice.

Changing pedagogies and classroom management

E-learning

In the 19th century the teacher was for most students the gatekeeper of knowledge, since learners had little or no independent, ready and inexpensive access to books. Some 150 years later, the teacher is no longer a gatekeeper, for the new technologies have made vast sources and quantities of information accessible to almost anyone, almost anywhere and at almost any time at the touch of a button. (Hargreaves, 2005: 22)

Information and communications technology is a major part of the lives of many young people, from use of games consoles to the use of mobile phones and the Internet. People live and learn in a multi-modal, digital world and classrooms are sites of multi-modal learning in which students should be enabled to develop their digital literacy. It is no surprise that there is an increasing desire to use a number of technologies within an educational context, which may offer certain advantages in a classroom context (Hargreaves, 2005).

Interactive whiteboards

Many schools now have interactive whiteboards as a standard element of the classroom environment. The essential feature of these is the projection of a computer screen image onto a large board, which is itself 'live'. Therefore, software packages or the Internet can be used, and navigated around as if it were a normal computer screen. This allows for you to use information interactively, as you and the students can browse for Internet information, play educational games or develop understanding through animated software, all directed from the board itself. This is the type of use that interactive whiteboards were designed for, although in some cases use is far more restricted, and a very technologically advanced piece of equipment becomes a normal whiteboard. Such restrictive use highlights the need for beginning teachers to spend time observing carefully and explicitly planned exemplar lessons which focus on the use of interactive whiteboards, and to ensure that use of the equipment is fully integrated into lessons where appropriate. However, it should always be the case that you have back-up resources for those lessons where the Internet might be used, as it is a fact of life that the school server can fail from time to time. If this happens, it can be very uncomfortable if an alternative exercise is not at hand.

Weblink: examples of the use of interactive whiteboards are available via the companion website.

The rise and rise of the socially networked classroom

Over the past decade, the use of the Internet by children has become increasingly ubiquitous, the result of the regular use of Web 2.0 media and social networking media. The development of such media has led to a continual expansion of free tools which can be used by teachers and students alike to support and extend their learning. Below are two examples of Web 2.0 tools which have become mainstream media through which students can develop their learning.

Blogs
Blogs (short for weblogs) are a rapidly expanding form of Internet communication, their success perhaps due to the fact that they are essentially an easily created, easily updatable website. They allow individuals to publish instantaneously on the web from any Internet connection point. As Richardson states: 'they are comprised of reflections

and conversations that in many cases are updated every day (if not three or four times a day). Blogs engage readers with ideas and questions and links. They ask readers to think and to respond. They demand interaction' (2006: 18).

Eide and Eide (2005) believe that blogging has a huge potential for a positive impact on students. They argue that blogs can:

- promote critical and analytical thinking
- be a powerful promoter of creative, intuitive and associational thinking
- promote analogical thinking
- be a powerful medium for increasing access and exposure to quality information
- combine the best of solitary reflection and social interaction

Within the classroom context, Ray (2006) sees four main uses of blogs:

1 *Blogs to communicate*: developing an electronic bulletin board as a fast means to communicate with other interested parties, such as students, other colleagues and parents.
2 *Blogs as instructional resources*: developing ways in which homework can be further supported, through the publishing of tips, explanations or samples of work. There might also be the development of hyperlink libraries to help structure the research of students.
3 *Blogs as collaborative tools*: students could set up blogs as groups so that they can work collaboratively on projects, such as field trips or enquiries/investigations. The blog allows the development of a meta-cognitive strand which allows for more explicit reflective opportunities for the students involved.
4 *Blogs as showcases for student projects*: a way of publishing student work to the Internet, which can be easily accessed by parents or other students.

Wood (2009) demonstrates that Geography teachers in the UK are using blogs for all of the purposes outlined above. The teachers involved in the research see the use of blogs as important to their work with students. It gives them an opportunity to communicate in more immediate ways beyond the classroom, as well as developing collaborative projects with schools in other regions.

However, there are potential problems with blogs. First, if core information and learning is to be transferred to the Internet, the teacher needs to ensure that all students have equal access to the information. Second, given that blogs are intentionally written to allow for discussion on the Internet, there is a need to ensure that students are safe and are not exposed to online bullying, or predators. Finally, there is the issue of time. It is very easy to begin to use a blog as a medium for learning, and find that increasing amounts of time are used to write, update and police the resource. This is something which must be carefully considered before developing this technology too far.

 Weblink: the companion website provides links to a variety of exemplar blog sites.

Wikis

Wiki is a shortened form of the Hawaiian word 'wiki-wiki', meaning 'quick'. First developed by Ward Cunningham in 1995, wikis were created to enable easy and quick publishing of information to the Internet. An example of this rapid and easy publishing of information can be seen from the aftermath of the Indian Ocean earthquake and tsunami. The event occurred just after midnight (GMT) on 26 December 2004. Within 24 hours of the event a wiki had been formed, had been edited 400 times and had expanded to a document of 3,000 words, supplemented with photographs, charts and other graphics. Within 48 hours, there were over 6,500 words, which had been edited 1,200 times (Richardson, 2006).

Wikis have therefore become a medium through which collaborative documents can be easily and quickly developed. This is the focus for potential uses in schools. It is very easy to set up free wikis on the Internet, and some VLEs (see Chapter 3) are now incorporating them into their structures. A template is then developed which acts as the 'content page' for the wiki which students can then be asked to populate. This allows students to work collaboratively to produce a form of publication together. The teacher's role needs to be carefully considered, as it is important that the resultant document is accurate and useable. However, it is also an ideal opportunity for peer assessment (see Chapter 5) as students can be asked to edit elements of the publication written by others. *Wikipedia*, the online encyclopaedia, can be used as a reference point when considering how a wiki might work in the classroom and the format that might be used.

Activity 4.12   Blogs

This activity can be completed individually but (b) should be discussed with your mentor.

(a) There are a number of blogs which are run by enthusiastic teachers in most subjects. Using the Internet, identify three blogs which focus on your subject. What are they being used for? How successfully do you think they are being used? Complete an analysis of each of the blogs using the framework created by Ray (2006; see page 156 in this chapter). What does tell you about the way in which blogs are developed and used?

(b) Once you have done this, try starting your own blog or wiki (there are a number of free providers which can be found through searching on the Internet). You might want to focus on a particular topic with a class. Be careful both to consider how you want the site to be used (that is, what you are trying to help

(Continued)

(Continued)

the students gain from the experience) and to discuss safety and access issues with your mentor *before* introducing the blog or wiki to your class.

(c) Once you have tried using the blog/wiki for a period of time, reflect on whether the students have gained anything from using these media and what positive impacts it appears to have on their learning.

Social media

Social media has become a controversial area in education. Media such as Facebook and Twitter are treated with suspicion by many schools, and in the majority of cases the use of social media with students is not allowed. However, there are other uses for social media which are becoming ever more popular. One example is the use of Twitter to create informal teacher networks and continuing professional development opportunities. '#ukedchat' is a weekly open forum conducted through Twitter, with each topic being chosen by individuals voting online through a wiki. Once the focus has been decided, an informal debate is conducted online for one hour with teachers and others interested in education tweeting ideas and comments about the focus which has been voted the most popular. Other educational uses of Twitter have been highlighted by McCulloch et al. (2011) who show how senior leaders and teachers are using social media such as Twitter to engage each and support each other in professional development.

Whichever the ICT medium used, there is no doubt that e-learning and the wider use of computers will play an increasingly central role in learning, both within and outside of the classroom. You will need to consider how you can best make use of these resources to serve purposes that you feel are important, rather than be carried along by technological experts who may not have an acute understanding of the needs and dynamics of the learning context in which you are working.

E-safety

In each of the above cases, the use of technology is allowing the classroom environment to extend beyond that of the physical walls of the school. Although there are issues of equality of access, if these can be positively resolved, then e-learning developments such as these can make the learning environment both broader and more flexible. However, the examples above also require teachers to reconsider their role in students' learning as being less of a transmitter of knowledge and more of an aide or mentor for students to help them to build their capacity for learning. This change of approach is very much in the spirit of social constructivist models.

There are also serious issues concerning **e-safety** which need to be considered to ensure that both teachers and students are safe in their use of the Internet and associated media.

E-safety highlights the need to keep children safe whilst educating them about the benefits and potential dangers of information technology. It is not merely concerned with the use of the Internet, but includes all devices which relate to the use and transfer of information including mobile phones and games consoles. Students are exposed to a bewildering spectrum of information on the Internet. They need to be able to develop the critical skills which allow them to use this resource in a positive and safe way. All schools have an e-safety policy which covers issues of professional conduct for teachers, child safety and e-bullying. This is a constantly changing area and you will need to regularly update your technological knowledge. The nature of the Internet tends to blur the distinctions between professional and personal 'spaces' and you will need to ensure that any personal use of social media you make is considered carefully to protect your privacy and personal integrity.

E-safety advice and guidance can be found at ICTCPD4FREE www.ictcpd4free.co.uk/ where there are two courses (one short and one long) focusing on embedding e-safety within the curriculum.

Critical reading at Master's level

Academic papers often take very different approaches to similar problems. Some may be heavily theoretical, whilst others might be located more within the practicalities of certain classroom practices.

1   Download or find the two references given below from your library service:

Taylor, S.S. (2011) 'Behavior basics: quick behavior analysis and implementation of interventions for classroom teachers', *The Clearing House*, 84: 197–203.
Hart, R. (2010) 'Classroom behaviour management: educational psychologists' views on effective practice', *Emotional and Behavioural Difficulties*, 15(4): 353–371.

Both papers focus on a common concern that many starting teachers have early in their training and career.

2   Read each paper, and consider what the main messages are and how well argued the main points are in each.

3   What are the similarities and differences in the main messages of each paper and how might their contents be synthesized to help you in developing your behaviour strategies?

4   What difficulties might exist in trying to take conclusions from academic papers and applying them in the classroom? Is this process important as a wider part of professional behaviour and development?

Conclusion

You enter a very complex and diverse situation when you first go into classrooms to teach. As suggested in the introduction to this chapter, you should not expect to find the experience easy, and you will only develop your ability as a teacher through careful planning and preparation, and through constant reflection on your experiences. However, by taking account of the issues raised here, you should be able to understand and develop your classroom practice. The last section of this chapter also demonstrates that classrooms are dynamic and open to change. Those of you who will become expert over time will be those who can critically assess the changes which you believe could enrich the experiences of your students, and act accordingly, rather than simply accepting national developments because the government states that they are the best approaches to take.

References

Association for Science Education (2004) *Laboratory Design for Teaching and Learning*, Secondary CD-ROM, Hatfield Association for Science Education.

Balshaw, M. and Farrell, P. (2002) *Teaching Assistants: Practical Strategies for Effective Classroom Support*. London: David Fulton.

Berne, E. (1966) *Games People Play: The Psychology of Human Relationships*. London: André Deutsch.

Betoret, F.D. and Artiga, A.G. (2004) 'Trainee teachers' conceptions of teaching and learning, classroom layout and exam design', *Educational Studies*, 30(4): 355–372.

Blatchford, P., Kutnick, P., Baines, E. and Galton, M. (2003) 'Toward a social pedagogy of classroom group work', *International Journal of Education Research*, 39(1–2): 153–172.

Bloom, B.S. and Krathwohl, D.R. (1956) *Taxonomy of Educational Objectives. Handbook 1: Cognitive Domain*. New York: Longmans.

Blum, P. (1998) *Surviving and Succeeding in Difficult Classrooms*. London: Routledge-Falmer.

Burton, G. and Dimbleby, R. (1995) *Between Ourselves – an Introduction to Interpersonal Communication*. 2nd edition. London: Arnold.

Butt, G. (2006) *Lesson Planning*. 2nd edition. London: Continuum.

Coffield, F., Moseley, D., Hall, E. and Ecclestone, K. (2005) *Should We Be Using Learning Styles? What Research Has to Say to Practice*. London: Learning and Skills Research Centre.

Consortium of Local Education Authorities for the Provision of Social Services (CLEAPSS) (2007) *CLEAPSS Science Publications*, CD-ROM. Uxbridge: CLEAPSS.

Cothran, D.J., Kulinna, P.H. and Garrahy, D.A. (2003) '"This is kind of giving a secret away …": students' perspectives on effective class management', *Teaching and Teacher Education,* 19(4): 435–444.

Cremin, H., Thomas, G. and Vincent, K. (2005) 'Working with teaching assistants: three models evaluated', *Research Papers in Education*, 20(4): 413–432.

Department for Education and Skills (DfES) (2004) *Pedagogy and Practice: Teaching and Learning in Secondary Schools. Unit 1: Structuring Learning Key Stage 3 National Strategy*. London: HMSO.

Department for Education and Skills and the Qualifications and Curriculum Authorities (DfES/QCA) (2002) *Training Materials for the Foundation Subjects: Module 3. Lesson Planning*. London: DfES.

Dobson, J. (1992) *The New Dare to Discipline*. Wheaton, IL: Tyndale House.

Duthie, J. (1970) *Primary School Survey: A Study of the Teacher's Day*. Edinburgh: HMSO.

Ecclestone, K. (2002) *Learning Autonomy in Post-16 Education*. London: Routledge-Falmer.

Eide, F. and Eide, B. (2005) 'Brain of the blogger'. http://eideneurolearningblog.blogspot.com/2005/ 03/brain-of-blogger. html (accessed 18 July 2007).

Hargreaves, D. (2005) *Personalised Learning – 3: Learning to Learn and the New Technologies.* London: Specialist Schools Trust.

Hart, R. (2010) 'Classroom behaviour management: educational psychologists' views on effective practice', *Emotional and Behavioural Difficulties*, 15(4): 353–371.

Haynes, M., Bowen, S., Tuxford, J. and Ridley, S. (1992) 'Give your room a face-lift! (classroom displays)', *Instructor*, 101(7): 38.

Ho, B. (1995) 'Using lesson plans as a means of reflection', *ELT Journal*, 49(1): 66–71.

Kerry, T. (2002) *Explaining and Questioning*. Cheltenham: Nelson Thornes.

Kerry, T. (2005) 'Towards a typology for conceptualising the roles of teaching assistants', *Educational Review*, 57(3): 373–384.

LeLaurin, K. and Risley, T.R. (1972) 'The organisation of day care environments: "Zone V", "Man to man assignments"', *Journal of Applied Behaviour Analysis*, 5(3): 225–232.

Mansaray, A. (2006) 'Liminality and in/exclusion: exploring the work of teaching assistants', *Pedagogy, Culture and Society*, 14(2): 171–187.

Marlowe, M., Disney, G. and Wilson, K.J. (2004) 'Classroom management of children with emotional and behavioural disorders', *Emotional and Behavioural Difficulties*, 9(2): 99–114.

McCormack, A. (1997) 'Classroom management problems, strategies, and influences in physical education', *European Physical Education Review*, 3: 102–115.

McCulloch, J., McIntosh, E. and Barrett, T. (2011) *Tweeting for Teachers: How Can Social Media Support Teacher Professional Development?* Pearson Centre for Policy and Learning (www.pearsoncpl.com/wp-content/uploads/2011/10/Tweeting-for-teachers.pdf, Accessed 21 November 2011).

Moore, A. (2000) *Teaching and Learning: Pedagogy, Curriculum and Culture*. London: Routledge.

Moran, A. and Abbott, L. (2002) 'Developing inclusive schools: the pivotal role of teaching assistants in promoting inclusion in special and mainstream schools in Northern Ireland', *European Journal of Special Needs Education*, 17(2): 161–173.

Morgan, N. (2005) *Blame my Brain*. London: Walker Books.

Newell, S. and Jeffery, D. (2002) *Behaviour Management in the Classroom: A Transactional Analysis Approach*. London: David Fulton.

O'Brien, T. and Guiney, D. (2001) *Differentiation in Teaching and Learning: Principles and Practice*. London: Continuum.

Porter, L. (2000) *Behaviour in Schools: Theory and Practice for Teachers*. Buckingham: Open University Press.

Radford, M. (2006) 'Researching classrooms: complexity and chaos', *British Educational Research Journal,* 32(2): 177–190.

Ray, J. (2006) 'Welcome to the blogosphere: the educational use of blogs (aka edublogs)', *Kappa Delta Pi Record*, 42(4): 175–177.

Richardson, W. (2006) *Blogs, Wikis, Podcasts and Other Powerful Web Tools for Classrooms*. Thousand Oaks, CA: Corwin Press.

Roberts, M. (2003) *Learning Through Enquiry*. Sheffield: Geographical Association.

Rogers, B. (1997) *The Language of Discipline: A Practical Approach to Effective Classroom Management*. 2nd edition. Plymouth: Northcote House.

Rogers, B. (1998) *'You Know the Fair Rule' and Much More: Strategies for Making the Hard Job of Discipline and Behaviour Management in Schools Easier*. Melbourne: ACER.

Supaporn, S. (2000) 'High school students' perspectives about misbehaviour', *Physical Educator,* 57: 124–135.

Taylor, S.S. (2011) 'Behavior Basics: Quick Behavior Analysis and Implementation of Interventions for Classroom Teachers', *The Clearing House*, 84: 197–203.

Theoharis, G. and Causton-Theoharis, J. (2011) 'Preparing pre service teachers for inclusive classrooms: revising lesson planning expectations', *International Journal of Inclusive Education,* 15(7): 743–761.

Thomas, G. (1992) *Effective Classroom Teamwork: Support or Intrusion*. London: Routledge.

Tizard, B. and Hughes, M. (1984) *Young Children Learning*. London: Fontana.

Wood, P. (2009) 'Advances in E-learning – the case of blogging in U.K. school geography', *Research in Geographic Education*, 11(2): 28–46.

Wood, P. and Patterson, C. (2004) 'Questions, questions, questions', *Teaching Expertise*, 5: 47–49.

Wragg, E.C. (1994) *An Introduction to Classroom Observation*. London: RoutledgeFalmer.

Zeidner, M. (1988) 'The relative severity of common classroom management strategies: the students' perspective', *British Journal of Educational Psychology*, 58: 69–77.

CHAPTER 5

ASSESSING STUDENTS

Tony Lawson

By the end of this chapter you will have:

- been introduced to the key issues concerning monitoring, assessment, recording, reporting and accountability
- begun to understand some of the theoretical background to assessment
- learnt about the terminology associated with assessment
- reflected on your initial experiences of assessing students

Introduction

Assessment pervades schooling and the curriculum. Like it or not, one of the main functions of secondary schooling is to grade, sort and make judgements about the knowledge, skills and attitudes of individual students, and it is one of your main responsibilities to assist your students to achieve the best that they can in a system which continually judges them, both formally and informally. Assessment is therefore about power – an **assessment regime** acts to privilege some and exclude others; it is the **gatekeeper** from the school to the wider world (Lingard et al., 2006).

This chapter is concerned with issues to do with monitoring, assessment, recording, reporting and accountability (referred to as MARRA). All these practical aspects of a teacher's job have complex theoretical backgrounds expounded in a range of weighty texts. The emphasis here is on equipping you with the knowledge and skills to meet your obligations and improve the teaching and learning in your classroom early in your teaching career. Practical considerations must, however, be informed by an understanding of some of the theoretical background and the terminology associated with assessment, as well as you reflecting on your initial experiences of assessing students.

A starting point for a critical look at the changing role of assessment in schooling might be the work of Lloyd-Jones et al. (1992: 6), in which the authors seek to identify trends in assessment (see Isaacs, 2010 for an account of the changing assessment regime in England). Some of their predictions have come to pass in full, for example, the move away from 'comparing pupils with each other to indicate final achievement and for ranking and selection purposes' towards 'comparing pupils' performance with predetermined criteria to provide feedback for improving performance' (Lloyd-Jones et al., 1992: 6). Others have been partially fulfilled, but perhaps in ways that the authors were not expecting, such as the move away from academic assessment towards 'recognition given to skills such as listening, speaking, practical skills, attitudes, personal and social development' (1992: 6). Some of their other predictions sound unbelievable when compared with current assessment arrangements, such as the move away from examinations towards 'continuous assessment, often as a normal part of the teaching/learning process' (1992: 6). The introduction of **Standard Assessment Tasks (SATs)** for the end of Key Stage test and modular examinations post-16 has intensified the formal examination experience of students to an unprecedented extent. Other developments were not anticipated by Lloyd-Jones et al. For example, it could be argued that the main purpose of formal assessment has shifted from the 'ranking and selection of pupils' (Lloyd-Jones 1992: 6) to the use of collective statistics for the ranking and selection of *schools*. Moreover, assessment arrangements are in a constant state of change, as governments introduce new or altered testing (for example, the proposal in 2010 by the coalition government to eliminate modular forms of GCSE).

These predictions raise a fundamental question in relation to any assessment regime, which is 'What exactly is being assessed?' If you think about the complexity of human characteristics, it is difficult to envisage any ways in which an assessment system can encapsulate all the aspects of the human condition without serious testing overload. For example, a prospective employer might want to know how good you were intellectually, practically, or at theoretical knowledge, but would also be interested in your character, your ability to work socially, your values and personal dispositions that might impact upon your ability to do a good job (see Pring, 1984). Watkins (1992) identified seven 'selfs' that might be subject to testing: the bodily self, including health and environmental impact; the sexual self; the social self which includes communication skills;

the vocational self and career trajectories; the moral self as a political actor; the self as a learner; and the self in the organization. Perhaps most influential on present-day schooling in the UK, the work of Howard Gardner (see Gardner, 1993, for example) on multiple intelligences (see Chapter 2) raises problematic questions for any assessment system. Gardner proposes that there is not a single 'intelligence' that therefore can be simply measured, but that there are a number of 'intelligences' existing in everyone, but developed to different levels depending on the individual. The difficulty Gardner faced was in devising measures that could assess and profile the intelligences of an individual in a way that was practical and not too time-consuming (see Gardner, 2006).

Before looking at each of the five MARRA elements, gather your own thoughts about what you think assessment is for and how it has affected you.

Activity 5.1   Why assess?

This activity can be completed individually or with other beginning teachers.

Before you look at the list below, try to answer the question 'Why assess?' With other beginning teachers you could 'brainstorm' lots of ideas.

Then read these 15 suggested reasons and indicate with '++', '+' or '−' those which are very important (++), fairly important (+) or least important (−) to you as a teacher and, in your view, to students.

	Teacher	Student
1 To monitor student progress of a whole class.		
2 To identify strengths and weaknesses of individual students.		
3 To find out how well individual students are assimilating what is being taught.		
4 To provide feedback to students in order to help decide what action should be taken next.		
5 To provide information to students about how well they are doing against national standards.		
6 To accumulate records of progress.		
7 To inform other teachers who have to make decisions about students.		

(Continued)

(Continued)

		Teacher	Student
8	To assess the benefits of a course.		
9	To evaluate the effectiveness of teaching methods.		
10	To provide motivation to students.		
11	To provide incentives to learn.		
12	To assist in guidance about choice of subject, course, career, and so on.		
13	To inform parents about progress.		
14	To provide information to employers, further and higher education for use in selection.		
15	To comply with statutory requirements about publication of results, which is designed to enable governors and parents to judge the effectiveness of the school.		

Monitoring

An essential part of the everyday activity of all teachers is monitoring students' achievements and progress. This is often done in an informal and impressionistic way to allow the teacher to decide what has been learned and where there are still weaknesses in students' understanding. One of the most important skills you can develop in this regard is always to be aware of what is going on in your classroom. This is described as 'withitness' by Kounin (1970). Picking up quickly on the individual needs of students has a direct bearing on the quality of their learning experience, their behaviour and their motivation, and, by doing this, you will be able to teach more effectively.

Wragg (2001) suggested that observing students in the classroom is a key aspect of this monitoring process. It allows teachers to link informal assessment to learning. By looking at the interactions and individual circumstances of the students, the teacher can distinguish between those who might be making progress and those who might be having problems with the learning. However, Wragg warned against making simplistic judgements about student behaviour on the basis of observation alone. For example, what might seem to be a student concentrating on the task could be a student daydreaming. Therefore to monitor effectively, he argued that the teacher needs to interact verbally with students, both in groups and as individuals. However, what is vital in the monitoring process is *how* the teacher enquires about the student's engagement, what he called 'the language of discourse' (Wragg, 2001: 39) of the interaction. To monitor students' learning in a meaningful way, the teacher has to find the form of question that allows *the student* to identify what they have learned and achieved over the immediately preceding segment of the session.

Despite the apparent informality and spontaneity of classroom monitoring, planning will improve its effectiveness. Four aspects are worth looking at:

1 Very many lessons start with a teacher-led introduction, which includes a few questions and answers by way of a recapitulation of previous lessons. This is a rough and ready form of 'baseline assessment' (see page 175). To teachers, its main advantage is that it is a quick and efficient way to start a lesson, which helps to focus students' minds on the forthcoming topic. The drawback is that it is easy to rely on a few students to supply all the answers and the rest of the class get used to opting out. As a tool for monitoring what students already know or have recalled from previous work, it therefore has limited benefits unless the teacher consciously plans a sequence of questions and involves most if not all of the class. The use of directed questioning in this circumstance helps to spread the range of those who answer the questions. More formal methods of monitoring may be employed at this point, for example, requiring every student to come to the interactive whiteboard (IWB) and contribute to a mind map or having a prepared written task on the desk as students come in to the class, which is designed to establish what the students have brought with them from a previous session.

2 The use of the 'three-part' lesson and its variations is one way in which monitoring student progress can have a built-in segment, usually called a plenary. While the use of the word 'plenary' would seem to indicate that it occurs at the end of a lesson, a plenary can occur at any stage, as it is the function that is important rather than its location. Plenaries are intended to provide an opportunity for students and teachers to review what has been learned in a previous learning episode and establish the foundations for future learning. They can be formal or informal, teacher- or student-led, and written or oral. Ofsted (2002) identifies the plenary as a way of ensuring that 'the whole class (is) moving forward together' (2002: 4) and teachers 'review with (students) the extent of their learning' (2002: 74).

3 Very many lessons also include a substantial amount of time when students are working on the task they have been set, with the teacher moving around the class responding to individuals. Beginning teachers are generally good at supporting students when they are working individually, but again practice could be improved by considering the nature of the questions asked in these interactions. Wragg (2001) distinguishes between lower-order and higher-order questions in which the former are concerned with asking students to give a factual response, that is recall a piece of knowledge, and the latter demanding some form of thinking beyond just remembering facts. The key skill of problem-solving is directly concerned with this higher-order

questioning. Observations of the classroom have shown that many teachers give a very limited time for students to think about their answers, before the teacher moves on to someone else, or answers the question themselves! While factual recall can be a quick-fire activity, the thinking processes in higher-order questions need time to be thought through. The format of the question will also differ according to what you want to elicit from the students. Higher-order questions are generally more open than factual recall questions (see also Chapter 2).

It is also worth considering why students may seem to be disengaged from activities in which you have planned for their active involvement. There is no one explanation for off-task behaviour. It may be that the student already knows a great deal about the topic or alternatively does not understand the task. It may that they have not had the chance to develop the skills to complete it or external factors may be affecting their performance. Some students for example are shy of engaging in public contributions in the classroom. As presentation is a central skill in many occupations, it is your responsibility to devise strategies that allow students to develop those skills in a structured and supported way, while monitoring their progress in this skill.

4 Teachers commonly attach considerable importance to written tasks such as homework or tests to judge how well students have understood a topic. The business of marking written work is looked at in the section on assessment (page 169), but it is worth considering its value as a way of monitoring students' progress. For the student who struggles with or dislikes writing, it has obvious limitations. A salutary experience is to observe and/or talk to an early years teacher who has to find ways of monitoring the progress of children too young to express themselves adequately on paper.

Over time, a good teacher also needs to monitor students' progress in terms of what kinds of task individuals find difficult and what skills they might be lacking. This should be closely linked to assessment, so that your mark book shows you significant ups and downs in a student's performance, and to planning, so that you can build in further opportunities for practice and improvement.

Activity 5.2   Definitions of assessment

This activity can be completed individually and responses shared with another beginning teacher.

Assessment and testing policies and practices are central structuring features of education systems, schools and classrooms, one important component of what Bernstein (1971) called the three message systems of schooling – curriculum, pedagogy and assessment. Assessment sits at the intersection of the educational field with its semi-autonomous character and the fields of the broader social arrangement. The varying forms of assessment and testing sit in different positions across these fields; compare, for example, formative assessment and summative assessment, or the distinctions utilized by the contemporary Scottish project 'Assessment is for learning' of *assessment for, as and of learning* (see Hayward et al., 2000; Hutchinson and Hayward, 2005). There are inherent tensions between assessment located within the educational field for educative purposes and that located at the intersection of that field and an unequally structured society for sorting and selecting purposes and within the bureaucratic state field for system accountability purposes (Lingard et al., 2006: 83–84).

In three sentences, distinguish between *curriculum*, *pedagogy* and *assessment* in schooling.

1   Providing examples, identify the differences between assessment 'for, as and of learning'.

2   In discussion with another beginning teacher, establish what you understand by the authors' view that there are 'inherent tensions between assessment located within the educational field for educative purposes and that located at the intersection of that field and an unequally structured society for sorting and selecting purposes and within the bureaucratic state field for system accountability purposes'?

3   Individually, decide which of the three fields you think is the dominant one in contemporary schooling. Justify your answer to the other trainee.

Assessment

Assessment is any method of obtaining information about the progress and performance of your students. It is a big and complex area of a teacher's work, yet one that is undertaken every day. The research basis for awarding bodies' and teachers' practices in assessment is fraught with uncertainty. Some areas of schooling are more amenable to accurate testing than others. The more complex the understanding to be tested, the more difficult it is to devise assessment tasks that can validly measure that understanding. Take, for example, the issue of key skills. The 'harder' key skills such as numeracy can have assessment activities that can be fair and reliable to all the students who take them. However, with the 'softer' key skills, such as 'working with others', it is difficult to construct assessment circumstances in which we could be confident that everyone who participated was awarded the grade that their performance deserved. Because of this problem, data about schools' performance is expressed as attainment and achievement data. Attainment is the level of knowledge and skills that can be formally tested and presented as examination grades or test scores. Achievement is the broader range of knowledge, skills and attitudes that students acquire in schools and which are often part of the social and personal development of an individual student.

There is no generally agreed model for assessment. However, most commentators would agree that a useful starting point would be Thomas's (1990: 128) definition that 'assessing learning should involve not only terminal or summative assessment, but should also be a diagnostic process embracing learning as it proceeds'. Issues concerning assessment have come to the forefront of debates about how to improve student attainment, as evidence from Ofsted has accumulated that suggests that 'good assessment practice in the schools visited derives from scrupulous attention to pupils' progress and draws teachers together in working systematically on achievement. It has been key to improvement in these schools' (Ofsted, 2003: 4).

You will need to develop an understanding of how formal and informal approaches can work; of how you elicit information and form judgements about cognitive development (knowledge, understanding) as opposed to affective development (attitudes), and, within the former, the difference between knowledge and skills; of differences between 'attainment', 'ability' and 'achievement', and the importance of recognizing 'effort' and of using assessment in a way which motivates students. Assessment should never be seen as the last 'add-on' stage in the process of teaching and learning, but as an integral part of the planning cycle. In the 'virtuous circle of teaching' (see Figure 5.1) learning is at the very heart of what teachers do, and assessment is one of the four planks of teacher activity that promotes student learning. Alongside planning, delivery and evaluating, assessing is a vital component of teaching and has to be integrated into teachers' practices seamlessly.

Some of the terminology associated with assessment may be unfamiliar to you. Key concepts include the following.

Summative assessment

This takes place at the end of a course or period of schooling and is largely concerned with reporting results to an external audience such as parents, carers or a potential employer. End of year examinations or GCSE or **level 3 examinations** (AS – Advanced Supplementary level taken at age 17, and A2 – Advanced level taken at 18, Applied A levels and the International Baccalaureate) are typical examples of summative assessment. While, historically, summative assessment has taken a particular form, it is not a fixed format at all. Traditionally, discursive subjects such as history have relied on the essay-type question for their major form of assessment; the scientific and mathematical subjects relied on working through set problems; and the more artistic subjects have used practical tasks, but usually time-constrained and in a more formal setting. In the

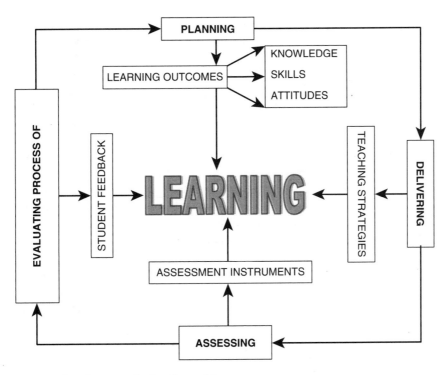

Figure 5.1   The virtuous circle of teaching

future, the involvement of ICT in summative assessment is likely to increase. Awarding bodies such as the Assessment and Qualification Alliance (AQA), Oxford, Cambridge and RSA (OCR) and Edexcel already use electronic marking and the virtual standardization of scripts in a wide range of subjects, including discursive ones, but there are also ways in which ICT can be utilized for direct assessment activities (see Richardson, 2003).

Since the 1980s, there has been a movement to less formal means of summative assessment, especially involving the project or coursework. The General Certificate of Secondary Education (GCSE) had a compulsory element of coursework in all subjects since the 1980s. However, coursework options were removed from most GCSE subjects in 2009 and replaced with 'controlled assessment'. This is a form of internal assessment, set and marked by the schools or by the awarding body, depending on the level of control determined in the specification of subjects that are allowed to include controlled assessment. The argument in favour of coursework was that it was a more 'authentic' way of assessing what students 'know, understand and can do'. It also allowed those students who did not perform well in the 'three-hour' examination format to have a different experience of assessment that might more closely fit their learning preferences. However, concerns about the reliability of coursework modes of assessment, in particular its potential for plagiarism with the rise of the Internet and the contributions that parents can make in a non-supervised mode of assessment, have led to a rethink about the efficacy of coursework and its replacement in some subjects by controlled assessment. At level 3, changes in coursework at AS and A2 introduced in 2008 include the introduction of a free-standing extended project qualification that could use techniques drawn from any subject (see www.thekjs.essex.sch. uk/yates/Documents/EPQ%20Project%20Ideas.pdf for some examples).

One of the perceived problems with summative assessment, where nationally validated, is that it becomes a 'high-stakes' assessment. By this is meant that, because success in examinations is a passport to higher study, better jobs, more money, higher status, and so on, the investment of students in education can be aimed at achieving the certificate rather than learning about the subject. If you add in the fact that teachers are judged on the results that their students achieve, there can be a bias towards performance in examination rather than understanding the complexities of an area of study. This is often referred to as a focus on 'shallow' rather than 'deep' learning (see Harlen and James, 1997). Teachers may be aware of 'teaching to the test', but may still find their classroom strategies and interactions with students leaning towards more passive modes of learning in order to secure the best examination results (see Harlen, 2006).

Activity 5.3   Assessing your subject

Parts (a)–(c) of this activity can be completed individually and discussed with other beginning teachers. Parts (d)–(f) should be discussed with your mentor or another experienced teacher.

The approach to assessment in each National Curriculum subject represents one view of the matter: that of the people who devised the Order. You may agree with it, or parts of it; you may not. The fact that there are marked differences in this respect between the 1990, 1995, 2000, 2008 and 2011 Orders suggests the difficulties and contentiousness of assessment issues.

(a) Before examining the National Curriculum, consider the following questions:

What should be assessed in your subject?

Are there aspects of your subject that should not or cannot be assessed?

(b) Now examine the National Curriculum document in your subject (or one closely related if yours is not part of the National Curriculum) with these questions in mind:

To what extent do the assessment arrangements in your subject reflect your own views?

Are there aspects of those arrangements you would modify or remove?

(c) Compare your views with beginning teachers from other subjects in order to decide whether some subjects are more problematic than others in the matter of assessment.

(d) Examine closely the wording of the level descriptions for your subject or a closely related one. What are their strengths and weaknesses? Do they cover everything that you value in the learning activities to which they relate?

(e) Carry out a marking exercise according to the marking criteria for your chosen subject to see how closely your judgements match those of a more experienced teacher. This will take you a long time, but is the best way of interpreting and applying National Curriculum assessment criteria.

(f) Carry out a similar exercise for work at GCSE or A2 and AS levels or for the International Baccalaureate. Do this as a 'blind' activity, marking work that a more experienced teacher has already marked but without knowing what mark it has been given.

Formative assessment

This is part of a continuous spiral of learning, the assessment of what has been learned in order to guide what should happen next, then more learning, more assessment, and so on. It is important to recognize that formative assessment can have negative as well as positive effects on achievement. Dweck (1986) distinguishes between 'mastery-oriented' responses to assessment, in which students seek challenge and deploy effort in pursuing goals, and 'maladaptive' responses, which are seen as a form of helplessness, where students avoid challenges and have low persistence when struggling with learning. Formative assessment is more diagnostic, should give more immediate feedback to student and teacher, and should be acted upon by them. Although allotting a mark to a piece of work does not seem to be as important in raising achievement as the provision of a commentary about how to improve it, Smith and Gorard (2005) showed that the students themselves valued a mark as a means of identifying where they were in terms of standards. Many would argue that self-assessment is an essential component of formative assessment. Theorists such as Earl (2003) argued that studies of assessment have concentrated on the assessment *of* learning, but that the investigation of assessment *for* learning and assessment *as* learning are equally important. Formative assessment is now most closely associated with the idea of assessment for learning (see page 177). Assessment as learning is used by teachers to gain access to students' understandings of an issue, to identify misunderstandings and plan for remedial action.

Normative assessment

This provides information about a student's ability or achievement compared with others in the same age cohort. Thus a mark or a grade tells us, for example, that a student is in the top 10 per cent for their age, or 23rd in their class. Much assessment has traditionally been of this kind. The advantage of this type of assessment is that it establishes the relative position of students in relation to their peers. When entry to higher education or more prestigious occupations was limited to a relatively small percentage of the population, then this was probably an appropriate way of sorting individuals into a normal distribution curve, where the top percentile alone would be most likely to be recruited into higher education. However, the weakness of norm-referencing is that it does not describe what an individual student can actually do, only their position in relation to others' performance. As social policies have shifted towards increasing the proportion of each age cohort which is to be recruited to further study, norm-referencing has fallen out of favour as a principle of national examinations in the UK.

Criterion-referenced assessment

This is where a student's performance is judged against a clear and concrete statement (the criterion) of what is expected. It requires a careful analysis of the course concerned and its learning objectives, leading to unambiguously stated criteria. These require the formulation of a set of statements that enable the assessment to be expressed as a 'profile' of achievement rather than, or as well as, a single overall grade or mark. In national examinations, criterion-referencing usually appears as a number of level descriptions, with each paragraph defining what might be expected of a candidate at grade E, C and A (for AS and A2 examinations).

The link with formative assessment can be seen, as criterion referencing should give a clear statement of what a student can do or has achieved, which can be built upon in the next stage of their experience. Whilst the benefits of criterion-referenced assessment are now widely accepted, there can be practical difficulties. In particular the production of unambiguous and acceptable criteria can be highly problematic and time-consuming. General Certificate of Secondary Education and Advanced level are criterion-referenced examinations, but there are difficulties in putting them into practice. For example, the complexity of the original National Curriculum assessment regime included several criteria at each level of each attainment target. The testing regime was supposed to be short tests, but they could not cover all the criteria at all the levels (see Cullingford, 1997, for an account of this issue). The level description criteria used in GCSE and Advanced level examinations often contain within them norm-referenced statements, so that for example, a C-level candidate might be described as having a 'satisfactory' grasp of a piece of knowledge, which is implicitly contrasted with those who have a less or more satisfactory grasp (see Wragg, 1997).

Baseline assessment

In general terms, this means finding out what your students know and can do before you teach them more. Since September 1998 it took on a particular meaning as a statutory requirement for all children starting school – teachers had to use an accredited baseline scheme, usually developed by the local authority, capable of producing numerical outcomes related to a specific range of achievements. This has been replaced by the coalition government of 2010 with the Foundation Stage Profile, which captures a more rounded picture of young children's abilities. Schools that have adopted a dense form of assessment activity use baseline-type assessments to inform their future policies. For example, in the Sacred Heart High School, 'a range of assessment information is considered, including Key Stage 2 test and teacher assessment data, and the outcomes of standardized tests in mathematics, reading and non-verbal reasoning. These are used to provide a baseline for individual pupils and benchmarks for the school' (Ofsted, 2003: 7). These baseline assessment measures are also used by schools to identify those who have particular learning needs, or who are gifted and talented, or 'most able and more able' (MAMA).

Validity

This and reliability (next section) relate to technical issues of assessment and researchers in the area of assessment emphasize their importance. Validity concerns the extent to which an assessment actually assesses what it is supposed to be assessing. Most commonly this is judged by the opinions of those knowledgeable in the subject area concerned, but it is also sometimes possible to judge validity by some external criterion: for example, do results from this assessment predict performance in a subsequent course? This occurs for example when schools generate '**value-added**' measures of attainment.

Students are given predictions of what they should achieve at the next level of assessment on the basis of a previous assessment. When students achieve higher grades than previous performance would predict, the school is said to have 'added value' to that student's education. Another way that external criteria might be use to judge the validity of an assessment task is where the results from a test agree with ratings of achievement given by a teacher. You may be asked to engage in this predicted grade activity on post-16 examinations such as AS and A2 examinations.

However, there are certain areas of controversy around validity suggested by researchers that have to be considered. Different experts emphasize different types of validity in approaching assessment. Awarding bodies are particularly concerned with content validity, that is, how closely an examination paper matches the assessment objectives of the specification. For example, it would be unfair if an area of the specification studied by a group of students never had a question set on it. Lloyd-Jones et al. (1992) describe construct-validity as an important element for those programmes that cover a variety of skills, as well as knowledge. Construct-validity refers to how well an assessment task can provide judgements about higher-order cognitive skills, such as analysis and evaluation, rather than just the recall of relevant knowledge. The problem here is not just that it is more difficult to devise tasks that give all students who take them the possibility of demonstrating these skills if they have acquired them. There is also the problem that areas of affective skills such as feelings and attitudes that a subject might engender have proved to be very difficult to assess in a valid way (Messick, 1994). The search for reliability in assessment can therefore lead to only assessing those aspects of education that can more easily be assessed reliably (see Stobart, 2006: 135).

Finally, criterion-related validity refers to the ability of an assessment task to cover all the level descriptions connected to a particular examination. The difficulty of devising questions that all levels of ability can access fairly has led, in some subjects only, to the tiering of GCSE examinations in which those who can access the higher criteria have additional or different assessment tasks to attempt.

Reliability

This relates to whether assessment results are consistent. Would the results be the same if the assessment was carried out on a different day, or in slightly different circumstances, or by a different teacher? Gipps (1994) distinguishes between consistency in student performance and consistency in assessing that performance. In the case of the former, reliability refers to how far the student would be able to replicate his or her performance on a different day with the same examination paper. The latter refers to whether different markers would arrive at the same mark for one candidate's paper. The awarding bodies try to achieve this through the technical device of defining reliability as all markers giving the same mark to a candidate's work that the principal examiner, who set the paper, would have given it. Reliability is clearly an important issue where results are for use outside the classroom, for example where they might influence selection for a job or for a place in higher education (see Black and Wiliam, 2006: 130–131). This is why all the awarding bodies are required by the Office of Qualifications and Examinations Regulation (Ofqual) to have appeals procedures in place, so that candidates can challenge whether their individual papers have been reliably marked.

The question of the reliability of end of Key Stage tests in the National Curriculum has also been raised. The problem is that the tests can either assess a relatively small area of a subject in some depth or take a broader view and assess a greater range of skills more superficially. Wiliam (2000) has calculated that over 50 per cent of students who take end of Key Stage tests at Key Stage 3 are classified at the wrong level. Similarly Massey et al. (2003) argued that much of the apparent gain in test results at Key Stage 2 was attributable to variations in the standards of the tests, rather than a measure of real progress (see Bew, 2011 for the coalition government's review of Stage 2 assessment).

Activity 5.4   Identifying good practice in assessment

All parts of this activity can be completed individually. Parts (c) and (d) can be shared with your tutor or mentor.

(a) On the companion website is a link to an Ofsted document entitled *Good Assessment in Secondary Schools*, published in March 2003. You will need to read this or download all or part of it.

(b) In Part 2, there are a number of vignettes of good assessment practice in various subjects. Choose a subject, *other than your own*, and select an account that you think has implications for good assessment practice in your own subject.

(c) Write a 250-word report on the specific practice(s) that you have chosen, showing how it/they would be useful in your own subject and how you will introduce it/them into your own practice.

(d) Choose another account from a different area of the curriculum where you think the assessment practice(s) is less useful for your subject and detail the reasons for your decision as another 250-word report.

Assessment for learning

An extension of formative assessment, this is one of the key thrusts of the National Strategy (see Ofsted, 2010) for raising standards of student attainment. It is defined as 'the process of seeking and interpreting evidence for use by learners and their teachers to decide where the learners are in their learning, where they need to go and how best to get there' (ARG, 2002: 1). This can be seen as an element of an action planning process, in which students and teachers together review the evidence of what has been achieved, identify what still has to be done in terms of **SMART** (specific, measurable, achievable, realistic, time-defined) targets, draw up strategies to move the student towards those targets and provide a time frame when progress will be next checked.

The impetus for work in this area was created by the research by Black and Wiliam (1998), in which they reviewed the research evidence for the effectiveness of formative assessment. Their starting point was that international research suggested that the existence of formal external tests dominated the classroom and led to a focus on the outcomes of schooling rather than looking at the processes whereby learning could be analysed to promote improvements in learning. They concluded that implementing formative assessment could produce substantial gains in attainment but that major weaknesses in classroom assessment would need to be tackled if the potential of formative assessment is to be realized.

Three main categories of weakness are identified: the quality of assessment tasks on which the process of feedback is based; teachers' grading of students' work as part of the feedback process; and a failure to actively involve students in their own assessment in order to help them become increasingly responsible for their own learning.

Assessment for learning has the greatest potential for advancing students' progress, because it has the potential to close the gap between the current level of achievement and the desired level. Two crucial ingredients can turn this into reality: high-quality assessment tasks, which do actually find out what you think they will; effective feedback, which acknowledges achievement to date and indicates ways to improve. It is essential that students understand the processes so that self-assessment and target-setting can start to operate; in other words, assessment is not something that teachers do to students' work, but something in which all parties are involved.

Researchers have shown that classroom practice often demonstrates weaknesses in each of these areas (see Black and Wiliam, 1998), and offer the following recommendations.

Assessment tasks should:

- be planned as part of a deliberate sequence to achieve progression in students' learning over a minimum of a Key Stage
- be enjoyable but reasonably challenging and differentiated
- develop thinking skills, for example the ability to synthesize or evaluate
- require students to transform rather than transfer information
- make students aware of how they will be assessed
- sometimes be devised for students working in groups
- sometimes enable teachers to observe the process of decision-making
- sometimes make possible more than one acceptable solution or answer
- sometimes permit the student to select the form of response

Feedback should:

- be directly related to the assessment task
- be related to the standards the teacher has set for the successful completion of the task
- concentrate on what the student particularly needs to do to improve which will make the most difference
- be communicated in a language the student can understand
- be positive but constructively critical
- be as immediate as is practical
- require action on the part of the student
- use consistent marking conventions across a department to acknowledge success and identify targets for improvement
- take advantage of a range of contexts, for example pair or group work or homework (see Spendlove, 2009 for ideas about how to put these into practice and Bennett, 2011 for a criticial review of AfL)

This last point can be extended to include the importance of self- and peer-assessment as important elements of assessment for learning. Black et al. (2003) argue that self-assessment by students is a difficult skill to develop, as students do not automatically have the necessary analytical know-how to identify what has gone wrong or the ability to set realistic strategies for improvement. However, they claim that peer-assessment can help the students to develop these skills, because it motivates them to work more carefully, gives greater power to the student voice, thus commanding more attention and uses more accessible language to offer criticism that may more readily be taken on board.

Activity 5.5   Self-assessment

You can complete activity (a) individually and (b) in a small group.

(a) Consider the experiences you have had of self-assessment. In what ways do you think they influenced your learning?

(b) In a small group:

 (i) List the possible benefits of students assessing their own work.

 (ii) Consider whether there are any drawbacks or potential difficulties.

 (iii) Drawing on experience from your own subject area collate ideas for supporting students' self-assessment.

 (iv) Discuss how schools can teach/encourage pupils to become autonomous learners.

 (v) Identify the skills you need as a teacher to help give young people the confidence to take responsibility for their own learning.

Marking

During the early part of your teaching career, the priority is to mark in a way which is in line with departmental or school policy and therefore familiar to the students. One of the first difficulties that you might face is how to mark non-written work in a way that accords with the standards in your department. For example, the English National Curriculum has attainment targets related to speaking and listening, as well as reading and writing. Other subjects, such as drama, design and technology and PE, are involved in the marking of practical and performance work. In addition, you will have to familiarize yourself with national standards of attainment for your particular subject or subjects, especially if you are involved in marking controlled assessment for national examinations or are preparing students for National Curriculum assessments. The difficulty that you face here is conforming to a standard that is fixed by remote awarding bodies and the Office for Qualifications and Examinations Regulation. These organizations are charged with the responsibility of ensuring comparability in national examinations. By comparability, they mean three related aspects of examining:

- Examinations in the same subject should be comparable in standard year on year, so that a student achieving a B grade at GCSE in one year is at roughly the same standard as a student in the subsequent year.
- Examinations in different subjects at the same level in the same year should be of a comparable standard, so that a GCSE grade B in Mathematics represents a comparable difficulty to achieving a grade B GCSE in English.
- Examinations in the same subject but offered by different awarding bodies should be roughly comparable in standard, so that a C in History with OCR is the same level as a C with AQA.

Of course, it is not an easy or simple process to ensure that these elements of comparability are achieved. For example, schools may switch the awarding body they use for a particular subject because of a perception that one examination is easier than the other. However, there are procedures in place to try and ensure that comparability is as real as the human dimension of marking allows. So, subjects at a specific level are regularly scrutinized by Ofqual to ensure that they are at a comparable level of difficulty and Ofqual runs constant checking projects to track standards over time and between subjects. However, the margin for error in marking remains a function of its human agency. As Sutton (1992: 2) puts it: 'Assessment is a human process conducted by and with human beings and subject to the frailties of human nature. However crisp and objective we might try to make it and however neatly quantifiable may be our results, assessment is closer to an art than a science.' The coalition government, which came into power in 2010, will require Ofqual to make international comparisons with British qualifications, to ensure that they are consistent with the highest global standards.

The difficulty that you will face in absorbing the national standards of marking is important because, when you mark your students' work, you need to give them a realistic assessment of where they stand in relation to the national standard. Giving a piece of work an accurate mark or grade is important for the students to understand where they are and the gap between that and where they want to be (for example, in terms of the grade they need to get to the course of their choice if they are going to go to university). It is also part of your job to support students with appropriate strategies to make that improvement – part of the assessment for learning agenda. There are a number of ways in which you can access the national standards. The awarding bodies offer training sessions for teachers to familiarize them with the processes of marking external examinations and internally assessed coursework. There are often clusters of schools that co-operate in moderating their own marking. In terms of your training year, the school or college department you are in will be the easiest place to access these standards.

Prompt, careful marking of students' work is one of the most important ways in which you can convey respect for their efforts and demand similarly high standards from them. It also has a special role in relating to parents/carers, who tend to make all sorts of judgements and assumptions about your teaching on the basis of the few comments they see on their child's work.

Marking is a form of assessment that gives teachers the chance to respond to an individual's work. It helps both teachers and students develop a shorthand language which facilitates efficient and clear communication. The problem is that marking is time-consuming and can easily feel burdensome. You will have to learn to fit marking into your working schedule, and plan the tasks which you set so that all your classes' work does not come in to be marked at the same time. Most departments select certain pieces of work – perhaps at the end of a topic – for careful assessment and prepare the students accordingly. You may need to target particular pieces of work for detailed marking and comments and treat others more superficially. Remember, too, the possibility of training students to use self- and paired-assessment.

Activity 5.6   Ways of assessing

Consider the following list of assessment strategies.

Oral evidence	Written evidence	Graphic evidence	Products
Questioning	Questionnaires	Maps	Models
Listening	Diaries	Diagrams	Artefacts
Discussing	Reports	Sketches	Games
Presentation	Essays	Drawings	Photographs
Interviewing	Notes	Graphs	Databases
Debates	Stories	Printouts	Dance
Audio recording	Newspaper articles	Overlays	Performance
Video recording	Scripts	Video clips	Theatrical show
Role-play		Spread sheets	PE or games exhibition

(Continued)

(Continued)

Oral evidence	Written evidence	Graphic evidence	Products
	Short answers to questions	PowerPoint presentations	
	Lists	Storyboard	
	Poems		
	Descriptions		
	Portfolios		
	Booklets		

1 Consider from your observation of others and your own experience of the classroom:

- Which of these are produced frequently in the classroom?
- Which of these are used infrequently?
- Why?
- Are any of the above under-used in your own classroom?

2 Choose at least one example from each column of the table and consider the positive and negative aspects for each, for example:

Wallchart or display	
Positive	**Negative**
Encourages discussion	Encourages copying
Co-operation	Assessing individual contribution difficult
Skills other than writing	
A guide to future lesson planning	Some pupils left out
Sharing ideas	Time-consuming
Demonstrates understanding	Has everyone a record of what they did?
Gives information about the topic for others to see	How do I record the work?
Interesting	Did everyone understand?

3 During your teaching experience, you must use a variety of teaching and assessment strategies. As part of your lesson evaluations, comment on the effectiveness of what you have tried and how this has informed your future planning to meet the needs of individuals.

Recording

Keeping tidy, accurate and informative records about students is a responsibility for every teacher and has become increasingly important as systems of public accountability for schooling have been refined. Records fulfil a number of functions for the individual teacher:

1 To support your memory and keep information for your own use, for example formative assessment purposes.
2 To enable information to be passed on within school to other teachers, for example as a student progresses up the school.
3 To inform contacts between school and parents/carers.

Records also provide functions for schools and colleges and the education system as a whole:

1 To provide information to other schools when children transfer.
2 To identify any patterns in a child's performance and thereby identify the need for intervention, in particular with regard to special educational needs, including gifted and talented students.
3 When aggregated, to provide information for outside agencies, for example inspection agencies, the national government, parents and the media.
4 To contribute to a school's improvement plans.

These different functions require varying amounts of detail and types of information. Good advice early in your career is to keep relatively full records, including notes and reminders to yourself from lesson to lesson. The mark book maintained by each teacher is an important record of student's work and progress. One of the problems with recording is that performance can be recorded in a number of forms (percentages, raw marks, grades, linear scales for effort – see Wragg, 2001: 76). You need therefore to organize your recording practice to fit in with the school's system of recording, but as long as it enables departmental records to be completed, it can be unique to each teacher. In addition, teachers are required to keep information about students' progress that contributes to the self-evaluation documents that departments and schools have to submit as part of their school-improvement procedures.

Many schools have sophisticated systems for building up a profile of each student and groups of students throughout the school career, and as a class teacher you will contribute to that. Increasingly, these profiles are based on ICT software that allows a sophisticated analysis of an individual's performance, attendance, punctuality and the like, with the capability of awarding red/amber/green status to individual students on the basis of their combined scores on these criteria. Ironically, one of the items of record-keeping that is often ignored is to build up a record of an individual student's exposure to various forms of ICT applications beyond the ICT classroom (see Comber et al., 2002).

This record-keeping will therefore involve your role as a classroom teacher but also your pastoral role (see Chapter 6). As learning support teachers and teaching assistants take on duties within the classroom, you will also take responsibility for their record-keeping. Your duties in this regard will include both the collection of appropriate data, and also its accuracy.

Records of achievement

The term 'records of achievement' first came into use in the 1970s. It developed from a concern to recognize the achievements of young people leaving school with no or few formal qualifications and primarily as an aid for employers to identify the skills of potential employees. However, the processes and principles of assessment that the term came to embrace steadily grew in their influence, and came to be seen as relevant to all students.

A large number of individual schools and local authorities developed their own versions of records of achievement, and in the mid-1980s the Department of Education and Science (DES) supported a number of pilot projects and a national evaluation (Broadfoot and Pollard, 1997) that resulted in a National Record of Achievement (ROA) in 1993. This was intended to have four purposes: documenting achievement; recognizing wider achievement; organizing the individual's curriculum; and motivating students towards personal development (see Latham, 1997).

Records of achievement record the result of the processes of education and activities such as profiling (see later in this chapter). They therefore had the following features:

1   They use largely criterion-referenced methods to emphasize positive achievements.
2   They assess a wide range of achievements; including subject specific achievements, but also cross-curricular skills and extra-curricular and out-of-school achievements (and sometimes personal characteristics and attitudes).
3   They result in a summative document for use by the student on leaving school.
4   They incorporate elements of self-assessment by the student.

Profiling

In developing ROAs, much emphasis was placed on the processes that resulted in the final document, as a way of students engaging in planning their own educational development (see Latham, 1997). That is to say, the formative processes of 'profiling' were seen, not only as a way of planning to achieve formal qualifications, but also as a means of promoting individual self-development in a number of areas. The central aspect of profiling includes discussions between individual teachers and students about each student's progress in relationship to desired outcomes (that could be a certificate or the development of skills and attitudes). These discussions would lead to targets being set for the student to focus on within a timescale, with strategies suggested for how the student could make progress in achieving these targets and evidence identified that would indicate when these targets had been achieved. Increasingly, these 'conversations' are being recorded and monitored using sophisticated software.

Therefore a process of individual action planning (IAP) lay at the heart of the profiling movement. The central theoretical idea behind action planning was the desire to engage students in their own learning and for them to take more responsibility for their progress. By encouraging a greater sense of ownership of learning, the intention was to 'empower' students, so that education was no longer something that happened to students, but became a process in which students were actively engaged in constructing their own profiles of achievements. The notion of empowerment is not without its controversies (see Lawson and Harrison, 1999; Lawson, 2011). It has been argued that individual action planning, rather than passing control to students, gives only the illusion of freedom and instead, gets students to manage their own educational development within strict limits, as the end results (recognized qualifications or skills and attitudes desired by employers) are predetermined and outside of their control (see Lawson et al., 2004).

Portfolios

In many areas of education, the development of portfolios has been significant. The portfolio is 'a purposeful collection of student work that tells the story of the students' efforts, progress or achievement in (a) given area(s)' (Arter and Spandel, 1992: 36). However, portfolios can be used for a variety of purposes connected with assessment. They have been particularly deployed in vocational qualifications as a summative document for accreditation purposes (see Wolf, 2011 for the coalition government's review of vocational qualifications). Criteria for making judgements about the level of performance indicated in a portfolio are usually built into the specification for the subject and identify, for example, the number and type of pieces of work to be included, the skills to be included and often a requirement of an element of self-evaluation as part of the content. Portfolios are increasingly used in professional courses such as the PGCE (see Groom and Maunonen-Eskelinen, 2006) or for threshold assessment for teachers as a means of logging evidence for the range of standards that they have to reach in order to pass the course or proceed to higher pay levels. Grant and Huebner (1998) argued that the most effective portfolios in teacher education are those designed to promote reflective practice. To do this, the structure and processes associated with these portfolios should encourage a habit of mind that sees teaching as a continuous process of self-reflection and changes in practice as a result of collaborative working among professionals (see Chapter 1).

One of the main problems associated with portfolios as a means of assessment is their contrast to more traditional approaches in which reliability was assumed to be superior. The development of portfolios resulted from the search for more 'authentic' forms of assessment than traditional examinations. That is, many teachers and educationalists argued that reliance on end-of-course examinations alone meant many of the skills and attributes that students might have acquired during a course were not being assessed. By moving to portfolios, the range of criteria could be extended and therefore students would be allowed to show what they actually could do. However, because there were fears that portfolios did not provide a reliable measurement of the desired characteristics, the criteria for assessment were often drawn very tightly, with such a prescriptive and extensive number of assessment objectives that the portfolio was reduced to a bureaucratic exercise rather than an educational experience (see Klenowski, 2002). In addition, unless portfolio assessment is linked to some sort of reflective practice, there is a danger that it is seen by students as a hurdle to be overcome rather than a helpful device for demonstrating what they have learned (see Fernsten and Fernsten, 2005).

Progress File

The Progress File was the planned successor to the National Record of Achievement. It supported the processes of planning, achieving and reviewing, which are at the heart of individual learning and development.

The Progress File aimed to serve as a tool for:

- recording achievements
- helping students plan their learning and career development
- recognizing the knowledge, understanding and skills they are acquiring

It consisted of guidance materials for students from age 13 to adults.

Many schools have embedded Progress Files in their tutoring, mentoring, target-setting and reviewing, key skills development, personal development via PSHE, careers education guidance, preparation for transition, and work-related approaches to learning. The DfE, under the 2010 coalition, does not support any specific approach to monitoring and no longer provides templates for Progress Files. The department argues that the processes underpinning Progress Files are well established and has encouraged schools to adapt 'official' templates for their own purposes.

Activity 5.7   Recording achievement

Part (a) of this activity can be completed individually. Part (b) should be completed in consultation with other teachers.

(a) In your school find out whether students have Records of Achievement or a Progress File. If so, what format are these in? How are they used? Who has overall responsibility for this in the school?

What achievement do you think should be recorded:

(i) in your subject area or one closely related to your subject?

(ii) generally for students?

(b) If possible discuss with experienced teachers and/or other beginning teachers:

(i) What does your faculty/department regard as achievement? How is this recorded?

(ii) Do you consider there is a relationship between use of Records of Achievement/Progress Files and styles of teaching and learning within a department?

(iii) Arrange to look at examples of Records of Achievement/Progress Files and, if possible, talk to students about them.

Reporting

There will be, during your career, various ways in which you may be asked to report on your work — to your head of department, to senior management, to visiting inspectors, awarding bodies and to parents or carers. Reporting to external agencies has become part of the accountability system in education (see a later section in this chapter), while reports to internal lines of authority such as department heads, heads of division, and so on are often part of the process of self-evaluation and improvement that all schools and colleges are expected to engage in.

The style and timing of reports to parents and carers vary from school to school, but there are certain compulsory requirements. Schools must send a written report to parents on their children's achievements at least once during the school year and convey the results of National Curriculum assessments no later than 30 September of any year. Reports must include brief comments on the student's progress in each subject and activity studied as part of the school curriculum, highlighting strengths and development needs; the student's general progress; arrangements for parents to discuss the report with a teacher at the school; the total number of sessions (half days) since the student's last report or since the student entered the school, and the percentage missed through unauthorized absence. Many schools report more frequently than required as they view it as part of building a partnership between home and school.

At the end of each Key Stage, Ofqual suggests including: the student's National Curriculum assessment levels; a statement that the levels have been arrived at by statutory assessment; a statement where any attainment target has been dis-applied for a student; the percentage of students at the school at each level of attainment at the end of the Key Stage; the most recent national percentage of students at each level of attainment at the end of the Key Stage. All reports written about a student must now be part of the student's educational record.

The purpose of reporting to parents in these formal ways is to provide parents with the necessary information so that a dialogue can take place about the best way forward for an individual child. As the personalized learning agenda (see Chapter 3) has been implemented in schools and colleges, this dialogue has become increasingly important when individual students are entered for formal assessments at different ages rather than an age cohort. However, as assessment information has become more technical, there may be an increasing gap between parents/carers and the school in terms of a common understanding of this information. For example, the complexities of the statements of attainment and the levels that students can achieve may obscure rather than illuminate the overall progress of an individual student.

Writing reports

Report writing is, quite rightly, a time-consuming business – there are no short cuts! The terminology of the National Curriculum and, in particular, its level descriptors give teachers a neutral context in which to couch their comments, but a good report should also convey your personal response to a student's efforts (or lack of them) and be distinctive to that individual. Many styles and presentational formats of report writing are currently used by schools; these include detailed prose, tick boxes, combination of tick boxes and prose, prose generated from statement banks and so on. Most would agree that there is no single format for what constitutes a 'good report'.

The following is a suggested list of contents of a good report from a subject teacher:

- brief outline of learning experiences
- what the child has achieved within the subject, especially in core/key skills
- overall National Curriculum working level or GCSE level
- where the student is in relation to the cohort/age-group
- overall progress – target level/grade if appropriate
- effort, behaviour, concentration, attitude
- homework
- examination/test results
- coursework
- future development and targets

It is unlikely that during your training you will be given sole responsibility for report writing, but it is an excellent time to gain some practice and see how more experienced teachers go about the task.

Consider the following checklist:

- Read some previous reports to familiarize yourself with the general style.
- Start to collect some useful phrases.
- Invite the students to assess themselves or write their own version of their report.
- Think of the overall message you want to convey.
- Avoid jargon (even the use of levels to label attainment is baffling to many parents).
- Find something positive to say about every child and start with that.
- Convey criticism clearly but in positive terms, with advice about how to improve.
- Double check for any spelling or grammatical errors.

Activity 5.8   Writing reports

In consultation with your mentor or a teacher whose class you teach, try writing some reports taking account of the advice given here.

The sites below provide additional guidance and examples of good report writing:

http://webarchive.nationalarchives.gov.uk/20110223175304/http://www.qcda.gov.uk/default.aspx.

www.completeteacher.co.uk/report_writing.htm.

Meeting parents/carers

Parents' evenings can be quite stressful events for all concerned. They are a very important point of contact between teachers and parents and so opportunities for fruitful exchanges of views should be maximized. They are situations in which you as a teacher can find out about your students rather than just a one-way flow of information (see Wragg, 1997: 77–78). Schools have tried out various formats to make the most of the occasion, and there may be variations in how they are handled for different age groups of students. It is always worth remembering that you are on familiar territory and that parents can be surprisingly anxious or reticent about visiting school, especially on formal occasions. Brooks (2002) argues that the teacher needs to pay particular attention to the language that is used at these events to avoid either oversimplifying information that will patronize parents or making it so complex that important messages about students' progress are lost to the parents/carers. She also suggests that parents/carers are as concerned about their child's social and personal development as they are about academic performance.

There are other occasions at which you will meet parents/carers, most notably at open or recruitment events. Here, your concerns are more likely to be subject based, in that you will be trying to engage students in the possibilities of your subject. Striking the balance between attracting the students themselves and keeping the parents/carers involved will be your most important consideration here. As you progress in your career, there may also be occasions when you carry out home visits to parents/carers, often in difficult circumstances, but you should be supported in your first forays into these activities.

Activity 5.9   Meeting parents/carers

Part (a) of this activity can be completed individually and part (b) discussed with your mentor or another teacher.

Reports very often lead towards a parents'/carers' evening. If the school's cycle of consultation evenings fits in with your time in school, be sure to take the opportunity to attend. Schools organize such events in different ways and you will no doubt form impressions about the value of the occasion. Try and see it from the parents' perspectives too.

The following comments were collected from parents after such an evening:

1 'The information given me was insufficient. The teacher did not seem to know my son very well and could not advise me on the best way of assisting him with his Mathematics, which he said was weak.'

2 'Some of the information given to me was inaccurate. I checked the marks which the teacher said that Debbie had gained in English this term with her exercise book and they did not match. Could more care be taken?'

3 'It would have been useful to have been able to ask questions. The teacher talked all the time and gave me so much information that I could not absorb it all.'

4 'I don't understand all this business about levels. What is a level 5c? Couldn't they simply tell us whether the children are doing better or worse than they should be?'

5 'I'm sorry we did not attend the meeting as the notice was too short. Delvinder only gave us the information about it the previous day.'

6 'Could the meeting be organized to give more privacy rather than in the school hall? My son was heavily criticized and I felt that other parents were listening. It was most embarrassing.'

7 'Many thanks to all the teachers for attending and giving me such a good report on Nivraj.'

8 'Mr Potter complained that John was lazy in class and also inattentive. John tells me that Mr Potter finds it difficult to control the class and that he cannot work with all the noise. Could something be done about this?'

9 'The time given on the timetabled meetings was too short. We need at least half an hour with each teacher.'

10 'It would have been a successful meeting if teachers and parents had kept to the timetable. I missed three appointments in this way.'

(a) Consider your response to some of the comments made above.

(b) Discuss advantages/disadvantages/possible improvements for such an event with your mentor or another teacher.

Accountability

Accountability – 'the public face' of assessment – was a relatively new feature of education in the late twentieth century, though a familiar one in the late nineteenth century! West et al. (2011) show that there are many forms of accountability in schools, such as professional, hierarchical, market and participative, amongst others, but in this section, we are concerned with the 'public' accountability of schools and colleges. The requirements for test and assessment data (Key Stage, GCSE and Advanced level results) to be made public have therefore made teachers much more accountable to a wider audience than their predecessors were. The publication of 'league tables' every year has resulted in a situation of competition between schools, as they seek to attract students to maximize their income. This means that every teacher has the burden of their students' results being part of the story of the success or failure of their school. The management of whole-school data and statistics is likely to be in the hands of a senior member of staff and to be more or less computerized. However, any teacher may be asked within school to account for a particular set of results (good or bad) and, in due course, the measurable results of your work may have a bearing on your career prospects and salary.

One of the problems with the publication of assessment data is that they can be represented in several different ways and different types of data can be used to 'spin' the story of the school. For example, statistics may be represented as a raw 'pass rate' for the whole school or for selected subjects (usually mathematics and English to the fore). The coalition government has introduced the English Baccalaureate at GCSE, in which students who achieve A*–C in a suite of subjects that includes English, Mathematics, a science, a modern or ancient language and a humanities subject such as history or geography will receive the 'E-Bacc'. This new requirement for published results will affect how schools are evaluated by parents and students. These pass rates may also be compared with the national averages in these areas, or against benchmark statistics for similar institutions, with the aim of showing better than average scores. Success might also be shown by the 'points scores' of individual students in the grades achieved across their examination subjects. Which of these is used can result in very different pictures of the work of the school (see Hewett, 1999). As statistical analysis of assessment data becomes more sophisticated, then the potential for public misunderstanding of their significance is increased. However, careful use of this assessment data can also provide a picture of the complexity of school provision, for example identifying 'coasting' schools – those that do not add much educational value to students who are already high attainers. **Performance data** can also be a 'tool in the service of school improvement' (Brooks, 2002: 144).

Activity 5.10   Accountability

Parts (a), (b) and (d) of this activity can be completed individually. Part (c) requires you to interview a specific member of your school or college staff.

(a) Inform yourself of the meanings of some of the key terminology in relation to assessment-related data collection, such as: raw scores, value added, average, mean, median, mode, ratio, centile, quartile, standardized, histogram, scattergram, whiskergram, variables, normal curve of distribution, YELLIS. You may find Google useful in this activity.

(b) Have a look at a sample numeracy test for beginning teachers (www.tta.gov.uk/skillstests). Many of the questions concentrate on the presentation and interpretation of data relating to student performance.

(c) Arrange to interview the person in school who has most to do with whole-school assessment issues. Explore with them how they use data to analyse performance and develop plans for future action on a whole-school basis. You may want to ask to look at the latest **Self-Evaluation Form (SEF)** to see how data is used.

(d) Reflect on the view that the drive for accountability presupposes wrong-doing, inadequacy or guilt.

The other main engine of accountability is the 'light-touch' inspection of schools (and including PGCE provision) carried out by the Office for Standards in Education (Ofsted). In making judgements about the effectiveness of schools, Ofsted makes use of a great deal of statistical data, which emerge from your activities as a teacher. These data are connected to student performance in tests and examinations and to the ability of schools and colleges to make accurate judgements about the learning that takes place in the classroom to generate strategies for future improvements. Analysing dense amounts of rich assessment data is seen as a key process in improving schools (Ofsted, 2008). In the first decade of the twenty-first century schools and colleges have had to complete a SEF (Self-Evaluation Form), in which the strengths and weaknesses of provision have to be identified. To do this, they made use of data about student performance contained in PANDA (Performance and Attainment) reports or their replacement RAISEonline (Reporting and Analysis for Improvement through School Self-Evaluation) The coalition government of 2010 signalled its intention to abolish Self-Evaluation Forms as part of its drive to cut down bureaucracy in schools and increase 'localism', where decisions are left to schools rather than local authorities (DfE, 2010). While your classroom performance may seem a small cog in the chain of inspection – and the 'light touch' involves fewer classroom observations of actual teaching – the effect may be to increase the pressure to shape your activities in the classroom to the achievement of national targets, rather than wider educational objectives you may have (see, for example, Lawson, 2005).

Features of good practice

The Office for Standards in Education (2003) has identified these features as being examples of good practice in the use of data by secondary schools:

- Key Stage 2 data are gathered as early as possible and analysed carefully (including analysis by gender, ethnicity and mobility), supplemented by other test data (such as in English, mathematics or verbal reasoning), when available, for cross-referencing.
- Students with special educational needs (SEN) or those learning English as an additional language (EAL) are identified through individual consultation to enable smooth transfer from their primary school.
- Data are used as a baseline to monitor and review each student's progress, especially to identify signs of underachievement or unusual potential, and to help set targets for the students and subject departments.
- An effective management information system allows individual departments and teachers to access information independently and in a way tailored to

their needs, and also allows new data to be easily entered and processed when required.

- Subject teachers and tutors use data and other assessment information to review the performance and expectations of students, maintaining a productive dialogue with the students about their progress.
- Test results and teacher assessments are analysed to illuminate aspects of students' performance and the extent to which progress is consistent with earlier data.
- Analysis of the performance of class groups is used to identify weaker aspects of teaching, which are then addressed through performance management and professional development.

Activity 5.11   Using data: aspects of best practice

Part (a) of this activity needs to be discussed with teaching colleagues in your department. Parts (b) and (c) can be completed individually.

(a) For each of the aspects of best practice identified by Ofsted, explore with your department how they seek to implement these. Be careful to maintain a professional attitude in discussing these matters – you need to learn about the departmental processes involved, not about the performance of the department in these regards.

(b) Place the list of features above in order of importance from your point of view, from 1 to 6. For the items you have decided are the *most* important and the *least* important, provide a rationale for your decisions.

(c) In relevant lesson evaluations, show where you have used data about performance with individual students to set targets and improve attainment.

Target-setting in schools and colleges

Target-setting to raise standards of student attainment became a statutory requirement for schools from September 1998 until 2011. In Circular 11/98, 'Target-Setting in Schools', the government set out the following requirements for school governing bodies.

At Key Stage 2 they set and publish targets for the percentages of pupils attaining:

- level 4 or above in English and Mathematics

At Key Stage 4 they set and publish targets for the percentages of pupils attaining:

- five or more GCSEs or equivalent at grades A* to C
- one or more GCSEs or equivalent at grades A* to C
- the average points score per pupil in GCSE or equivalent

However, in 2011, these targets were replaced by the coalition government with a new minimum or 'floor' standard, in which schools would be deemed to be performing poorly if less than 35 per cent were achieving grades A*–C in five GCSEs including English and Mathematics. This floor will be progressively increased over time and in the future will also include science.

The setting of targets by central government was seen by them to be a key mechanism for school improvement. By identifying realistic steps that individual schools could take to achieve the required standards, it was believed that national targets for the percentage of students achieving at particular levels could be met. The idea was that the targets would provide motivation, direction and a measure of 'success' for schools and teachers alike. However, critics of target-setting raise issues about who sets the targets, how realistic they are and, most importantly, what targets are appropriate for an education system. By concentrating on rather narrow ranges of targets, especially literacy and numeracy, critics argue that this has the effect of 'shutting down' other areas of the curriculum as teachers 'teach to the test' to meet the targets by which they will be judged (see Wragg, 2001: 85–86).

The government also provided schools and colleges with software called Pupil Achievement Tracker (PAT) or Learner Achievement Tracker (LAT) that allowed an institution or individual teachers to compare groups of students or even individuals with national and/or benchmark data as a basis for setting targets for the school, or an individual student. This software could also provide the school or teacher with value-added measures so that they can see how their students are doing compared to similar students elsewhere. RAISEonline replaced these tools in 2009 and this sophisticated software allows users to 'drill down' into data at the school and pupil level to provide a powerful means of analysing attainment and setting strategies for improving the achievement of individuals and groups of students.

The National Public Service Agreements (PSA) Targets for Education in England, which set targets for local authorities in terms of educational achievement, were abolished in 2011 by the coalition government. This was part of a series of measures designed to free up schools from what was seen as burdensome tasks. In the case of Assessing Pupils' Progress (APP), a structured approach to assessment within a school that enables teachers and parents to track pupil progress over time, the coalition government made APP a voluntary process for schools (see Ofsted, 2011 for an evaluation of the impact of APP on schools).

Activity 5.12   Analysing assessment data

All parts of this activity can be completed individually and then shared with your mentor in school or college.

The following tables are taken from anonymous PANDA (Performance and Assessment) data for secondary schools, published by Ofsted on the Internet. (Note that PANDA (and PAT/LAT) have been replaced by RAISEonline. This activity focuses on the skills of analysing data rather than the specific format it appears in.)

GCSE results for 2004 by subject.

School results against all maintained secondary schools.

First line is the school result, second line is the national result.

Subject Area	Percentage Achieving Grades									% A*–C grades	% A*–G grades
	A*	A	B	C	D	E	F	G	U		
Art and Design	0.0	11.5	17.3	42.3	9.6	3.8	7.7	5.8	0.0	71.2	98.1
	4.7	13.3	19.7	27.6	14.4	10.0	5.9	2.6	0.5	65.2	98.1
Combined Science	0.0	0.0	0.0	4.8	11.1	25.4	31.7	19.0	7.9	4.8	92.1
	0.2	0.7	2.0	12.1	18.0	23.7	21.8	12.2	8.5	15.0	90.7
Computer Studies	0.0	5.6	26.8	19.7	11.3	11.3	8.5	8.5	8.5	52.1	91.5
	3.6	10.5	16.9	24.1	15.5	10.7	8.2	5.4	4.6	55.1	94.7
Design and Technology	0.0	3.7	9.2	21.1	31.2	14.7	11.9	5.5	2.8	33.9	97.2
	2.9	12.0	15.0	24.8	19.8	11.4	6.6	3.6	3.0	54.7	96.2
English Language	0.9	6.1	14.0	36.0	19.3	8.8	2.6	6.1	6.1	57.0	93.9
	3.1	10.2	18.5	26.0	20.0	11.5	6.0	2.6	1.7	57.7	97.9
English Literature	0.0	1.3	16.3	51.3	17.5	5.0	6.3	0.0	2.5	68.8	97.5
	3.3	11.6	20.9	26.2	17.0	10.4	5.5	2.5	2.2	62.0	97.4
French	0.0	13.5	18.9	32.4	24.3	10.8	0.0	0.0	0.0	64.9	100
	4.1	8.2	13.1	21.5	19.8	14.9	10.4	5.7	1.6	47.0	97.8
Geography	0.0	20.0	25.0	15.0	10.0	20.0	5.0	0.0	5.0	60.0	95.0
	5.8	12.2	16.1	24.7	16.2	11.0	6.7	3.8	3.1	58.7	96.5
Maths	2.6	8.8	13.2	16.7	12.3	14.0	15.8	8.8	6.1	41.2	92.1
	3.3	7.2	17.3	22.3	17.5	15.5	9.3	4.0	3.2	50.0	96.3

PE	4.5	0.0	13.6	22.7	45.5	9.1	0.0	4.5	0.0	40.9	100
	3.8	11.9	19.8	21.5	24.3	12.4	4.5	1.2	0.3	57.0	99.4
RE	0.0	6.1	16.2	30.3	20.2	15.2	5.1	5.1	2.0	52.5	98.0
	6.8	16.0	20.4	19.0	13.9	9.8	6.7	3.9	2.5	62.3	96.6

AS and A2 results 2004 by subject.

School sixth form attainment summary against national figures.

First line is the school result, second line is the national result.

Subject	AS or A2	% A–B	% A–E	Average Points Score
Biology	AS	15.4	80.8	26.9
		10.4	63.5	19.8
	A2	39.1	100	80.6
		40.0	96.6	79.3
Business Studies	AS	11.1	61.1	22.2
		15.4	75.3	25.7
	A2	21.7	100	71.3
		39.4	98.9	81.8
Chemistry	AS	8.7	52.2	18.3
		13.2	70.3	23.0
	A2	36.5	100	80.6
		50.0	97.7	85.7
Communication Studies	AS	60.0	100	42.0
		24.9	87.2	32.8
	A2	47.5	100	87.5
		40.4	99.2	83.5
Drama	AS	0.0	100	30.0
		19.8	86.6	30.9
	A2	23.5	100	78.8
		42.8	99.6	85.1
Economics	AS	28.6	71.4	31.4
		28.6	71.6	25.8
	A2	25.0	100	78.3
		54.3	98.8	89.8

(Continued)

(Continued)

Subject	AS or A2	% A–B	% A–E	Average Points Score
History	AS	14.3	85.7	32.9
		20.8	82.2	29.2
	A2	68.8	100	99.4
		45.6	99.0	85.1
Information Technology	AS	6.7	73.3	22.7
		8.8	66.6	20.6
	A2	45.0	100	89.0
		25.7	96.3	71.1
Physics	AS	19.0	61.9	22.4
		14.8	66.4	22.4
	A2	56.3	100	88.8
		45.3	96.7	82.6
Psychology	AS	29.5	72.7	29.3
		15.1	67.8	23.2
	A2	42.4	100	85.5
		42.5	97.4	81.6
Sociology	AS	22.2	77.8	28.9
		19.6	72.1	25.9
	A2	31.3	100	82.5
		45.3	98.5	84.6

(a) Imagine that you are TIC (teacher in charge) of your subject (or a closely related one) at this school. You have been asked by the senior management to analyse the performance of students in your subject against the national statistics. Produce a report on this data for the senior management that highlights the strengths and weaknesses in your curriculum area.

(b) In the light of this analysis, you have to develop an action plan for your curriculum area for the next year. In your action plan, you have to suggest ways in which you will build on the strengths and address the weaknesses in your students' performance.

(c) Senior management is so impressed with your handling of this data that they have asked you to support another curriculum area that has the opposite characteristics to your own. Choosing such an area from the data, carry out a similar analysis and action plan for that department.

Critical reading at Master's level

Two of the most important characteristics of work at Master's level are the ability to be critical and the use of academic literature to support points being made.

1   Look at the webpages of the coalition's White Paper 'The Importance of Teaching', and in particular the pages on 'Curriculum', 'Assessment' and 'Qualifications'. You will find the start page at: www.education.gov.uk/schools/teaching andlearning/schoolswhitepaper/b0068570/the-importance-of-teaching/ curriculum.

2   Choose two of the proposals contained in these pages on assessment and qualifications and develop your own criticisms of them in no more than 250 words. You may want to start from first principles and ask yourself what assessment is for and whether the proposals you choose conform to your ideas. Or you may want to be critical of the specific practical implications of the proposal.

3   Using an educational research database such as the British Educational Index (BEI) or SCOPUS, search for academic articles that address the proposals you have chosen. Some useful search terms might be 'free schools', 'academies', 'English Baccalaureate', 'Teaching and Learning International Survey (TALIS)'. Another good place to start might be the special edition of *Forum*, 'In defence of state education', 53(2), especially the article by Stephenson (2011). Extract arguments from the articles that either support the proposal or support your criticisms of them. Use appropriate referencing when writing down these points from the article(s) you have found.

Conclusion

While the issue of assessment is fraught with difficulty, it remains true that a great deal of your professional life will be caught up with this type of activity. Indeed, the argument for increased teacher assessment, rather than national testing, has never gone away and seems to be having a resurgence in the early twenty-first century. However, national testing systems are not going to go away, as they represent a huge industry and encapsulate a long tradition of measures of success in curriculum subjects at all secondary levels, which are independent from schools. The challenge will be to combine testing and teacher assessments in ways that will command the confidence of the government, employers, teachers, parents and students that they produce reliable and valid data.

References

Arter, J. A. and Spandel, V. (1992) 'Using portfolios of student work in instruction and assessment', *Educational Measurement: Issues and Practice*, Spring: 36–44.

Assessment Reform Group (ARG) (2002) *Assessment for Learning: 10 Principles*. London: ARG.

Bennett, R.L. (2011) 'Formative Assessment: a critical review', *Assessment in Education: Principles, Policy and Practice*, 18(1): 5–25.

Bernstein, B. (1971) 'On the classification and framing of educational knowledge', in M.F.D. Young (ed.) *Knowledge and Control: New Directions in the Sociology of Education*. London: Collier-Macmillan. pp. 47–69.

Bew, Lord (2011) *Key Stage 2 Testing, Assessment and Accountability Review: Progress Report*. London: DfE.

Black, P. and Wiliam, D. (1998) 'Assessment and classroom learning', *Assessment in Education: Principles, Policy and Practice*, 5(1): 7–74.

Black, P. and Wiliam, D. (2006) 'The reliability of assessments' in J. Gardner (ed.) *Assessment and Learning*. London: Sage. pp. 119–131.

Black, P., Harrison, C., Lee, C., Marshall B. and Wiliam, D. (2003) *Assessment for Learning: Putting It into Practice*. Maidenhead: Open University Press.

Broadfoot, P. and Pollard, A. (1997) *National Record of Achievement Review: Report of the Steering Group*. London: Department for Education and Employment.

Brooks, V. (2002) *Assessment in Secondary Schools: The New Teacher's Guide to Monitoring, Assessment, Recording, Reporting and Accountability*. Buckingham: Open University Press.

Comber, C., Watling, R., Lawson, T., Cavendish, S., McEune, R. and Paterson, F. (2002) *Impact2: Learning at Home and School: Case Studies*. Coventry: Becta.

Cullingford, C. (1997) *Assessment versus Evaluation*. London: Cassell.

DfE (2010) The Importance of Teaching. White Paper Online. www.education.gov.uk/b0068570/the-importance-of-teaching/.

Dweck, C. (1986) 'Motivational processes affecting learning', *American Psychologist*, 41(10): 1040–1048.

Earl, L.M. (2003) *Assessment as Learning*. Thousand Oaks, CA: Corwin Press.

Fernsten, L. and Fernsten, J. (2005) 'Portfolio assessment and reflection: enhancing learning through effective practice', *Reflective Practice*, 6(2): 303–309.

Gardner, H. (1993) *Frames of Mind: The Theory of Multiple Intelligences*. New York: Basic Books.

Gardner, H. (2006) *Multiple Intelligences: New Horizons*. New York: Basic Books.

Gipps, C. (1994) *Beyond Testing: Towards a Theory of Educational Assessment*. London: Falmer Press.

Grant, G.E. and Huebner, T.A. (1998) 'The portfolio question: the power of self-directed inquiry', in N. Lyons (ed.) *With Portfolio in Hand: Validating the New Teacher Professionalism*. New York: Teachers College Press. pp. 156–171.

Groom, B. and Maunonen-Eskelinen, I. (2006) 'The use of portfolios to develop reflective practice in teacher training: a comparative and collaborative approach between two teacher training providers in the UK and Finland', *Teaching in Higher Education*, 11(3): 291–300.

Harlen, W. (2006) 'The role of assessment in developing motivation for learning', in J. Gardner (ed.) *Assessment and Learning*. London: Sage.

Harlen, W. and James, M. (1997) 'Assessment and learning: differences and relationships between formative and summative assessment', *Assessment in Education*, 4(3): 365–380.

Hayward, L., Kane, J. and Cogan, N. (2000) *Improving Assessment in Scotland: Report of the National Consultation on Assessment in Scotland*. Glasgow: University of Glasgow.

Hewett, P. (1999) 'The role of target setting in the school improvement', in C. Conner (ed.) *Assessment in Action in the Primary School*. London: Falmer Press. pp. 71–83.

Hutchinson, C. and Hayward, L. (2005) 'The journey so far: assessment for learning in Scotland', *The Curriculum Journal*, 16(2): 225–248.

Isaacs, T. (2010) 'Educational assessment in England', *Assessment in Education: Principles, Policy and Practice*, 17(3): 315–334.

Klenowski, V. (2002) *Developing Portfolios for Assessment and Learning*. London: RoutledgeFalmer.

Kounin, J.S. (1970) *Discipline and Group Management in Classrooms*. New York: Holt, Reinhart & Winston.

Latham, A.M. (1997) 'Profiling and self-assessment', in C. Cullingford (ed.) *Assessment versus Education*. London: Cassell. pp. 203–221.

Lawson, T. (2005) 'The new framework for the inspection of schools: implications for sociology teachers', *Social Science Teacher*, 35(1): 15–16.

Lawson, T. (2011) 'Empowerment in education: liberation, governance or a distraction?: A review', *Power and Education*, 3(2): 89–103.

Lawson, T. and Harrison, J.K. (1999) 'Individual action planning in initial teacher training: empowerment or discipline?', *British Journal of Sociology of Education*, 20(1): 89–105.

Lawson, T., Harrison, J. and Cavendish, S. (2004) 'Individual action planning: a case of self-surveillance?', *British Journal of Sociology of Education*, 25(1): 81–94.

Lingard, B., Mills, M. and Hayes, D. (2006) 'Enabling and aligning assessment for learning: some research and policy lessons from Queensland', *International Studies in Sociology of Education*, 16(2): 83–103.

Lloyd-Jones, L.J., Bray, E., Johnson, G. and Currie, R. (1992) *Assessment: From Principles to Practice*. London: Routledge.

Massey, A., Green, S., Dexter, T. and Hamnett, L. (2003) *Comparability of the National Tests over Time: Key Stage Test Standards between 1996 and 2001: Final Report to the QCA*. Cambridge: University of Cambridge, Local Examinations Syndicate.

Messick, S. (1994) 'The interplay of evidence and consequences in the validation of performance assessments', *Educational Researcher*, 23(2): 13–23.

Office for Standards in Education (Ofsted) (2002) *Good Teaching, Effective Departments*. London: Ofsted.

Office for Standards in Education (Ofsted) (2003) *Good Assessment in Secondary Schools*. London: Ofsted.

Office for Standards in Education (Ofsted) (2008) *Using Data: Improving Schools*. London: Ofsted.

Office for Standards in Education (Ofsted) (2010) *The National Strategies: A Review of impact*. London: Ofsted

Office for Standards in Education (Ofsted) (2011) *The impact of the 'Assessing Pupils' Progess' Initiative.* London: Ofsted.

Pring, R. (1984) *Personal and Social Education*. London: Hodder.

Richardson, C. (2003) *Whither Assessment?* London: Qualifications and Curriculum Authority.

Smith, E. and Gorard, S. (2005) '"They don't give us our marks": the role of formative feedback in student progress', *Assessment in Education*, 12(1): 21–38.

Spendlove, D. (2009) *Putting Assessment for Learning into Practice.* London: Continuum.

Stephenson, H. (2011) 'Coalition education policy: Thatcherism's long shadow', *Forum: for Promoting 3–19 Comprehensive Education*, 53(2): 179–194.

Stobart, G. (2006) 'The validity of formative assessment', in J. Gardner (ed.) *Assessment and Learning*. London: Sage. pp. 133–146.

Sutton, R. (1992) *Assessment: A Framework for Teachers*. London: Routledge.

Thomas, E. (1990) *Assessing Learning Unit 11 MA and Diploma Course in Distance Learning*. London: Institute of Education.

Watkins, C. (1992) *Whole School Personal and Social Education: Policy and Practice*. Coventry: NAPCE Publications.

West, A., Mattei, P. and Roberts, J. (2011) 'Accountability and sanctions in English schools', *British Journal of Educational Studies*, 59(1): 41–62.

Wiliam, D. (2000) 'Reliability, validity and all that jazz', *Education 3–13*, 29(3): 9–13.

Wolf, A. (2011) *Review of Vocational Qualifications – the Wolf Report.* London: DfE (DFE-00031-2011).

Wragg, E.C. (1997) *Assessment and Learning: Primary and Secondary*. London: Routledge.

Wragg, E.C. (2001) *Assessment and Learning in the Secondary School*. London: RoutledgeFalmer.

CHAPTER 6

PASTORAL CARE AND THE ROLE OF THE FORM TUTOR

Joan Smith

By the end of this chapter you will have:

- gained insights into the aims, definitions and purposes of pastoral care in secondary schools
- understood some of the ways in which pastoral care provision is organized in schools
- explored some of the key aspects of the form tutor role and considered how this fits into whole-school strategies for pupil welfare and achievement

Introduction

Ensuring the welfare, safety and emotional well-being of young people is fundamental to teachers' work and to the smooth, day-to-day running of schools. Pupils can only make progress if they are emotionally stable, cared for and secure, and systems need to be in place to ensure pupils' well-being. Pastoral structures therefore form an essential part of the fabric of an effective school. Pastoral care is a distinguishing feature of UK education, and a fundamental part of the life, work and culture of schools. In the course of your teaching career you will dedicate a vast amount of time and effort to ensuring pupils' stability, security and well-being. This is likely to be a very interesting aspect of your job, from which you will derive a great deal of enjoyment and satisfaction.

This chapter focuses on the aims and organization of pastoral care in UK secondary schools. Particular consideration is given to the highly complex role of the form tutor in ensuring pupils' well-being and progress, and to some of the multifarious aspects of the role, including fostering the form's identity, monitoring pupils' progress and attendance, liaison with other adults, pupil welfare and improving pupils' behaviour.

Aims and definitions: the changing role of pastoral care

There is no one fixed, shared, contemporary understanding of what is meant by 'pastoral care' (Calvert, 2009), a term that is thought to derive from early provision of formal education through the church schools of the nineteenth century. Rather, educators' understandings of the aims and purpose of pastoral care have evolved over time, in response to changing cultural, societal and policy contexts. Priorities, emphases and organizational structures for pastoral provision have changed over the years. Calvert (2009: 270) identifies seven 'ages of pastoral care', noting the shifts in priorities that have informed the practice of pastoral care over the last 50 years (for a summary, see Table 6.1).

The summary table provides an overview of the changing role of pastoral care. Although Calvert identifies seven 'ages', these are not distinct from each other with a chronological start and end point. Rather, in practice, the varying approaches have overlapped and co-existed as the educational culture has moved gradually from one phase to the next in response to the broader policy context, government imperatives and societal change. Moreover, as is discussed in Chapter 3, teachers do not operate in an ethical vacuum. Individual teachers bring their own values to the process, interpreting policy at national, local and institutional level, and translating it into action tailored to the needs of their own pupils, within the particular context of the school. Thus there is no one fixed model or interpretation of pastoral care. However, a useful working definition is that provided by the Department for Education and Science (DES/HMI, 1989: 3):

> Pastoral care is concerned with promoting pupils' personal and social development and fostering positive attitudes: through the quality of teaching and learning; through the nature of relationships amongst pupils, teachers and adults other than teachers; through the arrangements for monitoring pupils' overall progress; through academic systems; and through extra-curricular activities and the **school ethos**. Pastoral care, accordingly, should help a school achieve success.

The ways in which this is translated into action by different UK secondary schools vary considerably. In the next section of this chapter, some examples of how pastoral

Table 6.1   The seven ages of pastoral care (adapted from Calvert, 2009: 270–275)

The seven ages of pastoral care	Emphasis on	Characterized by
1. Pastoral care as control	power and control	• hierarchical pastoral structures; • an academic/pastoral divide; • heads of year/house seen as strong disciplinarians
2. Pastoral care as individual need	guidance and counselling	• widening of form tutor role; • awareness of need to develop the whole child; • individual support from form tutor for pupils
3. Pastoral care as group need	meeting individual needs via group work	• group counselling; • Active Tutorial Work (ATW) (Baldwin and Wells, 1979, 1980, 1981), undertaken during form time
4. The pastoral curriculum	holistic view of education and child development	• pastoral care seen as part of the whole school curriculum
5. Pastoral care after introduction of National Curriculum		
(i) 1988–1994	(i) traditional academic subjects, literacy and numeracy; performativity and marketization of schools	• centrally prescribed curriculum; • strengthened inspection regime; • non-statutory areas such as Personal and Social Education (PSE) neglected
(ii) post-1994	(ii) development of pastoral care and Citizenship	• National Curriculum is slimmed down following Dearing report (Dearing, 1994): more time and energy can be devoted to pastoral care and Citizenship
6. Pastoral care for learning	holistic approaches to pastoral care; emotional intelligence as central to learning; emotional and psychological well-being for learning	• recognition of the dangers of performativity and a restricted curriculum; • schools revisit pastoral provision
7. Pastoral care, the wider workforce and the Every Child Matters (ECM) agenda	academic output; interagency working; involvement of paraprofessionals	• increased diversity in schooling provision; • greater variation in school workforce; • increased deployment of paraprofessionals; • Heads of Year/House start to be replaced/ supplemented by Learning Managers; • aspects of pastoral role being picked up by others (e.g. Assistant Learning Co-ordinators, Teaching Assistants); • greater emphasis on multi-agency working; • services increasingly brought together under one roof (extended schools)

care might typically be organized and managed are discussed, although it is worth pointing out that you might also encounter interpretations which differ radically from the examples given. Before reading the next section, spend a few minutes completing Activity 6.1, below, in which you are asked to reflect on your own experiences of pastoral care provision.

Activity 6.1   Organization of pastoral care and PHSE

Discuss with colleagues and make brief notes in response to the following:

- What has been your experience of pastoral care and personal, health and social education (PHSE), both as a pupil and as an adult (if, for example, you have worked in a school as a teaching assistant or other role)?
- How was the pastoral management structure organized in the schools of which you have experience? For example, was there a hierarchy within the pastoral system of the school? How were pupils organized into groups (e.g. same age or mixed-age groups)? Was there a house or year-group system?
- Was PHSE timetabled or fitted into form time? Was it taught by form tutors or others? Did pupils have any say in determining the content and focus of PHSE sessions? What informal/spontaneous types of PHSE were undertaken? How and when? Who initiated these? What were the most effective PHSE sessions you experienced? Can you identify what made them effective?
- How do you feel you were treated in your own experience of pastoral care as a child? Did you feel a sense of belonging to a form or house? What contributed to the way you felt about your place in the school/pastoral system?
- What are the strengths and weaknesses of the pastoral management systems you have experienced?

Organization and management of pastoral care and PHSE in UK secondary schools

This section focuses on some fairly typical examples of pastoral management structures, arrangements for grouping of pupils and the organization of PHSE.

Pastoral management structures

Traditionally, a typical, hierarchical pastoral structure in a comprehensive school might feature a pastoral deputy headteacher, heads of each Key Stage, heads of year, assistant heads of year and teams of form tutors (see Figure 6.1). This structure, or a recognizable version of it, is in place in many schools. In this model, teams of form tutors are led by a head of year and assistant head of year, whose work is co-ordinated by the head of Key Stage.

A big part of the job of the head of year 7 and the year team is cross-phase transition, ensuring that primary school pupils are well prepared for their move into secondary education, and that appropriate support is in place. For this reason some schools prefer to keep the year 7 team as constant as possible, as experienced year 7 tutors have the

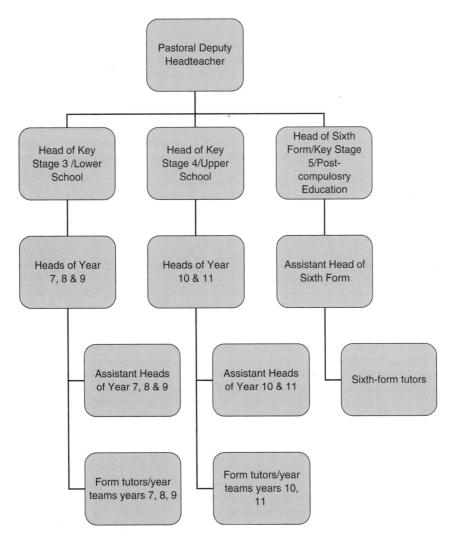

Figure 6.1   Traditional, hierarchical secondary school pastoral structure

necessary expertise in ensuring a smooth transition for pupils. In other schools, form tutors have the option of 'moving up' with their form, and staying with them throughout Key Stage 3 or even throughout Key Stages 3 and 4. Often, form tutors keep the same form for just two years, typically years 8 and 9 or 10 and 11, and the same year team remains together for that period under the leadership of the same year head, forming a two-year organizational cycle. If you are a form tutor under this system, you would normally have some say in whether or not to continue with the same group for more than one year. In general it is helpful to do so wherever possible. This gives the teacher and pupils improved opportunities to get to know each other, enabling form tutors to continue to be effective advocates for their pupils and to work to ensure their safety, well-being and academic progress. It also has obvious benefits for home–school liaison.

Another year team that often remains fairly constant is the sixth-form team. Again this is usually considered appropriate because students in the 16–19 age range have a specific set of needs, and it is helpful if they can be supported by tutors with the knowledge and skills to advise them on courses of study, applications to university, career options and so on.

In recent years, the traditional pastoral management structure exemplified in Figure 6.1 has been somewhat modified as a result of 'workforce remodelling'. The term 'workforce remodelling' refers to a long-standing change management programme which was intended to support schools in implementing the reforms outlined in 'Raising standards and tackling workload: a national agreement' (DfES, 2003). The stated aims of the reforms were to improve pupil outcomes and to reduce teachers' workload so that their time could be more effectively focused on teaching and learning and leading teaching and learning. Changes resulting from the agreement included amendments to teachers' contracts, a review of the roles of support staff and attempts to streamline unnecessary bureaucracy. This led to a considerable increase in the number of support staff and adults other than teachers in school, which has had a radical effect on the structuring and day-to-day operations of schools. In addition to the form tutor, head of year or Key Stage and senior pastoral care co-ordinator, a range of adults other than teachers have taken on some aspects of pastoral care in recent years. New roles have been created, including for example learning managers, higher-level teaching assistants, cover supervisors, **learning mentors** and parent support advisors (Edmond and Price, 2009).

Pupil groupings

Following the traditional model, pupils are organized into year groups (7, 8, 9, 10, 11) and organized into form groups within the year group. Often, post-16 provision runs quite separately from the rest of the school, with smaller sixth-form groups in which tutors offer support for 16–19 pupils with managing their studies and applying for higher education, training or employment.

In recent years, however, some schools have dispensed with year groups and moved to vertical groupings of children for the purposes of pastoral care provision. This means that form groups can include pupils from across the age spectrum of the school, with the result that you might find, for instance, pupils aged 11–16 in the same form. The idea of vertical groupings of pupils is not new: the notion of mixed age groups for learning is a key tenet of, for example, the Montessori approach to education (Montessori, 1912: 1949). However, although mixed-age groups are starting to be adopted for pastoral care purposes, it is interesting to note that as yet schools in twenty-first-century Britain have not, in general, extended the model to include vertical groupings for teaching and learning. Pressure on schools to perform in normative age-related external measures of performance, such as Standard Assessment Tasks (SATs) (Mansell, 2007) has resulted in children continuing to be taught in same-age groups, irrespective of ability and interests.

There are advantages and disadvantages to both 'horizontal' and 'vertical' systems for pastoral care. Whereas horizontal groupings mean pupils can form friendships with pupils of a similar age, vertical groupings enable friendships to be formed across the full age spectrum, and may serve to protect younger pupils from bullying (Kent and Kay, 2007), as well as to foster a sense of responsibility in older students. On the other hand it could be argued that older, disaffected pupils might have a toxic effect on the attitudes and behaviour of younger pupils. Horizontal groupings have particular advantages where the needs of an age group are specific and can be more effectively met via same-age tutor groups, for example, settling new year 7 pupils into the school, preparing year 9 pupils to make option choices or working with sixth formers applying to university. At the same time, vertical groups afford greater scope for friendships to be based on similarity of ability, which is again consistent with the Montessori emphasis on allowing children to develop at their own pace rather than in accordance with age-related norms.

In addition to and alongside vertically or horizontally organized tutor groups, some schools operate a 'house system'. This is a traditionally British notion, originally characteristic of public schools, where students might be allocated to a particular house in which they would have their dormitory. The term was adopted several decades ago by state schools, and used to create the notion of a broader group to which each pupil belonged. Typically a school might be divided into four 'houses', each with a name, and including pupils of all ages. Kent and Kay (2007) point out that where vertical form groups exist within such a structure, children's sense of house identity can be enhanced. The head of house and his/her team work to foster in children a sense of belonging and loyalty to the house, by, for example, encouraging their participation in inter-house competitions, which might typically be sporting in nature.

Personal, health and social education (PHSE)

Since the early 1980s PHSE, or its earlier equivalent, personal and social education (PSE), has been taught in most cases by form tutors. In some schools there has been a weekly or fortnightly timetabled slot for PHSE, supplemented by form activities during form time and registration periods. In other schools, dedicated PHSE teams have led the sessions, and more recently PHSE and Citizenship have been more closely linked so that in some schools PHSE, or parts of it, have been subsumed into Citizenship and taught largely by Citizenship specialists, with other teachers making contributions as needed. Health education, for instance, has been undertaken by a range of educational and health professionals, with considerable work being undertaken by Science teachers and teachers of Physical Education (PE). PHSE is currently a non-statutory subject, although schools have to ensure appropriate provision of sex education, careers education and work-related learning. Other than this, the content of PHSE varies from one school to another, but some of the likely topics include:

- health issues, for example healthy eating, alcohol and drugs, sexual health
- emotional well-being, for example conflict resolution, assertiveness, emotional intelligence
- human rights and responsibilities, for example, bullying, anti-racism, homophobia
- career choices, for example, Key Stage 4 choices, aspirations and the world of work
- the wider world, for example, globalization, the law, citizenship, ecology

A typical current whole-school model might include PHSE sessions offered at Key Stage 3, developing into Citizenship GCSE for most pupils at Key Stage 4.

Activity 6.2, below, offers you a structure for investigating PHSE provision in a school in which you are undertaking your Initial Teacher Education (ITE) placement, or in your first school as a Newly Qualified Teacher (NQT). Activity 6.3 takes this a stage further, as it requires you to undertake some PHSE teaching, reflect critically on it and consider next steps.

Activity 6.2   Organization and teaching of PHSE

During your school placement (or in your first school as a NQT) use the following structure to help you find out more about the way PHSE is organized and delivered in school.

1   If you are attached to a form, ask the form tutor to put you in touch with the person who co-ordinates PHSE for the particular year group/house/Key Stage. If you are not attached to a form, ask your school-based tutor either to arrange for you to be attached to a form, or to put you in touch with the school co-ordinator for PHSE. The form tutor or co-ordinator of PHSE will serve as a gatekeeper who can allow you access to PHSE provision.

2   Arrange a time to meet with the form tutor or co-ordinator of PHSE. Prepare some questions you want to ask them, relating to:

- how groups are organized for PHSE purposes
- who delivers PHSE sessions
- the resources available, and who designs/selects these

- when the PHSE sessions take place, how often, and how long they last
- who decides on the content of the sessions and on what basis
- whether different arrangements are in place for different Key Stages
- whether pupils have any say in the content of PHSE
- whether there are systems in place for evaluating the effectiveness of PHSE

During the interview, make notes on each of the above areas.

3   If possible, arrange to observe at least one PHSE session. Ideally, try to observe at least one at each Key Stage. Prior to the observation, decide on a specific focus for your observation. You might usefully discuss this with your co-tutor, the form tutor, ITE co-ordinator or PHSE co-ordinator. It is likely that the PHSE lesson will follow a very different format to subject-based sessions. You might find it useful, for instance, to look at how the teacher manages group discussion or handles potentially sensitive topics, or how they use questions and problem-based scenarios to stimulate discussion without drawing attention to individual pupils.

Following your observations, reflect on the following:

- What were the key differences between the way the teacher organized the group for PHSE as compared to the subject-based sessions you have observed/taught?
- What are the particular issues or challenges of which you need to be aware in planning a PHSE lesson? What are the potential pitfalls? How can you plan and organize to avoid these?

Activity 6.3   Reflective practice in pastoral care: a form tutor intervention

You will need to be attached to a form group in school in order to complete this activity.

After a period of observation, undertake this task at a stage at which the form tutor is happy for you to take the lead with the form, or a group of pupils in it.

In consultation with the form tutor, identify an area on which it would be useful to focus with the form/some members of the form. Some examples might be:

- A group of girls has been bullying/excluding one girl from the friendship group.
- Evidence of cyber-bullying has been brought to the form tutor's notice.

(Continued)

(Continued)

- Instances of racist/homophobic/sexist language and insults have increased.
- An anti-learning culture seems to have grown up amongst a group of boys in the form etc.

In consultation with the form tutor, devise some strategies (which might include designing resources/teaching materials for use in PSHE or form time) that can be used over a sustained period of time (e.g. two weeks) to try to tackle the area of concern.

Adopt the Action Research model summarized below in order to structure your reflection, planning, intervention and analysis. Keep notes and exemplar materials at all stages, so that you can report back to your colleagues/mentors/tutors. Bear in mind the need to anonymize pupils to whom you refer in your reports on the intervention, and that you should not discuss sensitive, personal or confidential information about pupils with anyone other than those adults directly involved in caring for the pupil.

An Action Research approach to reflective form tutoring

In undertaking your professional inquiry, work through the following stages:

Stage 1: Understanding background

This involves reading around the area on which you wish to focus in order to understand the theoretical background. There are some useful websites indicated throughout this chapter and a list of references at the end. In addition, useful, up-to-date information can be found in the weekly *The Times Educational Supplement*. To search for journal articles on recent research identify key words, e.g. bullying, pastoral, form tutor, pupil voice, homophobia, well-being, safeguarding. Useful journals include *Pastoral Care in Education* and the *British Educational Research Journal*, but it is also worth looking more widely. If you have an Athens account you can search databases such as the British Education Index for up-to-date sources.

Stage 2: Developing a focus

Drawing on your readings and your observations of the form group, identify a particular focus for the enquiry, for example tackling cyber-bullying amongst girls in the form.

Stage 3: Developing practice

Having selected the focus for the intervention, decide on the strategies you are going to trial. Design any resources you will need and think about how you will exploit them.

Stage 4: Reflecting on learning

Having developed your pastoral practice, reflect on what has been achieved, and what needs to be developed further.

Stage 5: Considering next area for development

Having reflected on what has been achieved, set out what needs to be developed next. This might include further development of the same focus, or extending the practice you have developed in some way. Ensure you report back your findings to the (usual) form tutor.

At the time of writing the Conservative–Liberal coalition government is planning a review of PHSE education. Further information is available from the following websites:

www.health-for-life.org.uk/
www.pshe-association.org.uk/
www.pshe-association.org.uk/
www.bbc.co.uk/schools/websites/11_16/site/pshe.shtml
www.tes.co.uk/pshe-secondary-teaching-resources/

Whilst the government agenda shifts and schools' interpretation and enactment of policy changes vary, a constant is that the form tutor remains a key person in ensuring pupils' pastoral needs are catered for. Some important aspects of the form tutor's role are discussed below.

The role of the form tutor

As a secondary school teacher in the UK, you can expect to be a form tutor for most, if not all, of your teaching career. Being a form tutor from the start has many benefits in terms of integrating new teachers into the school, allowing them to get to know pupils. It is also a highly enjoyable part of your job as a teacher, affording you valuable opportunities to work with young people in a different context to your subject teaching role.

There are numerous aspects of the form-tutor role, some of which are summarized in Table 6.2.

Form tutors are usually the people with the best overview of the children in their forms, often acting as funnels for information about children's welfare, behaviour and academic progress, and picking up any concerns. Thus they may frequently find themselves mediating between form members and subject teachers when issues arise. As such they are central to the work of the school in ensuring pupil welfare and discipline, working in accordance with school policies to ensure pupils are appropriately monitored and supported. They also carry out a number of daily administrative functions such as completing registers of attendance, chasing up absence notes, checking on punctuality, ensuring homework has been completed and so forth. In this section, some of the key parts of the form tutor's role within the school are discussed: fostering the

Table 6.2   Aspects of the form tutor role (adapted from Holmes, 2009: 182)

Aspects of the form tutor role:
Inspirer and morale booster
Counsellor
Communicator
Problem solver
Nurturer
Enabler
Monitor of academic progress
Monitor of social development
Manager of behaviour
Praise-giver
Motivator
Team-builder
Confidant

form's identity, monitoring pupils' progress and attendance, liaison with other adults, pupil welfare, and monitoring and improving pupil behaviour.

Fostering the form's identity

The form, the form room and the form tutor provide a physical and psychological base for children in school – a 'home', in a sense, to which they belong, contribute and are always welcomed. This is important for all children, but particularly so for vulnerable young people or those new to the school – year 7 pupils, for example, can find the transition from a small primary school to a huge and complex comprehensive school with over 1,000 pupils daunting and bewildering. The form base and membership of the form help pupils to have an anchor as they navigate the new secondary school environment. As a form tutor you are a very important adult in the lives of young people, and you can make a significant difference to the quality of their day-to-day experience of school. You are also an important role model for the children in your care, who look to you to exemplify your personal and professional values via your interactions with them and your expectations of them.

The effective form tutor is proactive in adopting strategies to build a sense of belonging and form identity to enable pupils to adjust to and feel they are a part of the school. It can be helpful and reassuring to pupils if form tutors arrange times when they can come and talk to them. Clearly the form tutor needs to be ready to *listen* – being approachable is an important part of being an effective form tutor. Some tutors keep their own notes on each pupil, to supplement what they have gleaned from official records. Learning the names of form members as quickly as possible is vitally important, crucial to making each member of the form feel valued. Encouraging pupils to participate as a form in school events (competitions, doing assembly, sports day and so forth) can help engender a sense of pride and belonging. Some form tutors like to take photos of pupils in the form and display these on the form notice board, along with other information, celebrations of achievements and form news. (It should be noted that parental permission must be sought before taking and displaying photos of children.) Some like to give the form notice board, or a section of it, to form members to take care of. Alternatively, they might have a rota of small groups of pupils taking care of it and deciding on themes for displays. This gives pupils a sense of ownership and responsibility.

Effective form tutors are proactive in seeking information from subject teachers about the progress and behaviour of their form and take every opportunity to praise form members, so that pupils are proud of their achievements as individuals and as a group. When you become a form tutor, you are in a unique position to know your pupils very well, especially if you stay with the same form for a number of years. This can be a very satisfying experience, allowing you to form lasting, positive, supportive relationships with and between members of your form. As a long-standing form tutor you are also in the best position to be alert to your form members' particular needs. This can be crucial if you are to act as advocate for them with the teachers and other adults who work with your form. Holmes (2009: 182) cites the case of an NQT who had been teaching a boy for a year before he realized the pupil had only one leg! She adds that he now makes sure he reads all of the information on his tutees very carefully. It is important to be proactive in getting to know pupils: to read available information and documentation about them, to chat to them during form time and to encourage them to chat to each other, perhaps via semi-structured activities or specific areas on which to focus during discussion time. In some schools PHSE is entirely delivered in this way, via form-time discussion and activities, often selected by the form tutor in response to issues that have arisen in the form, or to prepare pupils for a particular stage of their school career. The teacher–pupil relationship you enjoy in this context is quite different to that you will encounter in your subject teaching, and can be a source of great fun and satisfaction as you get to know the young people in your care in a more relaxed setting. Having a range of activities for pupils to engage in during form time allows you to work with pupils in an enjoyable and light-hearted way, involving everyone and celebrating their involvement. Little quizzes or question and answer sessions, looking at homework notebooks and reminding pupils about getting prepared for lessons, or just asking pupils about what they have been doing so far today, what went well, what they were proud of and so forth can be beneficial to pupils, whilst also setting a positive tone. It also provides a space for pupils to share concerns they may otherwise have kept to themselves. It offers opportunities for you to remind and reassure them about the small details that make day-to-day success possible for your form members, such as remembering equipment, ensuring they bring in completed homework and bringing their PE kit – these are all details that matter and that you can help pupils to get right. Remembering to congratulate form members and tell them when you have received good news about them from other teachers can boost the children's self esteem significantly. When this is also passed on to parents the benefits can be even greater.

Table 6.3   50 opportunities to say 'you're terrific' (adapted from Canter, 2002)

Praise students for:

1. Entering the classroom quietly	26. Good effort on a long-term project
2. Arriving on time	27. Sharing
3. Co-operating whilst the form tutor takes the register	28. Being sensitive to others' feelings
4. Returning forms on time	29. Learning a new skill
5. Transitioning into an activity	30. Appropriate use of school property
6. Following instructions	31. Returning borrowed books and materials
7. Saying 'please' and 'thank you'	32. Showing enthusiasm
8. Listening attentively	33. Being responsible for a classroom job
9. Helping a classmate	34. Offering help without being asked
10. Bringing necessary materials to school	35. Not wasting paper and resources
11. Handing in homework	36. Staying on task
12. Being a polite audience in assembly	37. Telling the truth
13. Beginning work right away	38. Accepting a new challenge
14. Asking questions when unsure	39. Behaving well when a guest is in the room
15. Good behaviour during a test	40. Reading at home
16. Participating in a form discussion	41. Participating in school events and activities
17. Walking appropriately in the corridors	42. Demonstrating a positive attitude
18. Working co-operatively with a partner	43. Making one's best effort
19. Taking part in a play or presentation	44. Participating in a community improvement project
20. Putting away resources and equipment	45. Participating in a group activity
21. Good effort on an assignment	46. Remaining calm during a problem situation
22. Assisting a new pupil	47. Showing creativity
23. Sharing school experiences with parents	48. Keeping busy when work is finished
24. Making up missed work	49. Taking turns
25. Making a new friend	50. Working co-operatively with a support teacher or volunteer

When things are not going so well for the form, the form tutor can play a crucial role in raising the group self-esteem and turning negative attitudes into positive efforts. Holmes (2009: 182) comments:

> There will be times when you will have to try to inject some enthusiasm into a demoralized group. Perhaps they are suffering under the pressure of exams, or have been reprimanded all morning for the poor behaviour of certain members of the group. Your role is to draw the group together and boost morale sufficiently for them to continue the day. Try to create in them a sense of enthusiasm for each other, and for learning.

It can be helpful to involve pastoral managers such as the head of year in congratulating the form or members of it when they have done something positive and praiseworthy. Effective form tutors (and indeed effective teachers) look for reasons to praise pupils, and steer clear of only ever celebrating the achievements of the most able. They might praise some improvement in a particular subject, improved behaviour, punctuality, attendance, taking part in an event and so forth, as well as academic achievements. Sincere praise and enthusiasm for children's achievements, no matter how small, will reap benefits. Canter (2002) identifies '50 opportunities to say "you're terrific"' (see Table 6.3). Insincere, condescending praise or sarcasm has the opposite effect, alienating pupils and destroying relationships of mutual trust and respect.

Your own teaching

Make a conscious effort during your own teaching to notice children who co-operate, and praise them for positive behaviour as well as for work. Think in advance about some of the types of behaviour you will look out for and comment on, using Table 6.3 to give you some ideas.

A useful technique in setting a positive tone is to make a conscious effort to comment on co-operation rather than non-co-operation. For example, when you give an instruction to the whole class, instead of commenting on pupils who have not followed the instruction ('John, you are looking out of the window instead of at the book!', 'Lee, stop talking and start reading!' 'Rajinder, put the phone away!', 'Anita, you weren't listening, as usual', etc.), look for those who *have* followed the instruction and comment on them instead, as shown in the table. Try to circulate in the class noticing and commenting on pupils who are doing as asked. Keep the pace brisk and the tone light. Observe the impact on other pupils as you do this.

After the lesson, reflect on how effective you were in praising co-operative behaviour, and not just recognizing high levels of achievement. Did you manage to praise every child? What was the impact of this positive recognition on individuals/the group? How could you improve further? Discuss with your colleagues.

The form tutor effectively acts as team-builder, helping the group to gel, to take care of each other and to have consideration for each other as individuals and as a group. These are important transferable skills that enable pupils to progress not just during their school career but beyond into adult life. Working to solve problems together can build a sense of unity in the form. For example, if a particular teacher is finding it difficult to work with the group, or vice versa, the form tutor might work with the group to find some ways of improving the situation, working towards a group strategy or solution.

Shared celebrations, such as simple form parties at the end of term or the year, or an end-of-term trip for the form, help to engender a sense of friendship and belonging. The knowledge that form tutors care enough to go to the trouble to arrange such events for their form members gives pupils a sense of being valued by their tutors, which can be beneficial to the tutor–form relationship. The shared enjoyment of a form outing or event can have a lasting, positive impact on your relationship with the form.

Activity 6.4   Use of praise

Observations

During your lesson observations, which might be PHSE or subject-based, make a note of how many times teachers use praise, the different forms it takes, and the impact on children's behaviour and achievement. (You could choose to focus on one child, and observe how often s/he is praised, why, and the impact of this on the child.)

Before embarking upon your observation, draw up an observation tool. For example, if you wish to look particularly at how teachers use praise to recognize appropriate behaviour as well as pupil achievement with a whole group, you might list examples of the two types of praise, e.g.:

Class 7B: Pupils receiving praise	Praise for positive behaviour	Praise for effort and achievement
John	'Nice to see you here on time, John, well done' 'You remembered your book, excellent!'	'Your last homework was really thorough, John, well done'
Rajinder	'Rajinder's ready to start, well done!' 'Rajinder, you put your hand up three times today, good girl, well done!'	'You've worked hard today Rajinder, and completed all your work. That's very good'
Lee	'Lee's put his pencil down and is ready to listen, as I asked. Thanks Lee' 'Lee has started right away without wasting any time. That's great Lee'	'Lee you got almost all of those problems right – you're making very good progress in this module'
Anita	'It's really nice to see you looking at me and listening Anita, well done. Keep it up' 'You're working well in your group today, Anita, you're listening to other people without interrupting. That's brilliant, well done'	'Your writing was very original and interesting Anita – I enjoyed reading it. Thanks for making such an effort with this'

You could also add a column in which you note and reflect upon how the children react to the teacher's praise, both immediately and during the rest of the lesson. What does this tell you? Were you surprised by the children's reactions?

Monitoring pupils' progress and attendance

Effective pastoral care is fundamental to pupil achievement, and effective form tutors ensure channels of communication regarding the progress of their forms are open.

They may be proactive in seeking feedback from subject teachers about the group as a whole as well as individuals in the group. For example, it may be that one teacher has noticed a deterioration in the attitude and behaviour of certain individuals, and it is of benefit therefore for the form tutor to find out whether this is across the board or subject-specific. Depending on school policy, the form tutor might ask teachers to give them verbal feedback, fill in a form or email comments to them, so that they can build up a picture of the group and pupils in it which they can then use as the basis for developmental work with the group. Such information might lead to the close monitoring of one or two individuals who are underachieving, for example. Form tutors have the best overview of the progress, attitude and welfare of the group of young people in their care. However, it is always wise to confer with pastoral managers about the best course of action to take in monitoring behaviour and acting on information, rather than taking unilateral decisions. Pastoral leaders are likely to be very experienced teachers with a wealth of expertise on which you can draw in your own work as form tutor. You are not expected to be the expert on everything so you need to adhere to school policy and consult your managers, informing them of details you have noticed about form members or issues that concern you. For example, changes in a pupil's behaviour, attitude, demeanour or appearance can denote problems which could have a range of origins, including family issues, problems outside school, bullying, neglect and so on. It is important to engage in level-headed monitoring and not to over-dramatize fluctuations in young people's attitude, while remaining alert to signs of more serious issues. Opening up dialogue with children as well as teaching colleagues is a good starting point, and sharing concerns with the pastoral manager, such as the head of year, always advisable.

As is explained in Chapter 3, some of the children you work with may have statements of special educational needs (SEN). For such children, annual reviews take place in school. These are intended to monitor the effectiveness and relevance of the provision specified in the statement. The child's form tutor may be asked to attend the annual review. The child will in most cases also attend, and his/her parents will be invited. The views of the child and his/her parents will be sought. A range of other professionals might be invited as relevant, including the Special Educational Needs Co-ordinator (SENCO), whose input will be of considerable importance. The child's progress in general will be discussed, as well as progress towards the specific objectives in the statement. Any changes in the child's needs are considered and any further necessary action clarified. If you are invited as the form tutor to take part in an annual review, you should meet with the head of year or pastoral manager and SENCO in advance of the meeting to find out how you can usefully contribute to the discussion, and prepare for it, by gathering relevant information about the child, with which you should familiarize yourself.

Consistent attendance at school is key to pupil progress: in order to achieve their full potential, pupils need to be in school every day. By law schools have to keep a register of attendance and it is usually the form tutor who administers this each morning. The vast majority of schools have adopted electronic systems for registering pupils' attendance (e.g. **Bromcom**). In addition, schools have adopted a range of strategies for following up on absences, using, for instance, telephone calls and text messages to parents on the first morning of absence so that reasons for absence can be cleared up and any unauthorized absence or truancy can be detected straight away. As mentioned above, it is always worth watching for patterns of absence. If a child is absent regularly at one particular time of the week, it may be that the cause for this is something of concern to the child. It may be that this is something the form tutor can help with; for example, the pupil may be avoiding a particular lesson, teacher or bully.

In trying to encourage punctuality in pupils, a good form tutor leads by example. Form tutors usually have a multitude of administrative duties to execute in addition to pastoral care of form members: it is essential therefore that, as form tutor, you arrive in good time in order to get everything organized, and to be there to greet pupils as they arrive. It is advisable to be very clear in your expectations of pupils with regard to punctuality as with everything else, and to be consistent in your own actions – so, for instance, if you make a rule that three late arrivals means a one-hour detention, it is important to carry out the sanction in order to underline to pupils the seriousness of the need to be punctual and self-disciplined.

Liaison with other adults

Adults working together for the benefit of the children in their care is vital to the pastoral work undertaken by schools, and communication between adults is a vital feature of ensuring pupils' welfare and progress. It is important to remember that as form tutor you do not work alone: you should liaise regularly with the person who acts as your line manager with regard to pastoral care, and you need to ensure you are familiar with related school policy so that you are confident that you are acting in accordance with agreed priorities and ways of working and that you have the support of your colleagues in this. As form tutor you should meet regularly with the head of year (or other pastoral manager) to discuss any concerns about the children in your care, and you should ensure you keep abreast of school policy as relevant to your daily work. In addition, though, as form tutor you are the hub of communication pertaining to the children in your form, and you will need to liaise regularly with a range of others, including, for example, subject teachers, parents, the head of year/ learning mentors, **Educational Welfare Officer (EWO)**, SENCO, and so on. Being an advocate for your form with other staff in school is an important aspect of the form tutor role. Making early contact with parents is advisable, be this via an early parents' evening, an introductory letter to parents or individual telephone calls, which can all help in your work to support the pupils. Some schools organize special pastoral parents' evenings – this is often the case for new year 7 pupils, for instance, or it may be that parents can make appointments to see form tutors as a part of an otherwise subject-based parents' evening. In any case, it is advisable to take all opportunities to talk to parents. This helps you to understand the needs of individual form members, strengthening your relationship with your form. It can be a source of strength on which to draw in learning how best to support individual form members. Adults working together and to the same end can have a very positive impact on children's progress and well-being.

The role of the school EWO is to promote school attendance and follow up on absenteeism. The school EWO is likely to be in regular contact with the head of year and other pastoral staff, so it is important as form tutor to pass on swiftly any concerns with regard to attendance, so that they can be followed up. In some schools form tutors liaise directly with the EWO. In such cases the form tutor needs to be prepared for the meeting with the EWO by having details to hand of attendance patterns, dates of absences and so forth. EWOs tend to work with families, so may collect information from the form tutors of brothers and sisters with regard to family patterns of absence so that this can be taken up with parents. Often the EWO knows particular families very well, and will normally make home visits. This can be a source of helpful information for the form tutor in making sense of what is happening in the lives of young people in their care. The EWO may also be able to advise on strategies for improving attendance.

Another important person in the school with whom the form tutor is likely to have direct contact is the SENCO, whose responsibility it is to assess the needs of children with learning difficulties, behaviour problems or physical and sensory difficulty, and to ensure appropriate provision for them. As a form tutor it is possible to be alert to the needs of children in your form either as a result of your own observations of them or from the information and concerns passed on by their teachers. It may be that the SENCO has no knowledge of the child thus far, so the form tutor needs to alert them to the child in question. Equally it may be that the SEN department are already working to support the child, but the form tutor's knowledge of the pupil can assist in ensuring provision is appropriately tailored to the child's needs.

Pupil welfare

Safeguarding and child protection

Schools have a duty to provide a safe environment in which children can learn. As adults who are in regular contact with children, teachers have a responsibility to ensure signs of abuse, neglect or need are picked up and acted upon. Form tutors are particularly well placed in this respect, as they will usually see the children in their form at least once and often twice per day. The form tutor may be the person to whom a child chooses to disclose an abusive situation. More often, though, the effective form tutor simply keeps a careful eye on the general well-being of form members, and is alert to signals that a child may be in need of support. It may be a question of spotting changes in behaviour, appearance or academic achievement, which may be symptomatic of a different, underlying problem. Often it is possible to spot a pattern in terms of lateness or absence. For example, a child may be arriving late every day in order to avoid bullies on the way to school, or taking every Wednesday afternoon off to avoid PE when they would have to undress and so show bruising or evidence of self-harm.

Whilst it is important to be alert to signs, it is also vitally important not to put pressure on children by asking leading questions. Instead of asking, 'Who has been hitting you and causing these marks?', you should use open-ended questions: 'How are things?'; or questions based on a statement of fact: 'I notice you've been late a couple of times recently. What happened?' Another tactic is to give pupils the opportunity to come and talk to the form tutor at a given time and place: 'I hope you're alright, but if you want to come and have a chat you know where I am don't you? I'm always in here at lunchtimes.'

In instances of disclosure it is absolutely crucial that the form tutor avoid asking leading questions and making judgemental statements: 'Your dad hits you, doesn't he? He's a bully and a horrible man.' Children's abusers are often people they love, and the child may fear that by telling another adult about it they will be taken away from parents and put into care. After the disclosure, it is the duty of the teacher to write down the details as soon after the event as possible, including time and date of disclosure. This written report should contain only facts, not opinions. No teacher should promise a child confidentiality. If there is even the slightest hint of abuse or risk the information must be passed onto the person responsible for safeguarding or child protection in the school. Information about who this is and what the procedures are should be made available to all staff on taking up a post in the school, and it is the duty of all staff to adhere to the guidelines. All teachers need to familiarize themselves quickly with the guidance as it cannot be predicted at what point and in which circumstances a child may share a concern with a teacher. For instance, PE teachers often pick up signs of physical abuse as children change for PE (or refuse to, saying they have forgotten their kit), but it is not unusual for the disclosure to be made to form tutors. It is not your role as form tutor to solve the child's problems yourself. Neither is it your job to decide whether or not the story is true, but to report it to the child protection or safeguarding officer for the school, who will then liaise with outside agencies so that appropriate action can be put in place to support the child. It is also advisable if placed in the position of hearing a child's disclosure to consider your own support needs, as it can be very upsetting after the event to have had to listen to a harrowing story of abuse.

Form tutors are sometimes asked to take part in case conferences for individual members of their form. These case conferences are normally organized by social services when there is a concern about a particular child, usually with regard to injury or harm. They are normally chaired by an independent person and attended by a range of people, which might include the child's parents, social worker, police, nurse, the child and so forth. The form tutor can be asked to attend as a representative of the school. The case conference is confidential, which means the details cannot be discussed with other people except those at work who need to know, such as your head of year and/or the person in charge of safeguarding/child protection. Decisions about the support that needs to be in place for the child will be made on the basis of the discussion at the case conference.

Dealing with bullying

Bullying in schools is a serious issue. A recent survey (Beatbullying, 2011) reports that more than a third (37 per cent) of young people have been physically attacked by or suffered inappropriate sexual behaviour from another young person. Vulnerable young people are at the greatest risk of physical violence: pupils with a statement of SEN were found to be twice as likely to have experienced physical abuse. Every year, several young people commit suicide because they have experienced bullying (Elliott, 2010). Even in less extreme cases, bullying can have a long-term effect on the victim, leading to absenteeism, under-achievement, childhood depression (Thorne, 1995; Stonewall, 2007), low self-esteem and loss of concentration on school work (Stonewall, 2007; Elliott, 2010). Some useful websites on dealing with bullying in general include:

www.bullying.co.uk
http://www.skills4schools.org.uk/
www.scre.ac.uk

Schools and teachers need to be alert to the diverse forms bullying can take, in and out of school. Although children can be bullied for no apparent reason, it is increasingly being recognized that it is not enough for schools to have a blanket anti-bullying statement, and that they need to be specific in stating the unacceptability of particular types of bullying, including racist and homophobic bullying (Parker, 1999; Stonewall, 2007; DCSF, 2008) and bullying in which children with SEN and disabilities are targeted.

Minority ethnic students can experience particular forms of bullying, and the racism that underpins it is not always recognized by schools. Both white and minority ethnic pupils in Osler et al.'s (2001) study had observed or experienced bullying based on ethnicity or country or origin, and South Asian pupils had been particularly targeted. Physical retaliation to racial bullying had resulted in disciplinary procedures for some pupils, and in some cases the racial element underlying their response to the bullying was not acknowledged or addressed. Websites addressing racial bullying issues in particular include:

www.antibullying.net/racistinfo3.htm
www.kidscape.org.uk/assets/downloads/kspreventingrascistbullying.pdf
www.insted.co.uk/race.html
www.egfl.org.uk/categories/behaviour/bullying/racbully.html#d

As well as physical bullying and intimidation, some pupils engage in the psychological bullying of others. Osler et al. (2001: 4) report that 'the verbal and psychological bullying more commonly engaged in by girls is more readily overlooked by school authorities than the physical bullying more typically engaged in by boys'. It is important that teachers are sufficiently vigilant that instances of bullying amongst girls are recognized and appropriately addressed. Although this form of bullying is less noticeable, it can lead to girls' decisions to self-exclude, and as a consequence, to underachievement. Psychological bullying might involve pupils excluding a child from friendship groups, making threats and personal comments, and more and more frequently it takes the form of cyber bullying, defined by the DCSF (2007: 2) as 'the use of Information Communications Technology (ICT), particularly mobile phones and the internet, deliberately to upset someone else'. Elliott (2010: 31) notes that this particularly insidious form of bullying is 'the fastest-growing type of bullying', making victims 'vulnerable 24 hours a day, 7 days a week'. It can be directed at pupils or teachers, and can take a range of forms, some examples of which are given in Table 6.4.

Table 6.4   Examples of cyber bullying (adapted from Elliott, 2010: 31; used with the permission of Teachers' Pocketbooks)

Cyber bullying: some examples
Nasty comments on Facebook, visible to all
Embarrassing and/or made-up photos posted on social networks
Hate websites and blogs set up to vilify the victim
Creating fake user accounts pretending to be a friend of the victims, then publicly dumping them saying they are ugly, stupid, disgusting, etc.
Sending horrible text messages and images to the victim and everyone else
Using chat rooms, instant messaging and gaming areas to harass victims

The following websites and resources focus particularly on cyber-bullying:

www.dfes.gov.uk/bullying/cyberbullying
www.digizen.org/cyberbullying
www.cybermentors.org.uk
www.beatbullying.org
www.beyondbullying.com/cyberbullying.html
DCSF 'Safe to Learn' guidance available at www.teachernet.gov.uk/publications
Information pack for secondary teachers available to download from www.stoptext
    bully.com
Lesson plans for teachers available at www.cybersmartcurriculum.org

Local police may organize training courses on e-safety for teachers, children and parents. For example see:

http://schools.leicester.gov.uk/home/jobs-careers-training/e-safety-and-online-child-
    protection-training/

Homophobic bullying is widespread. Homophobic attitudes have characterized UK schools for many years (Ellis and High, 2004). This has been linked by some researchers (e.g. Plummer, 1999) to the need for boys to project a heterosexual identity in order to maintain status amongst their peers and to avoid being subject to bullying themselves. Whilst McCormack (2011) argues that there has been some shift in attitudes and that homophobia is less significant than previous research suggests, the Stonewall report (2007), reporting on a survey of 1,100 gay, lesbian and bisexual young people, comments that almost two-thirds of those young people (150,000) have experienced homophobic bullying. The key findings of the Stonewall report are summarized in Table 6.5.

Table 6.5   Key findings of the Stonewall report (adapted from Stonewall, 2007)

School report: the experiences of young gay people in Britain's schools (2007)

65% of young lesbian, gay and bisexual pupils have experienced homophobic bullying

75% of young gay people attending faith schools have experienced homophobic bullying

Homophobic language and comments are commonplace: 98% of young gay people hear the phrases 'that's so gay' or 'you're so gay' in school

97% of pupils hear other insulting homophobic remarks

Less than a quarter (23%) of pupils have been told in their school that homophobic bullying is wrong

In schools that have said that homophobic bullying is wrong, gay pupils are 60% more likely not to have been bullied

Over half of lesbian and gay pupils don't feel able to be themselves at school

35% of gay pupils do not feel safe or accepted at school

Some useful resources for tackling homophobic bullying in school include:

Downloadable lessons and resources on theme of lesbian, gay, bisexual and transgender (LGBT) history month (available at www.lgbthistorymonth.org.uk/)

Stonewall 'FIT' movie (available at www.stonewall.org.uk/at_school/education_for_all/quick_links/education_resources/fit/default.asp)

Stonewall 'Spell it out' training DVD for teachers (available at www.stonewall.org.uk/at_school/education_for_all/quick_links/education_resources/4008.asp)

Channel 4's 'Gay to Z' programmes for schools (available at www.channel4.com/programmes/gay-to-z)

Schools Out information and resources (available at www.schools-out.org.uk/)

Inclusive schools cannot tolerate bullying: there is a clear legal obligation to keep children safe from harm (Davies, 2010). All schools are legally obliged to have an anti-bullying policy and all teachers have a responsibility for ensuring this is adhered to consistently. Incidences of bullying have to be logged and dealt with effectively. The policy should outline the steps to take, but if in any doubt, it would also be advisable, as form tutor, to discuss the issue with the head of year or other pastoral manager. Some schools employ other staff such as counsellors to work with children on bullying issues, so it may be appropriate to involve them.

Form tutors are in a good position to be alert to instances of bullying and to act upon them swiftly. There are also positive actions schools can take to pre-empt, limit and act upon bullying. The most effective schools in terms of addressing bullying have a number of things in common, summarized in Table 6.6.

Table 6.6   Strategies adopted by effective schools to address bullying, adapted from Elliott (2010: 15–16; used with the permission of Teachers' Pocketbooks)

How effective schools address bullying:
They have an anti-bullying policy that states, 'This is a telling school' and 'Bullying of any kind is not tolerated'
They ensure the pupils take in this message through assemblies, classroom work, computer use, contracts and posters
They involve students in writing anti-bullying codes
They conduct surveys to find out where, when and how bullying is occurring
They inform parents that bullying will not be tolerated
They ensure the consequences for bad behaviour and rewards for good behaviour are clear, known to all and reinforced
They ensure something is done to stop the bullying and to protect victims
They give pupils access to help privately, so that victims can tell in safety
They talk about anti-bullying strategies in lessons and assemblies
They train all staff to recognize signs and symptoms of bullying
The teachers have the proverbial 'eyes in the back of their heads'
They monitor computer use in the classroom

It is incumbent upon form tutors to reflect on the actions they can take in order to be an effective part of the whole school anti-bullying strategy, and to take the initiative to enact these. For example, a pupil survey might identify the bullying 'hotspots' around the school. At whole-school level, steps might be taken to ensure staff presence in the high-risk areas at key times of the day, as well as identified 'safe areas' in which pupils can choose to spend breaks and lunchtimes. As a part of this, some form tutors might voluntarily stay in their form rooms at lunchtimes so that form members have a safe place to go.

As well as taking steps to restrict opportunities for bullying in school, there is a need to foster an atmosphere in which pupils are encouraged to talk:

> Children need to know that they have a right to talk and that they do not have to suffer; that they can talk about their problems; that it will help to talk; that they will not suffer more because they have talked; and that they will be given strategies to help them. (Thorne, 1995: 176)

Jolly (1995) adds that if bullying is to be eradicated, it is essential that we look also at what motivates bullies:

> Beyond the school gates, teachers cannot control pupils' opportunities for bullying, and this makes it doubly important for schools to try to tackle motive, whether it be racial, religious, gang rivalry, or simply a matter of the strong preying on the weak. Students should be taught about equality of treatment, about standing up for others, about peaceful conflict resolution, and that force and violence are bad ways to solve disputes. (Jolly, 1995: 53)

Jolly (1995) argues that there should be guidelines in school such that 'both bully and victim can explain their case in a calm atmosphere'. It is important to recognize, however, that it is not easy for victims of bullying to talk about it. They may be reluctant to report it because they are feeling ashamed in some way as though they are to blame for the bullying, or they may be afraid of making the problem worse by reporting it (Osler et al., 2001). Homophobic bullying may be the type victims feel least able to speak up about, fearing social stigma and isolation (Intercom Trust, 2003). There is a need, therefore, for the school to be proactive in finding ways to reassure victims and encourage them to come forward. Suggested strategies schools could adopt in tackling homophobic bullying in particular are addressed in the Stonewall report (2007). As discussed earlier, however, approachability and availability of the form tutor are fundamental necessities in encouraging pupils to report instances of bullying. Pupils need to know where to find their form tutor and when they can talk to them safely. They may also need reassuring that they have done the right thing by talking about it, and to be encouraged to come back and report it again if it persists after an intervention by the tutor or the school.

A useful strategy to encourage more reticent pupils to 'tell' about bullying is that of the 'problem box' (Thorne, 1995: 176), suggested by pupils in a school-based action research project on bullying. This has become an established means for encouraging children in the school to bring attention to their problems. The idea is that pupils write down the problems or issues they wish to raise and put these in the box. These are then dealt with individually, but also provide the basis for a half-termly problem-box assembly. This idea could be adapted so that recurrent issues form the basis of form-time discussions or PHSE sessions. This would of course require some sensitivity, such that attention is not drawn to individuals in the form. One way to do this might be to plan group work based around semi-fictional case studies and scenarios, requiring pupils to discuss possible courses of action. It can also be useful to involve pupils in role-plays about bullying or discussing case studies and moral dilemma stories which are fictional but realistic. This encourages students to think about '*reasons for and solutions to* bullying' (Watson-Davis, 2005: 77). Engaging in the discussion of moral dilemmas relating to bullying situations fosters empathy in children as well as promoting an anti-bullying ethos and a sense that even the 'innocent' bystanders in bullying incidents have a responsibility.

Counsellors, mediators or other outside agencies are sometimes involved in dealing with serious bullying (Davies, 2010). In cases where the bullying occurs outside school, police might be involved, as well as school mediators and pupil counsellors (Elliott, 2010). The local authority may also have behaviour support specialists or PHSE teams who can help (Elliott, 2010). Some schools make use of 'peer support' schemes that involve pupils in sharing their concerns and exploring their own solutions, which can have a positive effect in reducing bullying in schools (Noaks and Noaks, 2009; Elliott, 2010). The schemes might include:

- **peer listeners**, who provide a confidential service as active listeners and facilitators, offering a safe place for pupils to share their concerns and explore solutions
- **peer mediators**, who are trained in conflict resolution strategies and may act as intermediaries in response to bullying situations
- **peer mentors**, who are often given a specific focus, such as acting as a befriender to pupils in a new school or as a support for pupils who are vulnerable; peer mentors are paired with another pupil for a specific reason, and intended as a source of support for them (Elliott, 2010: 109)

The form tutor is a key player both in helping to prevent children from being bullied and in helping bullies to take responsibility for their actions and change their behaviour. Being observant as a form tutor is possibly one of the most important skills. Noticing a change in a child's attitude, appearance, habits, friendship, demeanour, behaviour and achievement can be the first, crucial step in ensuring that appropriate support is provided. In addition to fostering a 'telling' and 'listening' culture (Thorne, 1995), therefore, it is helpful to be alert to some of the classic signs of bullying. These are summarized in Table 6.7. All of the signs in Table 6.7 can equally be indicative of other problems, but it may well be that by asking the child if they are being bullied the form tutor is able to ascertain the root of the problem.

Table 6.7   Signs of bullying (adapted from Elliott, 2010: 11; used with the permission of Teachers' Pocketbooks)

Sign	Notes
The child seems upset or secretive when using or looking at their mobile phone or computer	There may be cyber bullying going on, hurtful text messages, etc.
The child appears depressed or anxious	
The child is fearful of certain places and/or people	Certain areas of the school may be bullying hotspots, out of sight of duty staff and a popular place for bullies to wait
The child does not eat lunch	The child may be avoiding the school dining area in order to avoid the bullies, and/or their money may have been taken by bullies (this can go on for a sustained period in some cases)
The child starts to write stories or talk about suicide	This must be taken seriously and passed on to the member of staff in charge of safeguarding/child protection
The child regularly has books/homework/clothes go 'missing'	The child may be routinely targeted by bullies taking belongings to taunt and terrorise
The child becomes frightened of or unwilling to go to school, walk home or catch the school bus	The form tutor might pick this up from absence records or notice the child hanging around at the end of the day/lunchtime. It can help to reach an agreement whereby the child is allowed to leave five minutes earlier than other pupils, if handled sensitively and in conjunction with other measures
The child becomes aggressive, angry and disruptive and may lash out	A change in behaviour may be noticed by the form tutor/other staff/pupils

Activity 6.5   Whole-school approaches to bullying

Drawing on your experiences in your current or most recent school, make brief notes and/or discuss the following with your peers or school-based tutors:

- What do you understand to be the school policy on bullying?
- Are there, as far as you are aware, specific references in the policy to homophobic or racist bullying?
- Does the policy refer to the need to address bullying directed at children with SEN or disabilities?
- Does the school have a specific policy on dealing with cyber bullying?
- Are children involved in strategies to tackle bullying? How? What has been the impact?

(Continued)

(Continued)

- Are there peer mediation schemes in place of the sort described in the 'dealing with bullying' section of this chapter? What do pupils think of these?
- Are there ways you can think of to tackle bullying that are not already in place in school? How might these be introduced?
- Are there features of the building, or the access to it, which make it more or less likely that bullying can occur? What steps could be taken to improve the building in this respect?
- If you were advising an architect designing a new build school, what features would you suggest need to be planned in terms of ensuring the building limits the possibility for bullying to occur?

Monitoring and improving pupil behaviour

Much of the day-to-day liaison between form tutors and other teachers in the school relates to the behaviour and progress of form members. Often it is as form members' behaviour begins to give cause for concern, or starts to impede their own or others' progress in some way, that subject teachers will raise the issue with form tutors. It is imperative that the form tutor follows the school procedures for monitoring and following up on pupil behaviour, and it is advisable to work in tandem with the pastoral manager to do this. Use of daily/weekly report cards, target-specific monitoring systems and other tailored approaches to monitoring and improving behaviour varies a little from one school to another but in general serves to remind the pupil of the changes that need to be made. These tools also serve to make the child accountable at the end of each day or week, when they report back to a designated person (form tutor, head of year, learning manager, deputy headteacher and so forth), showing the completed report card containing comments from subject teachers throughout the day or week. This then provides the basis for discussion between the pupil and the pastoral teacher.

As a new teacher in a school it is clearly important for you to become familiar quickly with the school's policy on and approach to discipline and behaviour management. A common approach for the last 10–15 years has been that of 'positive discipline' or 'positive behaviour management', based on the principles of assertive discipline (Canter and Canter, 2001), in which positively worded classroom rules (see the example in Table 6.8), rewards (see Table 6.9) and consequences (see Table 6.10) are the key principles.

Some schools build into this system an automatic report to the form tutor if a child has broken rules more than two or three times in a particular lesson. This enables the

Table 6.8   Example of positively worded classroom rules (based on Canter, 1992: 6)

1. Follow instructions

2. Arrive on time

3. Bring equipment

4. Keep hands, feet and objects to yourself

5. Speak respectfully to others

Table 6.9   Example of rewards for positive behaviour (adapted from Canter and Canter, 2001)

Praise from the teacher

Positive notes sent home to parents

Positive notes to the students

Positive phone calls to parents

Vouchers

Raffle tickets

Student chooses where to sit in class

Participation in a school trip

Table 6.10   Example of a set of agreed consequences for breaking the rules (adapted from Canter, 1992: 6)

First time a student breaks a rule	Warning
Second time	Stay in class one minute after the bell
Third time	Stay in class five minutes at break
	Teacher alerts form tutor
Fourth time	Teacher calls parents and alerts form tutor
Fifth time	Referred to head of year
Severe clause (for serious offences)	Referred directly to head of year

form tutor to follow up on this by discussing the incident(s) with the child. It also allows the form tutor to gain an overview so that it is clear whether the child is misbehaving in more than one subject or whether the problem is confined to one area. In such cases it can be helpful for the form tutor to take on a mediator role, working with the teacher and the child to broker agreements about behaviour and suitable targets. In cases where the child is being referred in several subjects, there is a need for more targeted, personalized action, which is likely to require some liaison between the form tutor, pastoral manager and possibly parents.

Activity 6.6   Reflection on managing behaviour

Why should relationships and fair process be given such prominence when it comes to managing pupils and behaviour? Reflect on the following questions. You should discuss and debate these with your student teacher colleagues and the teachers with whom you work in school, before making brief notes in response:

1 What is the purpose of 'discipline' in schools?

2 What are we trying to teach our young people?

3 What are the most effective ways to achieve long-term behaviour change? Is punishment effective?

4 Is it important to us that young people feel safe at school?

5 What is our role as teachers in the development of social and emotional competencies in learners?

6 How important is the relationship between teacher and learner, and how important are the relationships between learners?

7 To what extent are relationships placed at the centre of your disciplinary philosophy and practice? Can you give examples from your practice about how you manage behaviour through positive relationships?

8 Is it possible that a punitive philosophy informing practice may be counter-productive? For example, what is the long-term impact of punishment on children's social and moral development? Are there more effective ways to enable children to develop a sense of responsibility? (Adapted from Thorsborne and Vinegrad, 2009: 22–25; used with the permission of Teachers' Pocketbooks)

More recently, restorative practice is becoming more and more prevalent in schools. Based on the principles of restorative justice, the focus is on repairing relationships. It is increasingly recognized that punishment is not the most effective way to change behaviour, and schools are moving towards restorative approaches in which strong messages are conveyed about what types of behaviour are acceptable and unacceptable (Thorsborne and Vinegrad, 2009). Restorative practice involves both those responsible for and those affected by the behaviour in finding solutions to the problem, with support provided for both parties. Drawing on the work of Wachtel (1999), Thorsborne and Vinegrad (2009: 16–20) identify four types of response a teacher might make having witnessed a bullying incident, for example witnessing one child tripping up and pushing another. These are summarized in Table 6.11.

Table 6.11   Four types of teacher response in dealing with a bullying incident (adapted from Thorsborne and Vinegrad, 2009: 16–20; used with the permission of Teachers' Pocketbooks)

Type of response	Use of authority	Description
Neglectful	The teacher chooses not to use their authority	The teacher ignores the problem and walks away. Pupils are not held to account. No support is offered. No reminders are given about behavioural limits and boundaries. The message is conveyed that the teacher does not care and cannot be trusted to keep children safe
Permissive	The teacher chooses not to wield their authority appropriately	The teacher excuses or downplays the wrongdoer's harmful behaviour with a mild admonishment. A high level of support is offered to the perpetrator, but inappropriate support to the victim. There is a very low emphasis on reinforcement of expectations. Wrongdoers are not confronted with the impact of their behaviour. This can result in victims feeling that the teacher does not care enough about what they have experienced
Punitive	The teacher chooses a top-down authoritarian approach where non-compliance must be punished	The teacher reprimands the wrongdoer loudly, criticising and/or applying a sanction with no constructive input from the victim. The emphasis is on non-compliance with a rule, and the punishment this incurs. Little or no support is provided for either party and no input is invited from them. Wrongdoers can be humiliated and victims disempowered through this process. This can increase the likelihood of 'payback' by the bully to the victim later on
Restorative	The teacher chooses to take an authoritative approach, making constructive use of their authority	The teacher brings together the students involved and creates a space for respectful dialogue in which the teacher acts as facilitator, working *with* the children. Via this approach the teacher signals that the behaviour is unacceptable, but engages both parties in helping to sort out the problem constructively. There is a strong emphasis on meeting the parties' needs with a fair process and support. There is recognition that harm has been done and needs fixing. Perpetrators are held accountable. Victims are empowered and given voice. The process exemplifies the value the teacher and the school place on healthy relationships between key parties. The emphasis is on relationships and fair processes

In order to adopt effective restorative practices the reflective practitioner needs to be able to re-examine and question taken-for-granted assumptions about strategies for changing pupil behaviour. The strong emphasis on fairness that characterizes restorative practices also fosters reflection in pupils. Children's ability and readiness to reflect on their own behaviour can be impeded if they feel they are being treated unfairly, and there is therefore a need to avoid causing this kind of resentment:

> One way to do this is to move away from consistency of consequence (predetermined sanctions) and focus on **fair process**. When young people experience fair process, they will more readily accept the consequences. It produces meaningful compliance and increased co-operation. (Thorsborne and Vinegrad, 2009: 30)

Table 6.12   Stages in the process of constructing a restorative conversation (adapted from Thorsborne and Vinegrad, 2009; used with the permission of Teachers' Pocketbooks)

Stages	Details
Engagement	Both pupils are invited into the dialogue, of which the focus is problem-solving, not blame – 'No-one is in trouble, but we need to talk about what just happened'
Reflection	Thoughtfulness and empathy are encouraged. This needs to be handled with care, and the opportunity for reflection should not be rushed – 'When you tripped x and pushed him over, what were you thinking?' The question contains an unambiguous statement of what happened, and should be delivered in a tone of polite but firm enquiry. If the child struggles to answer the question, some alternatives might be: • What were you hoping would happen? • What was the purpose of doing that? • What were you expecting would happen? • What did you want when you did that? • What was going on in your head when you were doing that? • What made you decide to do that? These 'thinking' questions avoid the use of the word 'why', which is less effective. It is important to remain neutral throughout and to allow the time for the pupil to collect their thoughts. The teacher should not restate or rephrase what is said, so allowing the people involved to make their own sense of what they hear
Understanding	Pupils are helped to understand how people have been affected, and what harm has been done. This is to enable the child who has done wrong to understand the harm they can do to others, so that they make better choices in the future. So the teacher might then ask: 'How do you think x has been affected? What's it like for him?' This question is aimed at promoting the perpetrator's level of empathy and compassion. Reflection on who is harmed is broadened: 'Has what you've done affected anyone else? Who? How?' The teacher then turns to the victim and invites them to contribute to the conversation: 'What did you think when y first tripped you and then pushed you over?' 'What was that like for you? What was the worst of it?' The purpose of these questions is to establish what harm has been done. It can be useful then to ask some questions about the impact this has had on the teacher: 'Do you have any idea of the impact this has on me?' This is intended to encourage both parties involved to think more broadly
Acknowledgement	The harm done is acknowledged. The attention returns to the perpetrator: 'Since we have been talking and we have listened to x, what have you been thinking about?' If the child has difficulty answering this, alternatives might be: 'Now we are here talking about what happened, what is going on in your head?' or 'Now we are here talking about what happened, what have you thought about?' or 'What do you think now about what you did? Was it helpful?' The questions require the child to reflect on what happened so they need to be asked after they have had time to think and reflect on their behaviour and its impact on their peers and others. Finally the teacher asks: 'What could you say to x right now about what happened? What does he need to hear from you?' An apology may feature
Agreement	A plan is agreed to fix things. The teacher asks the victim, 'What could x do to make things right for you?', then checks his suggestions with the perpetrator: 'Would that be OK with you?', and asks both of them, 'Do you have any other suggestions?' The parties involved contribute to their agreement with the teacher acting as facilitator
Arranging for follow-up	In order to make sure the plan is working, the teacher asks the parties involved 'How should we follow this up? Any suggestions?', then says, 'I'll just make a note of what we've agreed. Shall I check with you tomorrow at the end of lunch to see how the agreement is going? Shall we meet here? Thanks both for helping sort this out.' The certainty of the follow-up puts teeth into the process and gives valuable feedback about the action taken

This implies involving the pupils in resolving the problem. To return to the bullying example mentioned earlier, both the bully and the victim would be involved in the process, with the teacher acting as facilitator. Both parties are involved in discussing the incident and have a say in how to put things right, which is very different to the teacher making decisions about how to deal with the incident. This provides an opportunity for pupils to reflect on their behaviour and develop social skills. Importantly, once the particular issue has been resolved, it is not discussed again. There is also a strong emphasis on separating the particular unacceptable behaviour from the person doing it – the implicit message is that whilst the behaviour is unacceptable, a regard for the person is maintained.

Thorsborne and Vinegrad (2009) identify six stages in the process of constructing a restorative conversation. These are summarized in Table 6.12.

Restorative practices can be used more widely and to deal with more serious disciplinary issues. There is insufficient space here to go into detail, but useful references for those interested in pursuing a restorative rather than a punitive approach to managing pupil behaviour include Hopkins (2004) and Thorsborne and Vinegrad (2008a, 2008b, 2009). The key point is:

> the community responsible for and affected by the behaviour deliberate and decide on consequences aimed at making things right. This is in direct contrast to the punitive continuum where the sanctions are predetermined, and the community of people affected has no say in the outcomes. (Thorsborne and Vinegrad, 2009: 59)

If you work restoratively with your form members this could be time well invested, as gradually pupils become more aware of others' needs and the impact of their own behaviour on others. They become reflective about their own conduct and decisions.

Critical reading at Master's level

1   Read the following article, which reports on two anti-bullying programmes in Norway:

Stephens, P. (2011) 'Preventing and confronting bullying: a comparative study of two national programmes in Norway', *British Educational Research Journal*, 37(3): 381–404. Make notes on the implications of the findings for:

- school-wide strategies for drawing up, implementing and evaluating anti-bullying policies
- tackling bullying as an individual teacher, within and outside of the classroom

(Continued)

(Continued)

2 Read the following article, in which the author argues for a re-conceptualization of bullying:

Walton, G. (2011) 'Spinning our wheels: reconceptualising bullying beyond behaviour-focused approaches', *Discourse: Studies in the Cultural Politics of Education*, 32(1): 131–144.

Summarize the assumptions on which Walton argues anti-bullying strategies are currently founded.

What are the implications of this for the work of schools? How will this inform your work as a form tutor with regard to tackling bullying?

3 Which of the two papers was the most thought-provoking for you? Which do you think was most informative and most likely to influence your practice? Why? Finally, identify two further references (one from each article) that you would like to follow up, and explain why.

Conclusion

In this chapter you have learned about the aims and organization of pastoral care in British secondary schools. You have gained insights into the multifarious aspects of the role of form tutor and how this role fits into the broader school strategies to ensure pupils' well-being and progress. Particular consideration has been given to the part played by the form tutor in fostering the form's identity, monitoring pupils' progress and attendance, liaison with other adults, pupil welfare and improving behaviour.

Pastoral care is complex and difficult to describe, varying in nature from school to school in accordance with needs and priorities. In many schools, though, it is the foundation on which teaching and learning can be built. The form tutor is central to this, but does not work in isolation, harnessing the support and advice of colleagues to act in pupils' best interests. As a good form tutor, you really can make a difference to children's lives, affecting not only their academic progress but also their social and emotional development. Whilst there can be, on occasions, difficult and upsetting issues that have to be tackled, the majority of your work as a form tutor will be brisk, business-like and fun. Working daily as form tutor for a group of young people you know well is one of the greatest sources of satisfaction in teaching, and an aspect of the job you can look forward to enjoying throughout your career.

References

Baldwin, J. and Wells, H. (1979) *Active Tutorial Work Books 1, 2*. Oxford: Basil Blackwell in association with Lancashire County Council.

Baldwin, J. and Wells, H. (1980) *Active Tutorial Work Books 3, 4*. Oxford: Basil Blackwell in association with Lancashire County Council.

Baldwin, J. and Wells, H. (1981) *Active Tutorial Work Book 5*. Oxford: Basil Blackwell in association with Lancashire County Council.

Beatbullying (2011) *Child-on-Child Violence in the UK: A Retrospective Survey*. Available at: www2.beatbullying.org//pdfs/CoCV%20Evaluation.pdf (accessed 12 May 2011).

Calvert, M. (2009) 'From "pastoral care" to "care": meanings and practices', *Pastoral Care in Education*, 27(4): 267–277.

Canter. L. (1992) *Assertive Discipline Secondary Workbook*. California: Lee Canter & Associates.

Canter, L. (2002) *Assertive Discipline Secondary Workbook*. Bloomington, IN: Solution Tree.

Canter, L. and Canter, M. (2001) *Assertive Discipline: Positive Behaviour Management For Today's Classroom*. 3rd edition. Bloomington: Solution Tree Press.

Davies, S. (2010) *The Essential Guide to Secondary Teaching*. Harlow: Pearson Education Ltd.

DCSF (2007) *Cyberbullying: A Whole-School Community Issue*. Available at: www.education.gov.uk/publications/eOrderingDownload/Cyberbullying-leaflet.pdf (accessed 7 March 2011).

DCSF (2008) *Bullying: Don't Suffer in Silence*. Available at: http://webarchive.national-archives.gov.uk/20050302035856/http://dfes.gov.uk/bullying/pdf/dfee%20bullying%20insideNEW.pdf (accessed 1 April 2011).

DES/HMI (1989) *Report of Her Majesty's Inspectors on Pastoral Care in Secondary Schools: An Inspection of Some Aspects of Pastoral Care in 1987–8*. London: DES.

DfES (2003) *Raising Standards and Tackling Workload: A National Agreement*. Available at: http://education.gov.uk/publications/eOrderingDownload/DfES%200172%20200MIG1975.pdf (accessed 27 January 2011).

Edmond, N. and Price, M. (2009) 'Workforce re-modelling and pastoral care in schools: a diversification of roles or a de-professionalisation of functions?', *Pastoral Care in Education*, 27(4): 301–311.

Elliott, M. (2010) *Stop Bullying Pocketbook*. 2nd edition. Alresford: Teachers' Pocketbooks.

Ellis, V. and High, S. (2004) 'Something more to tell you', *British Educational Research Journal*, 30(2): 213–225.

Holmes, E. (2009) *The Newly Qualified Teacher's Handbook*. 2nd edition. London: Routledge.

Hopkins, B. (2004) *Just Schools: A Whole School Approach to Restorative Justice*. London: Jessica Kingsley Publishers.

Intercom Trust (2003) *Joint Action Against Homophobic Bullying Project: Practical Guidelines for Schools and Colleges in the South West*. Available at: www.intercom-trust.org.uk/resources/JAAHBGuidelines.pdf (accessed 1 April 2011).

Jolly, A. (1995) 'Tolerance: implications for educators', in A. Osler, H.F. Rathenow and H. Starkey (eds) *Teaching for Citizenship in Europe*. Stoke-on-Trent: Trentham Books Ltd. pp. 47–54.

Kent, P. and Kay, S. (2007) 'The strength of vertical tutor groups', *Principal Matters*, 73: 17–18.

Mansell, W. (2007) *Education by Numbers: The Tyranny of Testing*. London: Politico's.

McCormack, M. (2011) 'The declining significance of homohysteria for male students in three sixth forms in the south of England', *British Educational Research Journal*, 37 (2): 337–353.

Montessori, M. (1912) *The Montessori Method*. London: Heinemann.

Montessori, M. (1988; first published 1949) *The Absorbent Mind*. Oxford: Clio Press.

Noaks, J. and Noaks, L. (2009) 'School-based peer mediation as a strategy for social inclusion', *Pastoral Care in Education*, 27(1): 53–61.

Osler, A., Street, C., Lall, M. and Vincent, K. (2001) *Not a Problem? Girls and School Exclusion*. Leicester: National Children's Bureau and Joseph Rowntree Foundation.

Parker, J. (1999) 'School policies and practices: the teacher's role', in M. Cole (ed.) *Professional Issues For Teachers and Student Teachers*. London: David Fulton. pp. 69–84.

Plummer, D. (1999) *One of the Boys: Masculinity, Homophobia and Modern Manhood*. New York: The Haworth Press.

Stephens, P. (2011) 'Preventing and confronting bullying: a comparative study of two national programmes in Norway', *British Educational Research Journal*, 37(3): 381–404.

Stonewall (2007) *School Report: the Experiences of Young Gay People in Britain's Schools*. Available at www.stonewall.org.uk/at_school/education_resources/4121.asp (accessed 5 April 2011).

Thorne, S. (1995) 'Children's rights and the listening school: an approach to counter bullying among primary school pupils', in A. Osler, H.F. Rathenow and H. Starkey (eds) *Teaching for Citizenship in Europe*. Stoke-on-Trent: Trentham Books Ltd. pp. 169–180.

Thorsborne, M. and Vinegrad, D. (2008a) *Restorative Practices and Bullying*. Milton Keynes: Speechmark.

Thorsborne, M. and Vinegrad, D. (2008b) *Restorative Practices in Classrooms*. Milton Keynes: Speechmark.

Thorsborne, M. and Vinegrad, D. (2009) *Restorative Justice Pocketbook*. Alresford: Teachers' Pocketbooks.

Wachtel, T. (1999) 'Restorative justice in everyday life: beyond the formal ritual', paper presented at the Reshaping Australian Institutions Conference: Restorative Justice and Civil Society. The Australian National University, Canberra, 16–18 February. Available at www.iirp.org/library/anu.html (accessed 18 January 2012).

Walton, G. (2011) 'Spinning our wheels: reconceptualising bullying beyond behaviour-focused approaches', *Discourse: Studies in the Cultural Politics of Education*, 32(1): 131–144.

Watson-Davis, R. (2005) *Form Tutor's Pocketbook*. Alresford: Teachers' Pocketbooks.

CHAPTER 7

DIVERSITY, SOCIAL JUSTICE AND GLOBAL ISSUES IN EDUCATION

Chris Wilkins

By the end of this chapter you will have:

- engaged with a range of specific social contexts of education
- reflected upon your life experiences and personal values – and how these impact on your developing professional identity
- challenged your existing preconceptions of issues of social justice
- developed your understanding of the statutory duties schools have in respect of equality and diversity, and the implications for you as a beginning teacher
- engaged in wider debates about the future of education

Introduction: why is diversity important?

Earlier chapters in this book have stressed the importance of understanding and responding to each individual student's needs. Chapter 3 introduced issues of inclusion in respect of special educational needs, gifted and talented students and English as an

Additional Language, and Chapter 6 explored the pastoral care of students. This chapter explores the wider social context of working with students from diverse backgrounds, and the legislative framework that determines the responsibilities that schools and teachers have in respect of these issues. It considers complex and sometimes controversial issues around diversity and social justice, and encourages you to reflect on your own background and the ways in which you respond to these issues. In doing so, it leads you to consider how your attitudes and values influence your teaching, and how you engage with students.

Schooling as a socio-political process

Ever since the Education Act of 1870 introduced state control of schooling in the UK, education has been explicitly recognized as being a social and political process. The Act was a consequence of social *and* economic matters; the need for 'civic education' for voters newly enfranchised by the 1867 Reform Act, and concern about declining UK competitiveness in an increasingly global industrial market. Both concerns seem familiar today, with successive prime ministers talking of the importance of education in the 'global skills race' (Gordon Brown, quoted in Brown et al., 2008: 4) and in creating 'better citizens' (David Cameron, 2011a).

However, given that everyone has different aspirations for social change, it is not surprising that the precise social purpose of education, and how it can best be achieved, remains the subject of controversy. Schooling can be viewed either as a process of social reformation (or transformation), or alternatively as a means of *resisting* change, of preserving 'the social order'. This, perhaps, lies at the heart of the ideological divide in the politics of schooling between 'liberal-progressives' and the 'traditionalist-conservatives'.

This divide came to a head in the UK in the 1970s and 1980s, with traditionalists claiming that education was dominated by 'loony left' Marxists committed to social engineering, using 'pseudo-subjects' such as anti-racist education and world studies (Jones, 1989) for the promotion of 'impractical utopian values that will destroy all that is most valuable in our culture' (Scruton, cited in Hill, 1994). Progressives countered by labelling traditionalists as elitists determined to maintain the class divide and resist the encroachment of a civil rights agenda into schools (Whitty, 2002).

Prime Minister James Callaghan's 'Great Debate' speech at Ruskin College (1976) brought education policy to the centre of political debate. No serious consideration had previously been given to any national control over the curriculum (often referred to as 'the secret garden'). Schools were broadly free to determine what was taught, and regulation was minimal compared to that which followed the establishment of the Office for Standards in Education (Ofsted) in 1992.

Before the events of this period are dismissed as being of marginal historical interest, it is worth considering the changes that emerged and their impact on what it means to be a teacher. The 1988 Education Reform Act not only established the National Curriculum, but began the processes of devolving the management of schools from local authorities to governing bodies and of increased parental choice that continue almost a quarter of a century later. The establishment of Ofsted led to a increasingly rigorous regime of the regulation of teachers' work, and professional standards for teacher competence were introduced in 1998; the pace of change being such that 2012 will see the fourth generation of these come into force (TDA, 2011).

Amidst this constantly evolving landscape, the traditionalist–progressive debate about the extent to which teachers engage directly with social and political issues has been ever present. Activity 7.1 asks you to reflect on your views about the social context of schooling; whether you see teaching as a process of overt socialization (either aimed at *conserving*, *reforming* or *transforming* the social order), or an activity sitting outside the socio-political sphere.

Activity 7.1   Views about the social context of schooling

Read the following quotations and use the scale to indicate your response. (Avoid reading the sources of the quotes below until you have completed the activity and do not think too long about each statement – go with 'gut instinct'.) Then, share your responses to these quotations with another teacher or colleague.

1 'There is no virtue in producing socially well-adjusted members of society who are unemployed because they do not have the skills'

Strongly agree   Agree   Neither agree nor disagree   Disagree   Strongly disagree   Not sure
| | | | | |

2 Teachers '... should not waste their time on the politics of gender, race and class'.

Strongly agree   Agree   Neither agree nor disagree   Disagree   Strongly disagree   Not sure
| | | | | |

3 Teachers must '...demonstrate consistently the positive attitudes, values and behaviour which are expected of pupils' and must not undermine 'fundamental British values ...'

Strongly agree   Agree   Neither agree nor disagree   Disagree   Strongly disagree   Not sure
| | | | | |

(Continued)

(Continued)

4   'Education has an emancipatory, liberating, value ...[it is] ... the means by which individuals can access to all the other goods we value – cultural, social and economic – in their own terms'

Strongly agree   Agree   Neither agree nor disagree   Disagree   Strongly disagree   Not sure
| | | | | | |

5   '... despite a rhetoric of standards for all, education policy in England is actively involved in the defence, legitimation and extension of white supremacy... The racist outcomes of contemporary policy may not be coldly calculated but they are far from accidental'

Strongly agree   Agree   Neither agree nor disagree   Disagree   Strongly disagree   Not sure
| | | | | | |

6   'The school is an institution in which children are initiated by teachers, who are authorities in their subjects, into a body of knowledge which has no immediate connection to their lives or necessary relevance to the problems of society'

Strongly agree   Agree   Neither agree nor disagree   Disagree   Strongly disagree   Not sure
| | | | | | |

7   'There is no doubt that in our headlong rush to educate everybody we are lowering our standards and more and more abandoning the study of those subjects by which the essentials of our culture ... are transmitted'

Strongly agree   Agree   Neither agree nor disagree   Disagree   Strongly disagree   Not sure
| | | | | | |

Now share your responses to these quotations with another teacher or colleague. Whether you agree or not does not matter, but try to explore together why you responded the way you did:

- Did you draw upon your own life experience (your family background, gender, ethnicity, etc.)? If so, how?
- What about your own experience of education (from primary school right through to university)?
- How has your time in teacher education influenced your responses?
- Having discussed your responses, have you changed your views, or did the discussion reinforce your position? Now look below at the source of the quotations. Does this knowledge change your views in any way?

Key questions/thoughts to take away from this exercise

- Where do you think your responses place you on the spectrum of 'traditionalist–progressive'?
- Is that how you would have expected to see yourself when you first thought of becoming a teacher?
- What impact do you think this may have in the way you approach your teaching in the future?

Sources for Activity 7.1

1   Prime Minister James Callaghan, Ruskin College lecture (1976)

2   Prime Minister John Major, Conservative Party Conference (1992)

3   *Teachers' Standards* (2011)

4   Michael Gove, soon to be Secretary of State for Education, Royal Society of Arts speech (2009)

5   David Gillborn, sociologist (2005)

6   Chris Woodhead, former Chief Inspector of Schools (2009)

7   T.S. Eliot, writer, quoted in Goodson (1985)

Diversity: teachers' responsibility

A core principle of UK equalities legislation is the legal duty on public-sector bodies and workers to challenge discriminatory behaviour and practices, and to actively promote positive attitudes towards diversity.

This has significant implications for the way teachers need to approach diversity and social justice issues, as can be seen in quotation number 3 in Activity 7.1. The requirement that teachers demonstrate *positive values and attitudes* (and uphold *fundamental British values*) suggests that it is not enough for teachers to 'leave their values and attitudes outside the classroom door'. The notion that teachers must *promote* positive attitudes to diversity also suggests that remaining neutral on social issues in the classroom is insufficient.

The proactive principle of equalities legislation largely results from the Macpherson inquiry (1999) into the racist murder of London teenager Stephen Lawrence in 1993. The subsequent Race Relations (Amendment) Act (2000) led to 'establishment' acceptance of the notion of **institutional racism**, and extended the duty of public bodies beyond challenging discriminatory practices to include the promotion of positive values. This principle was reinforced by the Equality Act of 2010, bringing together existing legislation under a single Act (and embedding the UN Convention on Human Rights and wider European Union equalities legislation); Table 7.1 summarizes the key features of the Act. This legislative framework makes it clear that it is a core duty of schools to promote diversity and equality, and we must therefore consider carefully the implications for teachers' work with students.

For the beginning teacher, responding to these issues can seem an overwhelming challenge on top of everything else you have to address, and you may come across the view that early in your career you need to 'concentrate on getting the basics right'. This chapter is not designed to provide easy answers, but an overview of the key issues, and opportunities for you to reflect on the issues, as well as some sources of practical support. Through reflection it will become clear how effective teaching and productive learning places diversity and equality at its core, not at the periphery.

Table 7.1   The Equality Act 2010 – a summary

- intended to strengthen protection against discrimination and promote equality in respect of the following 'characteristics':
  - age
  - disability
  - sex
  - sexual orientation
  - gender reassignment
  - marriage and civil partnership
  - pregnancy and maternity
  - 'race'
  - religion or belief
- acknowledges the concept of 'dual discrimination'; where an individual is discriminated against on the basis of a combination of two or more 'characteristics'
- incorporates the Public Sector Equality Duty (PSED), explicitly framed to go beyond changing policy and practice to 'drive culture change'
  - key duties enshrined in the PSED:
    - eliminate discrimination, harassment and victimization;
    - advance equality of opportunity;
    - foster good relations.
  - also included are specific duties to regarding the monitoring of policy and practice, including:
    - setting equality objectives;
    - reporting on and publishing data relating to performance in meeting objectives.

Socio-economic class

Trying to unpick the impact of diverse social contexts on educational outcomes is never easy. In complex and changing societies, the relationship between students' identities and affiliations and their engagement and attainment seems almost impossible to pin down. However, the role of socio-economic class as the biggest single factor in determining educational outcomes stands out (Cassen and Kingdon, 2007; Mongon and Chapman, 2008). Numerous studies have supported the view that 'social background really matters' (Hills, 2010: 22) in determining **social mobility**, and the link between family income and education outcome in respect of:

- 'school readiness'
    - o each additional £100 income per month equates to an additional month in children's development
    - o the children of mothers educated to degree level are six months ahead in development of children of mothers without qualifications above a Grade D at GCSE

- 'progress in schooling'
    - o between the ages of 3 and 14, the attainment gap associated with parental income and education levels actually widens

- 'access to higher education'
    - o students from low-income families are less likely to go to university than peers from higher-income families even where they gain the same grades at GCSE and A level
    - o students from low-income families who do go to universities are proportionately under-represented at 'prestigious' universities (Hills, 2010)

Perhaps the most worrying trend is that not only is social mobility in the UK lower than the global average, it is in many respects more restricted than in the middle of the last century. Whilst education is supposedly a key social change agent, the attainment gap between children from low-income families and their peers from average or above-income families actually *widens* during the period of compulsory and post-compulsory schooling. This evidence of reduced social mobility is reinforced by research into the intergenerational links between educational outcome levels (Sutton Trust, 2010). This is not to say that schools are necessarily the *cause* of this widening gap; many complex factors are at work. It does mean, however, that as teachers we need to reflect upon how we respond professionally to the evidence presented to us. Before we do this, we need to first understand what we mean when we talk about 'social class' or 'socio-economic class'.

What is social class?

This chapter cannot provide a detailed account of social class. However, in order to reflect upon the role of class in education, we do need a brief overview. The 'three-tier society' (upper/middle/working-class) is essentially derived from the work of eighteenth-century political philosophy. Marx's analysis of the sociological and political implications of the Industrial Revolution delineated society into *capitalists,* the owners of the means of production, and *proletarians* who 'owned' only their labour (Cohen, 1979). The intermediate 'middle class' has always been a more fluid concept, sometimes referring to an urban merchant and professional class, sometimes to those possessing 'human/cultural capital' rather than economic capital (but economically mobile by virtue of education and/or skills).

Social-class categorization has become increasingly complex, and in recent times it is common to hear social class being described as being an outdated concept (more than one prime minister has talked of Britain becoming a classless society). Public discourse, however, seems to suggest that class does still matter, with the language of popular culture frequently being imbued with notions of class or social status; the proportion of Old Etonians and/or Oxbridge graduates in parliament/cabinet is frequently used as a barometer of social mobility (Curtis, 2005; Beattie, 2010).

Whatever your views on the validity of social class as a means of categorizing society, the relationship between family income and educational outcomes means we need to explore more deeply what the barriers to achievement are for students from low-income families.

It has become common to see social class as something defined by a complex set of 'lifestyle' indicators; occupation, income, political beliefs, cultural preferences. However, for analytical purposes, this produces an imprecise picture, and so social class as a 'fixed' political or economic classification has been superseded by 'socio-economic classification'. The difficulty of doing this is such that the Office for National Statistics regularly revises its classification model, with the latest version, the Standard Occupational Classification (SOC), introduced in 2010. This model places more emphasis on the educational implications of different types of occupation, with nine 'major categories' merged to produce four overarching 'skills levels'. Table 7.2 sets out the main categories.

Table 7.2   Standard Occupational Classification (SOC) 2010

Major group + qualifications, training and experience		Skill level + typical occupations	
1	Managers, directors and senior officials	Significant knowledge/experience of production processes and service requirements associated with the efficient functioning of organizations/businesses	**4**	Professional occupations high-level managerial positions in corporate enterprises or national/local government
2	Professional occupations	Degree or equivalent, some occupations requiring postgraduate qualifications and/or a formal period of experience-related training		
3	Associate professional and technical occupations	Associated high-level vocational qualification, often involving a substantial period of full-time training/study. Additional task-related training usually provided through formal induction	**3**	Technical occupations variety of trades occupations proprietors of small businesses
4	Administrative and secretarial occupations	Good standard of general education. Certain occupations require additional vocational training to a well-defined standard		

Major group + qualifications, training and experience		Skill level + typical occupations	
5	Skilled trades occupations	Substantial training, often through work-based programme	
6	Caring, leisure and other service occupations	Good standard of general education. Certain occupations will require additional vocational training, often through work-based programme	**2** Machine operation driving caring occupations retailing clerical and secretarial occupations
7	Sales and customer service occupations	General education/programme of work-based training. Some occupations require additional specific technical knowledge but primary task involves selling	
8	Process, plant and machine operatives	Knowledge/experience necessary to operate vehicles and other mobile/stationary machinery, to operate and monitor industrial plant/equipment, to assemble products from component parts according to strict rules and procedures and subject assembled parts to routine tests. Most occupations specify minimum standard of competence and a period of formal training	
9	Elementary occupations	Minimum general level of education (i.e. that generally acquired by the end of compulsory education). Some occupations will also have short periods of work-related training (e.g. health and safety, food hygiene, and customer service requirements)	**1** Postal workers hotel porters cleaners catering assistants

Adapted from Office for National Statistics classification guidance (2012)

Social class and schooling

Whilst the evidence linking social class/income to educational outcomes is overwhelming, this does not help us understand why it should be the case. (For instance, why are the educational aspirations of students from low-income families restricted even when they perform well at school?)

When we consider the impact of 'extreme' poverty, things appear straightforward. Being homeless or living in inadequate housing creates obvious barriers to performing well at school. Accessing schooling at all is a challenge; of the 130,000 homeless children of school age in UK in 2011, only 40 per cent actually attended school regularly (Cundy, 2011). Those who do attend probably have no suitable place (or the resources) to do homework effectively, and suffer through lost sleep and ill-health caused by their living conditions and diet. One study of homeless school students found that practical difficulties may be exacerbated by the feelings of insecurity caused by living in unstable circumstances (Baker and Credland, 2004).

Income alone, however, does not fully explain the impact of social class on achievement, and so attention has focused on social reproduction, through what French sociologist Pierre Bourdieu called 'cultural capital'. Bourdieu, in his exploration of the relationship between the 'objective' and 'subjective' (what he termed structure and agency) argued that individuals' chances were largely shaped by objective structures (Bourdieu, 1977). This is significant when individuals internalize structural circumstances in ways in which manifest themselves through individual attitudes, values and dispositions; or *habitus*. However, Bourdieu also argued that *habitus* is shaped by more personal, subjective factors (family relationships, everyday life experiences). So, although social class might be largely determined by structural factors (income, social networks), individual agency also plays a part. Bourdieu argued that dominant groups in society determine *habitus*, and so their social and cultural norms become seen as high status and desirable. When embodied in school systems, schools become sites of social reproduction that reinforce and extend class divisions rather than overcome them. If schools are seen as representing 'middle-class values', students who are familiar and comfortable with these values are more likely to be successful than those who are not.

The effects of social reproduction can be traced in the findings from many studies of education and class. One investigation of teachers' perceptions of 'underachieving' students found that many held stereotypical views of working-class students and their parents, and tended to view middle-class pupils and parents more positively (Dunne and Gazeley, 2008) (Table 7.3). Ofsted has acknowledged the intractable nature of the social-class divide in educational outcomes (2007) and this perhaps inevitably means that access to higher education is similarly affected (Reay et al., 2005).

Table 7.3   Key findings of *Teachers, Social Class and Underachievement*

- Teachers were uncomfortable talking about social class even though inequalities relating to social class and education are widely recognized.
- Some teachers held deficit views of working-class pupils and parents and located the causes of underachievement in the individual pupil or the home rather than in the classroom or the school.
- Pupils identified positive relationships with teachers as crucial to their learning.

(Dunne and Gazeley, 2008)

Activity 7.2   Reflecting on class identity

It is likely that most of you reading this book will have grown up in the era dominated by politicians denying that class is a significant issue in modern-day Britain – in fact, it seems to be mandatory for prime ministers to make this claim (a phenomenon almost exclusive to the UK).

John Major claimed that 'we are all middle-class now' (1992), Tony Blair that 'the class war is over' (1999) and David Cameron has continued the theme of 'the classless society' (2006). Together with Margaret Thatcher's famous claim that 'there is no such thing as society' (1987), talk of social class as being important to everyday life appears an unfashionable idea, so this may be something you have not given much thought to.

Given the evidence about how teachers perceive social class, it is important to reflect on how we see ourselves, and on how this might influence the way we perceive (and respond to) students.

1 Use the SOC model in Table 7.2 to identify where you (and your immediate family) fit.

   • You may find this quite straightforward – but does this really tell you any-thing significant about your own 'class identity'? You might have a 'gut instinct' about your class identity – but how is this formed?
   • This exercise is designed to help you go beyond how you see yourself in class terms, to reflect on your perceptions of class as a factor in education, and what it means for the expectations you have of students, their families and their communities.
   • In categorizing your social-class identity, what factors are particularly significant? Your own educational background, or your family's? If family background is important, how many generations can you go back before it becomes irrel-evant to your own class identity?
   • What about income?
   • Does ethnicity and/or nationality play a part?

Now think about values and attitudes to schooling. As someone entering the teach-ing profession, it is evident that you have been successful in educational terms – and the fact that you have chosen teaching as a career suggests you feel comfortable in the environment of a school.

• Think about what has made you successful, and what makes you feel 'at home' in a school.

Follow-up group discussion:

• Share your reflections on class identity and values in groups.
• Discuss the key influences in your own schooling:
   o What made you 'successful' – innate ability, your attitudes and feelings about the value of education, or your parent's/family's attitudes?
   o What might you have to think about when working with students whose attitudes do not match your own?

Socio-economic class and schools' policy

Addressing the class-based attainment gap has long been a contentious issue for UK governments. When the 1944 Education Act established compulsory free education for children aged 5–15, it was based on a two-tier, selective system in which testing at the end of primary schooling (the '11+') was used to select approximately 20 per cent of students to follow a traditional academic curriculum at grammar schools, with the remainder studying a vocationally oriented curriculum at secondary modern schools. Supporters continue to argue that this two-tier model enhanced social mobility by raising aspirations and providing a route for academically able working-class students to attend grammar school. Opponents point out that grammar school intake was in fact overwhelmingly dominated by the middle classes, and with little opportunity for students to move between grammar and secondary modern schools after the 11+, irrespective of their longer-term performance. The fact that each sector generally steered students towards different examinations, no matter how well secondary modern students performed, meant they were much less likely to gain access to higher education.

A small but significant element of the UK school system is the independent, fee-paying sector – commonly but confusingly known as 'public schools'. Despite the fact that only around 7 per cent of students attend public schools (ISC, 2011), there has been a long-standing and acrimonious debate about the impact this has on class division, social mobility and the achievement gap (Blanden et al., 2004). For critics, public schools create social segregation and a 'two-tier' system of schooling, perpetuating class division and reinforcing the achievement gap between rich and poor (Millar, 2011); in the 1980s, Neil Kinnock, leader of the Labour Party, described private schools as 'the very cement that divides British society' (cited in Hagan, 2001: 304). For supporters, they contribute to the diversity of provision necessary for meaningful parental choice, provide excellent education for students, including many from less-privileged backgrounds through scholarships and community outreach (Stafford, 1985).

By the 1970s the anti-selective education argument had overwhelmingly won the day; only a handful of local authorities have retained the selective system. This does not mean that the social class and schooling debate is over. The 1980s saw the beginning of a shift in the argument. Whilst many in the Conservative governments of the decade lobbied hard for a reintroduction of grammar schools, it was judged to be politically (and economically) impractical, so ministers instead focused on promoting diversity of school provision by other means.

Central to Margaret Thatcher's education policy was the theme of parental choice, with parents given greater opportunities to select their children's school rather than being forced towards the nearest 'catchment area' school. Adopted and extended by Tony Blair's 1997 Labour government, this has become an established element of schools policy; the coalition government legislated to add further diversity into the school system almost immediately after its election in 2010 (see Chapter 3). The 'free school' system, loosely based on the US Charter School and the Swedish Friskola, is intended to provide a 'third way' between state and independent schooling. Set up by groups of parents, teachers, charitable organizations or businesses, free schools are non-fee-paying and funded by public finance, but are independent of local authority control, can set their own admissions policy (although cannot select by academic attainment) and are largely exempt from the many prescriptions imposed on state schools regarding the curriculum.

The debates about diversity of school types are fiercely fought, but whatever the particular topic under discussion, be it the status of fee-paying schools, selective versus comprehensive schooling, academies and free schools – or simply how parents choose state schools – the argument generally comes back to the issue of social class. Those supporting parental choice and liberalizing legislation in order to provide a greater diversity of schools argue that this drives up quality as schools are forced to compete for resources, and that it increases social mobility by providing opportunities to bright, working-class students to find a route to success. Those arguing for more state control and more uniformity of school argue that the market-led approach that has developed in recent decades simply provides further opportunity for middle-class parents to use, in Bourdieusian terms, their 'cultural capital' to further their children's cause (Ball, 1993). More colloquially, Prime Minister David Cameron has referred to the phenomenon of the 'sharp-elbowed middle-classes' who find ways to benefit from social projects designed to help the less privileged. Recent research has found that the motivation of parents in choosing schools is sharply divided by social class (Burgess et al., 2009).

Activity 7.3   Parental choice in schooling (group debate activity)

'The policy of parental choice of schooling creates social class and faith group ghettoes, and reinforces the attainment gap between working-class and middle-class students.'

Divide your group into two debate 'teams' to argue for and against the proposition above.

- You might all start by agreeing or disagreeing with the motion – but sometimes it is a really useful exercise to adopt a position you do not actually agree with. Try to get 'inside the head' of the opposition viewpoint.

The diversity of schools available presents a choice for teachers as well as parents. Still in your groups, discuss the sort of school you might feel comfortable teaching in – and say why you see yourself 'fitting in' at:

- a state community school
- a state faith school (voluntary-controlled, voluntary-aided)

(Continued)

(Continued)

- an academy
- a free school
- an independent school

What do you base this on – your own school experience, or your views about the issues of choice and equity raised by the diversity of schools?

Measuring deprivation

Successive governments have attempted to close the class-based attainment gap, including providing additional funding for schools with high proportions of students from socio-economically disadvantaged backgrounds – and there is strong evidence that additional funding has a significant positive impact on student outcomes (DfES, 2006). However, the ways in which deprivation is calculated are complicated – and vary with different local authorities. A combination of measures are used, including the number of students in receipt of free school meals (because of a low level of parental income), the proportion of minority ethnic students, and an index of deprivation based on postcode (see Activity 7.4).

Activity 7.4   Measuring deprivation (individual reflection/research)

Local authorities use a number of different methods for measuring the level of deprivation in schools, with the main ones being:

1   proportion of students in receipt of free school meals (entitlement is for children with parents on benefits or very low income)

2   Income Deprivation Affecting Children Index (IDACI) – this index is based on census data analysing the average household income in schools' catchment areas

(a) Think about schools you have experience of – and about the way admissions policies work. Which of the above measures might produce the more accurate measure of deprivation – and therefore provide the fairer way of allocating resources?

(b) What do you think might be the main advantages and disadvantages of the two measures?

Web-based information and resources for teachers: general equality and diversity issues

Anti-Defamation League teaching resource lists for teaching about a wide range of equality/diversity issues (US-based): www.adl.org/education

Barnardo's teaching resources/research publications supporting teachers on issues of child poverty/homelessness: www.barnardos.org.uk/what_we_do/policy_research_unit/research_and_publications.htm

BBC London information about cultural and religious diversity focusing on London, but generally more widely relevant: www.bbc.co.uk/london/yourlondon/unitedcolours/index.shtml

Gender

Since the introduction of universal free education in the UK (and in many other countries), the issue of the different educational needs of boys and girls, and their different levels of attainment, has been the focus of as much attention and debate as the issue of social class.

This next section will examine the background to how gender impacts on education policy, practice and outcomes, and provide you with an opportunity to reflect on your own perceptions of gender in the context of your own teaching. First, however, we need to be clear what we are talking about when referring to gender.

Gender is a social construct, encompassing the ways in which society or groups within society view characteristics of people as either masculine or feminine, whilst *sex* describes biological differences between men and women. An individual's sex, therefore, is a biological fact; they are male, female or transsexual. Gender is a much more complex concept, and the cultural values by which individuals live have a significant impact on how 'masculinity' and 'femininity' is viewed; this in turn impacts on how individuals see themselves in gender terms. Whilst sex is broadly fixed (only being changed through complex physiological 'reassignment' treatment), gender is fluid. It is not uncommon to hear both sexes described in divergent gender terms. Women and girls may described either as feminine ('girly') or masculine ('tomboy', 'butch'), men may be 'macho' (masculine) or a 'wuss' (feminine). Significantly, however, in almost all societies the terms for masculine women and feminine men are generally considered derogatory, indicating the importance attached to 'conventional' notions of gender roles. This is the case even in societies (such as the UK today) considered to be relatively progressive in its views of gender.

This is not an abstract concept for teachers in secondary schools. Working with adolescents means you are engaging with emerging gender identities at a crucial and frequently stressful time, and so you need to consider how this impacts on your interactions with students.

Activity 7.5   Shared reflective 'life stories'

In order to stimulate a discussion with peers, write a short reflective account drawing on your recollection of how you became aware of your gender identity as a child and/or an adolescent.

Think particularly about:

- the messages you perceived when you were young about 'being a boy' or 'being a girl'
- who gave you these messages (parents/carers, siblings, other relatives, friends, teachers or others?)
- how these messages were given (explicitly/covertly?)
- how they made you feel

Now share your 'gender reflections' with your group. Try to maintain a focus in your group about the 'experiences of self' rather than being drawn into your 'perceptions of others'. Some prompt questions are set out below.

You might want to use the following prompt questions:

1   Have you ever systematically considered how you developed your gender identity?

2   How is your gender identity still affected by your experiences growing up?

3   What messages do you think you send to others regarding what it means to be a 'boy' or a 'girl' or a 'man' or a 'woman'?

4   How have your experiences of schooling shaped your understanding of what it means to be a man or a woman?

5   Have you ever been ridiculed or denied an opportunity for doing or saying something that others didn't consider 'masculine' or 'feminine' enough? How did that make you feel? How did you react? How did it affect your life beyond that single incident?

6   Have you ever ridiculed someone else for doing something you didn't consider 'masculine' or 'feminine' enough? (Adapted from Critical Multicultural Pavilion: Awareness Activities (Gorski, 2011))

When viewed in the context of social class, it is clear that educational outcomes are key to social mobility. However, when we look at gender, the picture suddenly looks much more uncertain. You can get a sense of this every year by looking at the front page of newspapers in the summer when public examination results are released. The photographs of students celebrating their multiple high grades seem to be overwhelmingly of girls. Read the accompanying stories, and once you are past the inevitable stories about whether the increasing success rates are due to brighter students, better teaching or 'dumbed-down' exams, you will probably read of the achievement gap between girls and boys. Whereas through the latter part of the twentieth century, debate about gender and education focused on how schools could be more supportive of girls' learning needs, it now is more common to read of boys' underachievement.

Various explanations for this surface at regular intervals; sometimes wider social breakdown is blamed, with increased single-parent households leading to a lack of suitable male role models for boys. At other times the 'feminization' of schools (the increasing proportion of women in the teaching profession and the shift to assessment based on coursework from traditional examinations) is the cause. The notion that boys want and need male teachers as 'role models' is so widely propagated that it is often considered an unquestionable truth, and the UK government has supported various initiatives to increase male recruitment into primary teaching (Skelton, 2007: 681–683). However, the evidence base for this notion is uncertain. Critics argue that it is based on a discredited 'essentialist construction of gender as polarized and homogenous' (Skelton, 2007: 687–688) that assumes boys and girls always respond more positively to teachers of the same sex, and that male teachers 'share something quite similar and unique in terms of masculinity' (p. 688). In fact, research has shown that students do not see the gender of their teaching as being as important as their individual qualities (Francis et al., 2006). Put simply, boys do not particularly want *male* teachers, girls do not want *female* teachers – boys *and* girls just want *good* teachers.

You will have learnt from Chapter 2 that it is crucial for teachers to develop an understanding of the different learning styles of their students, but although there is strong evidence suggesting that boys and girls do tend to prefer different approaches to learning, many researchers have argued that this is simply a reflection of socio-cultural expectations (Coffield et al., 2004; Skelton and Reid, 2006).

The problematizing of boys' achievement is also reflected in wider political debate. In 2011, David Willetts, the Minister for Universities and Science, caused controversy by appearing to suggest that the increase of well-educated women in the workforce was damaging to social mobility because it reduced opportunities for 'aspiring working class men' (Mulholland, 2011). For many this exemplified a misrepresentation of the real issues about gender and educational outcomes. Hopefully some of the contradictions behind the debate about gender and education will emerge from Activity 7.7, which will help you see that lying behind the apparently straightforward evidence of attainment data is a more complex story.

Table 7.4   Percentage of pupils in England reaching or exceeding expected standards,[1] by Key Stage and sex

	1999		2009	
	Boys	**Girls**	**Boys**	**Girls**
Key Stage 1[2]				
English				
Reading	78	86	81	89
Writing	75	85	75	87
Mathematics	84	88	88	91
Science	85	88	87	91
Key Stage 2[3]				
English	62	74	75	84
Mathematics	69	70	80	80
Science	75	76	85	87
Key Stage 3[4]				
English	55	73	71	84
Mathematics	63	66	79	80
Science	59	62	76	79

Source: DfE, 2011
Notes:
1 By teacher assessment. See Appendix, Part 3: The National Curriculum.
2 Pupils achieving level 2 or above at Key Stage 1.
3 Pupils achieving level 4 or above at Key Stage 2.
4 Pupils achieving level 5 or above at Key Stage 3.

Table 7.5   Percentage of population holding no qualifications, by sex and age (UK, 2009)[1]

Age	Men	Women
17–19	7	6
20–24	8	7
25–29	8	8
30–39	8	8
40–49	10	11
50–59/64[2]	17	20

Source: Labour Force Survey, Office for National Statistics
Notes:
1 Data are at Q2 (April–June) and are not seasonally adjusted.
2 Men aged 50 to 64 and women aged 50 to 59.

Table 7.6   Pupils achieving five or more GCSE grades A* to C or equivalent, by sex

Year	Male	Female	All
1995/96	40.6	50.5	45.5
1996/97	41.4	51.3	46.2
1997/98	42.3	52.8	47.5
1998/99	43.8	54.6	49.1
1999/2000	45.0	55.9	50.4
2000/01	45.7	56.5	51.0
2001/02	47.2	58.0	52.5
2002/03	48.3	58.8	53.5
2003/04	49.2	59.3	54.2
2004/05	52.1	62.1	57.0
2005/06	54.3	63.9	59.0
2006/07	56.9	65.8	61.3
2007/08	60.0	69.0	64.4

Source: Department for Education, 2011
Notes:
1 For pupils in their last year of compulsory education. Pupils aged 15 at the start of the academic year; pupils in year S4 in Scotland. From 2004/05, pupils at the end of Key Stage 4 in England.
2 From 1990/91, National Qualifications were introduced in Scotland but are not included until 2000/01.

Table 7.7   Higher education qualifications attained in UK, by sex and class of qualification (2007/08)

First degree	Men	Women	All
First class	12.8	11.9	12.3
Upper second	41.0	46.8	44.3
Lower second	29.8	27.3	28.4
Third class/Pass	8.7	6.0	7.2
Unclassified	7.6	8.0	7.8
All (=100%) (thousands)	**143.7**	**191.0**	**334.9**
Other undergraduate	**Men**	**Women**	**All**
Professional graduate certificate in education	3.7	4.8	4.4
Foundation degree	12.1	10.0	10.7
HND/DipHE[2]	19.6	23.7	22.3
Other undergraduate	64.6	61.6	62.6
All (=100%) (thousands)	**49.1**	**90.4**	**139.6**

(Continued)

Table 7.7   (Continued)

Higher degree	Men	Women	All
Doctorate	13.4	11.0	12.3
Other higher degree	86.6	89.0	87.7
All (=100%) (thousands)	**68.3**	**67.2**	**135.6**
Other undergraduate	**Men**	**Women**	**All**
Postgraduate certificate in education	25.8	37.1	33.0
Other postgraduate	74.3	62.9	67.0
All (=100%) (thousands)	**23.7**	**42.7**	**66.4**

Source: Higher Education Statistics Agency

Table 7.8   Percentage of population in employment, by sex and occupation (2009)[1]

Occupation class	Men (%)	Women (%)	All (%)
Managers and senior officials	19	12	16
Professional	14	13	14
Associate professional and technical	14	16	15
Administrative and secretarial	5	19	11
Skilled trades	18	2	11
Personal service	3	16	9
Sales and customer service	5	11	7
Process, plant and machine operatives	11	2	7
Elementary	12	11	11
All occupations[2] (=100%) (millions)	**15.4**	**13.4**	**28.8**

1 Data are at Q2 and are not seasonally adjusted. People aged 16 and over.
2 Includes people who did not state their occupation.

Table 7.9   Pay gap between men's and women's median hourly earnings (UK)[1]

Positive numbers indicate % gap between male and female pay (male higher than female)
Negative numbers indicate % gap between male and female pay (female higher than male)

Year	All employees		Full-time		Part-time	
1998	27.3		17.4		−4.0	
1999	26.9		16.4		−2.6	
2000	26.7		16.3		−3.5	
2001	26.3		16.4		−3.7	
2002	26.9		15.5		−0.6	
2003	25.1		14.6		−1.3	
2004[2]	25.0	24.7	14.1	14.5	−3.0	−2.6

Year	All employees		Full-time		Part-time	
2005	22.6		13.0		−3.0	
2006³	22.3	22.2	12.6	12.8	−2.1	−2.2
2007		21.9		12.5		−2.2
2008		22.5		12.6		−3.7
2009		22.0		12.2		−2.0

Source: Annual Survey of Hours and Earnings, Office for National Statistics, 2012
Notes:
1 All full-time and part-time employees on adult rates at April each year, whose pay for the survey period was unaffected by absence. Excludes overtime.
2 Higher percentage includes supplementary information.
3 Discontinuity in 2006 as a result of further methodological changes.

Activity 7.6   Analysing the gender achievement gap

Tables 7.4 to 7.9 present data comparing the sexes' attainment at different stages of school, and employment and earnings outcomes.

Examine the data, bearing in mind some of the arguments this chapter has presented about 'the achievement gap'. Does this data help you clarify your thinking about the arguments? Which arguments appear to be supported by the data, and which appear to be contradicted?

A final conundrum. For approximately three decades, from the 1944 Education Act until the spread of the comprehensive school system across most of the UK, despite the pre-comprehensive school system in the UK, whatever the variance in performance, the ratio of boys and girls obtaining a grammar school place remained equal. Why do you think this was the case? *[see footnote for the answer]*.

Activity 7.7   Reflection on observation of learning

You can do this either individually or with a peer – and you can either make this the specific focus of a planned lesson observation, or based on a recent observation.

(Continued)

Answer: The reason for there being equal numbers of boys and girls attending grammar schools between 1944 and the 1970s was that the criteria for selection ensured the ratio remained equal. In order for this to be the case, girls had to achieve a higher score to obtain a grammar school place than boys (Gender Education Association, 2010).

(Continued)

- Do boys and girls contribute in similar ways to classroom discussions?
- Do they participate equally in 'active learning' activities?
- What other things do you notice? What about the ways in which boys and girls behave when not focused on task, and how teachers manage these?

Now think back to Activity 7.5 ('Shared reflective "life stories"'), and reflect on how you see gender identities playing out in the classroom setting you are observing.

- Do you see predictable patterns of behaviour and response, or does what you see confound your expectations?
- How do you think you might respond as a teacher to the situations that arise in the classroom?

How might an increased awareness of your own gender identity affect the way your act as a teacher?

Web-based information and resources for teachers: gender education

Feminist Art Resources in Education US-based portal to teacher guides/curriculum ideas bringing feminist perspective to art education: http://feministart.rutgers.edu/resources/fare/

Gender and Education Association news/teaching support/academic articles on gender and education: www.genderandeducation.com/

The Women's History Network academic publications and networking: www.women shistorynetwork.org/index.html

Sexuality

Whilst the ways in which schools address gender issues have been widely acknowledged for some time as a matter of crucial importance for teachers, sexuality has received much less attention. In fact, for many, until recent decades social and cultural norms meant that issues of sexuality – and particularly homosexuality – were treated as 'taboo' in schools. Indeed, during the period of 1988 to 2003 in England, the Section 28 amendment of the Local Government Act (1988) took this taboo status a stage further by stating that a local authority 'shall not intentionally promote homosexuality or publish material with the intention of promoting homosexuality' or 'promote the teaching in any maintained school of the acceptability of homosexuality as a pretended family relationship'. The impact of Section 28 is difficult to judge even at a distance; it only resulted in one (unsuccessful) prosecution, and arguably raised the profile of gay rights campaign groups such as Stonewall and Outrage in the UK, but it also created a widespread culture of 'self-censorship' as teachers adopted 'risk-averse' approaches for fear of prosecution and/or negative publicity (Nayak and Kehily, 1996).

Chapter 6 has highlighted the diverse forms of bullying that occur in schools. The mounting evidence of widespread homophobia in schools (Rivers, 2006; Stonewall, 2007) together with the apparent reluctance to challenge it, has led some to portray schools as environments where heterosexuality was normalized in the 'heterosexual matrix' (Butler, 1993). Feminist writers have theorized gender as a social construct rather than a biological determinant (so establishing the distinction between gender and sex). In the gendered social world, masculinity and femininity are learned not 'born into'. At a very simple level, this means that girls are not born to like wearing pink and playing with dolls, boys are not born to wear blue and play football.

For beginning teachers, challenging often entrenched attitudes about sexuality, and particularly dealing with incidents of homophobia, can create a great deal of anxiety. Recent research has shown that whilst 65 per cent of lesbian, gay and bisexual young people experience homophobic bullying and 98 per cent report hearing the term 'gay' used in a derogatory context, only 23 per cent report receiving a clear anti-homophobic message in school (Hunt and Jensen, 2007). Stonewall's research also makes it clear that whilst an overwhelming majority of teachers want lesbian and gay issues addressed in schools, they generally lack the confidence to do this (Guasp, 2009). Stonewall has played a significant role in addressing the scarcity of practical guidance and support for teachers (certainly support has been harder to access that that relating to wider gender issues, or 'race'). There may also be a lasting legacy of the Section 28 era in the persistence of the notion that any reference to homosexuality in schools is going to be controversial and 'unwelcome'. However, Activity 7.8 will help you gain confidence in this area by asking you to locate sources of guidance about sexuality through your teaching without putting yourself into difficult situations. This is an area where there has been a significant growth in the amount, and quality, of guidance and teaching resources available in recent years.

Activity 7.8   Individual resources/teaching support search

Spend some time researching the support and guidance for teachers in dealing with sexuality issues in general and challenging homophobia in particular. Use the web-based information in Table 7.10 as your starting point.

NB: Stonewall is a particularly good place to start, but don't restrict yourself to this – or to UK-based resources; you might find a particularly rich variety of sources based in the US. Obviously some of the specific curriculum and pastoral contexts will be different – you might find it interesting and useful to reflect upon the different approaches to gender and sexuality in the UK and the US.

Table 7.10   Challenging homophobic language (excerpt from Stonewall Education Guide, downloadable from Stonewall/Education for All website, see below)

Stonewall's top ten recommendations

1   *TEACHERS AND SCHOOL STAFF MUST CHALLENGE HOMOPHOBIC LANGUAGE EVERY TIME THEY HEAR IT*
Language such as 'lezzer' and 'gay boy', as well as 'gay' as a term of disapproval of someone or something, must be challenged in each and every instance to send the message that homophobic language is unacceptable.

2   *MAKE SURE THAT PUPILS UNDERSTAND WHY HOMOPHOBIC LANGUAGE IS OFFENSIVE* Pupils will be less likely to use homophobic language when, like racist language, they understand the implications of what they say.

3   *INCLUDE HOMOPHOBIC LANGUAGE IN ANTI-BULLYING POLICIES AND PROCEDURES* Teachers are able to challenge homophobic language more effectively when it is included in school policies.

4   *INVOLVE SENIOR MANAGERS IF HOMOPHOBIC LANGUAGE PERSISTS* The involvement of head teachers and senior management proactively as well as in response to the use of homophobic language sends a strong anti-homophobia message to the school.

5   *INVOLVE PARENTS IF PUPILS PERSIST* It is important for parents to help ensure that all school policies are upheld. All pupils deserve to feel safe at school. Whatever their attitudes towards lesbian, gay and bisexual people, parents can play an essential role in ensuring young people are protected from homophobic bullying.

6   *INCORPORATE LESBIAN, GAY AND BISEXUAL PEOPLE INTO THE CURRICULUM* Including themes around LGB people in lessons makes young people more aware of the LGB community and reduces homophobic behaviour.

7   *ADDRESS HOMOPHOBIA AND LGB EQUALITY IN YOURLESSONS* Teaching about homophobia and equality will discourage homophobic language and bullying in schools.

8   *USE ASSEMBLIES TO ADDRESS PROBLEMS OR PROMOTE POSITIVE MESSAGES ABOUT GAY PEOPLE* Assemblies can be an ideal opportunity to tackle issues regarding homophobic language or bullying particular to your school or to incorporate positive messages about gay people, for example during LGBT History Month.

9   *USE POSTERS AND PUBLIC DISPLAYS* Poster and public display campaigns can be used to communicate positive messages regarding lesbian, gay and bisexual people and to tackle homophobic language and bullying.

10   *INVOLVE PUPILS* Pupils want their schools to be safe and welcoming places. Ask pupils how they feel about homophobic language and bullying in their school and involve them in initiatives to tackle the problem.

Web-based information and resources for teachers: sexuality, LGBT issues and challenging homophobia

Gay, Lesbian and Straight Education Network (GLSEN) US-based information, campaigning and teaching resources: www.glsen.org/cgi-bin/iowa/all/home/index.html

LGBT Youth Scotland teachers' anti-homophobia toolkit: www.lgbtyouth.org.uk/schools-and-education/toolkit.htm

www.teachersmedia.co.uk/videos/gay-teachers

Schools Out support network, research and campaigning on LGBT issues in education: www.schools-out.org.uk/

Stonewall/Education for All publications/resources/support in challenging homophobia in schools: www.stonewall.org.uk/education_for_all

'Race' and ethnicity

The second half of the twentieth century, alongside the growing awareness of the impact of gender and social class on educational outcomes, saw a growth in immigration to the UK, in particular from the 'New Commonwealth'. The way in which schools respond to the needs of black and minority ethnic students and communities has been a subject of intense and sustained controversy ever since – perhaps the most emotive issue in relation to schooling and society of all. Before we look at some of the reasons for this, however, we need to start again by defining terms.

Given the sensitivities of the topic, many beginning teachers entering schools for the first time may feel insecure even about the language they use. Should we talk about *race*, or *ethnicity* – or *culture*? Should we refer to pupils from particular backgrounds as being *black*, *black British*, *Asian*, *Afro-Caribbean*, or *minority ethnic*? What about terms such as 'mixed race', *dual heritage, bilingual, EAL (English with an Additional Language)*? To complicate matters further, language changes with time – language seen as socially and professionally acceptable may not remain so. There are a number of useful sources of guidance around terminology (see the 'Web-based information and resources for teachers' list at the end of this section); but it is important to acknowledge the fluidity of language; context and time changes meaning (in Dr Martin Luther King's civil rights speeches in the 1960s his use of the term 'negro' was appropriate; it would certainly not be today). Guidance, therefore, is presented with this in mind rather than being prescriptive.

To begin with, although the terms 'race' and 'ethnicity' are frequently used interchangeably, it is important to acknowledge the distinction between the two. 'Race' generally refers to distinguishable physical differences of phenotype, whilst 'ethnicity' refers to cultural distinction, so that an *ethnic* group is generally considered to be a society/community sharing a common cultural heritage (based on language, history and/ or religion) (Gillborn, 1995: 4). From a biological perspective, race has no meaning when talking about humans – other than, of course, when we are referring to the human race. 'Race' has become generally accepted to be a purely socially or culturally constructed concept (Miles, 1993: 3), and so is a convenient term to use when we are discussing social phenomena such as racism. However, it must used with care, and this chapter adopts the convention common to many writers in this field of placing the term 'race' in inverted commas – as a reminder to the reader that we are not talking about race in a biological, scientific context.

Education policy has always been at the centre of the wider debate on the nature of the 'multicultural' Britain developed. Until the mid-1970s, there was a political consensus that the most effective way for public policy (including schooling) to accommodate large-scale immigration was through *assimilation*, with its expectation that immigrant communities should adopt the ways of the 'host community'. However, evidence of a significant level of under-attainment by immigrant students in schools began to appear in the early 1970s (DES 1971, 1975) alongside evidence of racial discrimination in schools and wider society (Coard, 1971; Mullard, 1973). Successive governments commissioned a serious of reports investigating black and minority ethnic underachievement and racial discrimination (Rampton, 1981; Swann, 1985), and education policy shifted to *integration* (the acceptance of incomers' distinctive cultural heritage within the perceived common culture of the 'host community'), then to *cultural pluralism*, in which difference is celebrated as a positive aspect of a rich and diverse society (DES, 1981). In this era, schools were explicitly viewed as agents for fostering understanding, tolerance and respect for 'other' cultures (Tomlinson, 2008: 83). However, the notion of cultural pluralism in education, commonly termed *multicultural education,* was criticized from all sides. From the conservative/traditionalist right-wing perspective, it was emblematic of a left-wing ideology (Palmer, 1986); for left-wing critics multicultural education as actually practised in schools was no more than 'cultural tourism', memorably satirized as 'the 3 S's: *Steel bands*, *Saris and Samosas*' approach (Bhavnani and Bhavnani, 1985: 203); at best patronising and tokenistic, at worst, perpetuating and reinforcing stereotypes (Wilkins, 2001). Critical Race Theory (CRT), a sociological perspective on 'race' of growing influence in recent years, analyses how the discourse of 'race' in dominant white societies (such as the UK) 'normalizes racism' and how education policy in such societies, in effect if not intention, can be conceptualized as 'acts of white supremacy' (Gillborn, 2005: 498). The Critical reading at Master's level section of this chapter asks you to examine this perspective in detail.

Throughout the 1980s and 1990s, the debate about the effectiveness of multicultural education continued. Educators such as Barry Troyna (1987) argued from a sociological background that multiculturalism's fundamental weakness was its concentration on the personal aspects of racism, at the expense of institutional/structural racism (see Table 7.11). Anti-racist education was intended to challenge discrimination at the institutional/structural level as well as the personal (Cole, 2005). Throughout this period, the notion of institutional racism was a deeply controversial one, but as noted earlier (page 243) the Macpherson inquiry into the murder of Stephen Lawrence in 1993 led to it being embedded into the legislative framework.

Whilst the 'direction of travel' of policy and practice regarding 'race' and education appears to have been largely one-way, recent years have seen some evidence in the public and political discourse of the potential for some reversal of this. Under the later years of the 1997–2010 Labour governments, the language of diversity and multiculturalism started to shift towards that of community cohesion, carrying connotations of a possible return to integrationist or even assimilationist policies. David Cameron, soon after becoming Prime Minister in 2010, stated that 'the doctrine of multiculturalism has failed' (Cameron, 2011b), and many of his government's policies (such as the revisions to Ofsted's inspection framework and Teachers' Standards) reflect on on-going shift in social policy from 'diversity' towards 'cohesion'.

As a backdrop to the debate about this debate, evidence of how ethnicity impacts on attainment shows an ever more complex interaction between ethnicity, social class and gender. Until the 1980s the issue seemed simple; minority ethnic students appeared to be underachieving, and policy and practice focused on attempts to address this problem. However, as schools produce more sophisticated attainment data, the patterns emerging show that some minority ethnic groups (particularly Chinese and Indian) outperform white students, but that both social class and gender influenced the impact of ethnicity (Connolly, 2006). In other contexts, ethnicity still appears significant; black Caribbean boys under-perform academically (and are disproportionately represented in school exclusions) even when gender and social class are taken into account (Gillborn and Mirza, 2000).

Table 7.11   Discrimination matrix (adapted from Gaine, 1989)

Type of discrimination	Social class	Gender	'Race'/ethnicity
Personal	Active use of stereotypes Demeaning language Lower expectations	Sexual harassment Patronising behaviour Lower/differing expectations	Insults/'jokes' Physical harassment/violence Derogatory language/ stereotypes
Cultural	Assumed superiority of Standard English Disapproval of particular clothing	Biased depiction in classroom materials 'Male' model of discipline 'Man-made' language	Biased depiction in classroom materials Eurocentric values in teaching practice Ignoring 'other' languages in classroom
Institutional	Letters home in overly formal Standard English Recruitment policy Staff recruitment	Segregation (in classroom/ lunch breaks) Staffing structures Timing of parents' evenings	Use of 'Christian' names Lack of multilingual information in school Inability to provide for cultural needs (dietary/religious)
Structural	Determination of curriculum Catchment area Wider media representation	Career structure of teaching profession Wider media representation	Non-recognition of overseas qualifications Wider media representation

Activity 7.9   Role-play activity, adapted from *The Stereotype Game* (Social Psychology Network (SPN)), 2011

Write a series of different stereotypical attributes on post-it notes:

- examples might include violent, good at sport, cute, overemotional, incompetent, good at maths/science, lazy, untrustworthy, unclean, musical, materialistic, diseased, unintelligent, exotic and frail

(Continued)

(Continued)

One person acts as a facilitator – the facilitator should *randomly* attach a 'post-it note' on each person's back so that the label is not visible to the wearer.

The facilitator now chairs a 15-minute discussion on 'my professional goals as a teacher'. Everyone should circulate to talk to as many people as possible – *and you must treat one another according to the other person's labelled attribute* (e.g. someone labelled *'forgetful'* might be repeatedly reminded of the instructions).

After this discussion, take off the post-it notes and discuss your feelings about the experience.

- Were you able to guess the label you were wearing?
- Were you able to disregard others stereotyping you?
- Did you try to disprove the stereotype – and did this work?
- How did you feel toward the person stereotyping you?

When stereotyping others, how easy was it to find confirming evidence – and how did you react to *disconfirming* evidence?

Activity 7.10   Group discussion scenarios

Below are a number of scenarios (adapted from the Multiverse web archive recommended at the end of this section). Discuss how you might advise a peer in this situation. When necessary, use the relevant guidance to help you. Further guidance may be found via the 'Web-based information and resources for teachers' list at the end of this section.

Scenario 1: I am in a predominantly white primary school on final placement. The school is keen to address community cohesion and 'race' equality as they feel that these are areas that have been neglected in the past. What can I do?

Scenario 2: I have overheard some overtly racist comments made by students to their peers, particularly when they are away from the classroom. I have mentioned it to my co-tutor she has advised me that as long as they don't do it in the classroom it is best to ignore it as 'they don't mean anything by it'. This doesn't feel right to me, but I can't challenge my co-tutor, can I?

Scenario 3: I told my professional tutor about a student in my previous placement; she told me she'd been teased about being a Muslim (9/11 jokes, calling her dad 'Taliban'). I found it hard to respond, particularly because she was Asian, but not actually Muslim. She hadn't told her teacher, and I said nothing to anyone as it was my last day in school. My professional tutor says the incident was 'unfortunately' quite common in that school, but that I should 'move on'. Should I just 'move on'?

Responding to Scenario 1

You can be encouraged that the school is looking to improve its approach to community cohesion. For a school located in a predominantly white location, this kind of work is particularly important as students' misconceptions and stereotypical assumptions may be more likely to go unaddressed.

As a beginning teacher, reflecting on your own planning would be a good starting point. Do they provide an opportunity to go beyond immediate curriculum objectives and bring students' attention to the diverse, multicultural society in which they live? This could be through your choice of texts, the images and resources in your classroom – but don't forget that simply by demonstrating the importance you attach to such work, you are acting as a role model.

A whole-school approach will always be more effective than working in isolation: talk to your school-based tutor/mentor to find out what colleagues are doing – and share *your* ideas. Use the 'Web-based information and resources for teachers' sites listed below to get practical examples of how to demonstrate your valuing of diversity across the curriculum.

Responding to Scenario 2

It is never appropriate to 'ignore' any possible incidence of racism, whatever the location; this would allow all those involved (including bystanders) to assume that there is nothing wrong with such behaviour. It sounds as though your co-tutor could be seriously underestimating the possible impact, and it is a professional duty to challenge and address racist language.

Schools have a legal responsibility to monitor and record such incidents. As a student teacher, although constrained by school policies, you are within your rights to question the view that such behaviour 'doesn't mean anything'. The school's race-equality policy will set out how to respond appropriately, and although you cannot know exactly *how* to respond until the facts are known, it is important that you *do* respond. As a student teacher, this might include passing on your concerns to the school's senior management team, who are obliged to investigate. In this scenario, it is important that:

(Continued)

(Continued)

- teachers and schools make it explicit that such behaviour is wrong, and will be taken very seriously
- students understand why it is wrong – and that they are not just 'told off'; this may simply silence perpetrators without addressing the causes of the behaviour
- perpetrators are given support in developing both an understanding of the impact of their behaviour, and in developing an active responsibility for their actions

In the longer term, and particularly when you qualify, think about how such incidents can be prevented through bringing issues relating to 'race' and diversity into cross-curricular planning.

Responding to Scenario 3

Given the difficult timing it is understandable you did not raise the matter in school – and it is a particularly complex issue.

Apart from the obvious offensiveness of the comments, there is an elision of Asian culture, Islam and terrorism that clearly needs addressing in the school; not to do so would be a neglect of community cohesion obligations (and additionally, the Racial and Religious Hatred Act (2006) that makes intent to stir up religious hatred an offence, even if as in this case the perpetrators are mistaken about religious identity of the person they threaten).

A further complication is the response of your tutor. Teacher educators have a similar duty to teachers in respect of diversity issues. She should not have told you to 'move on' – and the suggestion that these incidents are common in the school is worrying. If teacher educators are aware of an on-going problem in a partnership school they have a professional obligation to raise it. Talk to your course leader (or, alternatively, your university/training provider should have a named person with specific responsibility for equality issues – you may prefer to raise it with them). Either way, senior managers have a duty to support you by investigating this issue.

Web-based information and resources for teachers: race equality and multicultural education

Achieve good practice network on race equality/diversity (hosted by GTCE): www.gtce.org.uk/networks/achieve/

Antiracist Toolkit guidance/case studies for teachers on challenging racism, promoting positive school ethos: www.antiracisttoolkit.org.uk

BBC multicultural history teaching resources, background materials on black, Asian and Jewish history:www.bbc.co.uk/history/society_culture/multicultural/index. shtml

Black Information Link archive of newspaper articles/ reports: www.blink.org.uk/

Blacknet news items/articles on issues affecting black British communities: www.black net.co.uk

Multiverse teaching resources, professional/scholarly articles on supporting learning for pupils from diverse backgrounds: http://webarchive.nationalarchives.gov.uk/2010102 1152907/http://www.Multiverse.ac.uk

Race Equality Toolkit guide to terminology around issues of 'race', ethnicity, identity and equality: www.universities-scotland.ac.uk/raceequalitytoolkit/terminology.htm

Runnymede Trust scholarly articles, campaigning and teaching resources: www.run nymedetrust.org/resources.html

This chapter has given you an overview of the background to the some of the key social contexts of education that you will need to engage with in order to effectively address issues of diversity and social justice. However, it is important to note that although social class, gender and ethnicity are of immense significance to teachers, the range of social contexts you will need to consider in your professional lives is much wider than this. This chapter is limited in size, and so cannot provide a comprehensive overview of this full range. However, Activity 7.11 gives you the opportunity to reflect yourself on what other social contexts might be particularly relevant to your professional practice.

Activity 7.11   Individual reflection/research

Having read about and reflected upon the social contexts set out in this chapter so far, try to think now about what other social contexts might be relevant in the classroom.

You might want to structure this by using Table 7.11 as your starting point. Add further columns, and try to think of how each new social context fits with the *personal, cultural, institutional* and *structural* matrix.

For instance, if you chose disability as a social context, think about how an individual might experience personal discrimination in different settings (e.g. because of the physical environment, or ways in which communications are handled in an organization). The personal dimension will almost always be the easiest to identify – you will have to work harder to identify the more fundamental dimensions to discrimination.

Global education (and globalization)

You may be familiar with the term 'global education' from your own schooling – or perhaps you are more familiar with World Studies, Development Education or Citizenship Education. These have all at different times established a presence in the curriculum, but have also been susceptible to falling out of political favour, hence their transitory status. It may well be that by the time you are reading this book, the terminology may have changed again.

Many educators would argue that global education is not a 'subject' but a 'theme/ dimension' threaded through the curriculum combining *methodology* (active/experiential discussion-based activities) and *core values* (learning about global cultures, inequality and environment issues) (Hicks, 2003).

For many educators, the boundaries of global education are blurred. The division between global and citizenship education is particularly contentious, with some arguing that a more productive conceptualization of these issues would be to align the two as 'global citizenship education' (Davies et al., 2005). At a time when citizenship education appears to be falling out of the National Curriculum entirely, and global education's place remains uncertain, this debate may seem arcane. When all such aspects of the curriculum appear vulnerable to being squeezed by the 'core' curriculum, it becomes all the more important for teachers to take opportunities to incorporate global, international, citizenship perspectives into their teaching. Whilst this might seem like yet another challenge piled on top of the demands on new teachers, there is a wealth of ideas and support available from the organizations in the 'Web-based information and resources for teachers' section below. The richness of resources to call upon means that adding a global (or citizenship) dimension to your teaching may actually come to seem easier than trying to restrict yourself to narrow subject-driven activities. Take some time to explore some of these sites, and it is certain you will come across ideas for enriching your planning; whatever your subject, whatever Key Stage you are teaching, and whatever the needs are of any given group of students.

The Oxfam Education website has a particularly wide range of teaching activities that you might wish to try out (for example, the Key Stage 3 activity 'Oxfam, buckets and climate change'), which gives students opportunities to explore practical interventions to address water and sanitation needs, the wider implications of the human impact of climate change – and how students can make a difference through their actions.

Teaching in a globalized society

As beginning teachers entering the profession in the early years of the twenty-first century, you may be teaching students who live to see the twenty-second century, and it is not hard to imagine that their world will be very different from the one we know today. If the trends of the last century are to continue, we will see a continuation of the progressive globalization of recent decades. Globalization is often narrowly defined as the interrelationship and interdependence of economics, the transfer of power from nation states to transnational corporations, yet it is a much broader political, techno-logical and cultural phenomenon as well (Osler and Vincent, 2002: 11).

In this era of profound social change, global and citizenship education play a vital role in developing the strong civil societies that could ensure that 'globalisation becomes a force for global sustainability and survival' (Olssen et al., 2004: 2). This goes beyond cur-riculum content, and Activity 7.12 asks you to reflect on your own role, drawing upon the qualities of the 'global teacher' (Table 7.12 and Table 7.13), able to prepare your students for living in a globalized world.

Table 7.12   Key definitions around global education (Hicks, 2003: 274–275)

Global Education The term used internationally to designate the academic field concerned with teaching and learning about global issues, events and perspectives. Note: during the 1970s–1980s this field was known as world studies in the UK

Development Education Originated with the work of NGOs that were concerned about issues of development and north–south relationships. Focus of concern has widened to embrace other global issues but development remains the core concept

Global Dimension Refers to the curriculum taken as a whole and the ethos of a school; those subject elements and cross-curricular concerns that focus on global interdependence, issues and events

Global Perspective(s) What we want students to achieve as a result of having a global dimension in the curriculum; in the plural refers to the fact that there are different cultural and political perspectives on global matters

International Dimension Literally 'between countries'—as in international relationships; also refers to the study of a particular concern, e.g. education, as it manifests in different countries. Note: international refers to the 'parts' and 'global' to the whole

Global Citizenship That part of the Citizenship curriculum which refers to global issues, events and perspectives; also being or feeling a citizen of the global community (as well as cultural or national communities)

Globalisation The innumerable interconnections—economic, cultural, technological, political—which bind the local and national into a global community; the consequence of neo-liberal economic policies which see everything, including education, as a commodity to be sold in the global market place

Activity 7.12   Individual reflection and 'confidence audit'

Reflect on and critique the contemporary relevance of Steiner's attributes of a global teacher (Table 7.13):

- You may think some irrelevant, or simply unjustifiable. If so, why do you think so?
- Are there attributes missing? The world has changed since 1996, so perhaps you can add your own attributes.

1 Carry out a self-audit of where you, as an individual and a professional, see yourself in respect of these attributes.

(Continued)

(Continued)

2   Think back to the earlier activities in this chapter (e.g. the scenarios in Activity 7.11) and ask yourself what 'taking a principled stance ... against injustice and inequalities' means in these contexts.

What support do you think you need in your professional context to enable you to be an 'agent for social justice' in the classroom?

Table 7.13   Characteristics of the 'global teacher' (Steiner, 1996: 21–22)

The global teacher:

- Is interested in local, national and global events and movements;
- keeps informed while retaining an objective stance;
- takes a stand against injustices and inequality and supports others who do so;
- is informed about the impact of environmental issues on local, national and global communities;
- believes democracy to be the best way to bring about social change.

Global teachers:

- model democratic values of fairness, justice and equal respect;
- adopt teaching styles which foster individual development and group cooperation and enable students to make the best use of their differing learning styles;
- encourage students to be reflective and questioning in relation to knowledge;
- go beyond the prescribed curriculum to address human rights, relationships, self-esteem and respect for diversity;
- are critical educators, maintaining a balance between a framework of basic values and sceptical reflection on any set of given norms – social, economic, political, cultural, pedagogic.

In the introduction, the possibility was raised that this chapter would challenge to you reflect and possibly reconsider the way you see yourself as a teacher and perhaps even your overall views of the purposes of schooling. To be critically reflective is to examine your own values as well as your practice, and the learning of your students, and through reaching a better understanding of your own 'world view' to enable you to engage with the social world of students – and so be better placed to respond to their needs, and the needs of a changing society. This chapter ends, therefore, by asking you to consider what schools of the future may look like.

Web-based information and resources for teachers: global education

Centre for Global Education campaigning/publishing organization offering resources/ guidance for teachers on global/development education and social justice: www. centreforglobaleducation

Citizenship Foundation training/resources for teachers in citizenship education: www. citizenshipfoundation.org.uk

Development Education Project training and resources for teachers: www.dep.org.uk/

Global Teacher Project practical/academic resources: www.globalteacher.org.uk

Oxfam Education teaching resources/support in global citizenship and social justice issues: www.oxfam.org.uk/education/

Practical Action resources/support for teaching sustainable development education in a global context: http://practicalaction.org

RISC training/resources for global education and global citizenship education: www.risc. org.uk/education

The future of schooling?

> If every secondary school and university in the kingdom were wiped out tomorrow, and their staffs buried amid the ill-concealed exultation of their unfortunate pupils ... there would be an immediate and enormous increase in the number of really educated persons in England, and a quite blessed disappearance of a mass of corruptly inculcated error and obsolescence. ... Until then we shall remain the barbarians we are at present.

> School has become a social problem; it is being attacked on all sides, and citizens and their governments sponsor unconventional experiments all over the world.... Our options are clear enough. Either we continue to believe that institutionalized learning is a product which justifies unlimited investment or we rediscover that legislation and planning and investment, if they have any place in formal learning, should be used mostly to tear down the barriers that now impede opportunities for learning, which can only be a personal activity.

Expressing dissatisfaction with the *status quo* is not new. The quotations above come respectively from George Bernard Shaw in 1918 (reproduced in Nordquist, 2011); the second from Ivan Illich (1971: 49). Shaw died in 1950, Illich in 2002, but it is worth reflecting upon what they might think were they alive to see today's classroom.

Illich envisaged a 'de-schooled society' in which the 'digital revolution' allowed individuals to set up learning webs, free from the constraints of compulsory schooling. However, whilst the Internet, interactive whiteboards, laptops, PDAs and digital cameras are commonly used in classrooms, schools look similar to those that Illich judged to 'impede learning' (1971: 49). The curriculum remains essentially unchanged; examinations are taken in a manner familiar to Shaw, and the school day is structured in a way recognizable to both. The classrooms you see as a beginning teacher probably look almost identical to the ones you worked in as a student.

Can it also be possible that the classrooms of 2040 will look broadly the same as those of today? Whatever the future holds, as a teacher your voice is crucial. The purpose of schooling, the *why* question, is as important as the questions of *what* to teach and *how* to teach it. So your final activity is to look to the horizon and consider what schools might look like as your career progresses. Ask yourself – *what will my role be in shaping the future of schooling*? Whatever governments might say or do to reform schools, the professional community of teachers of which you will be a member will play an important role in influencing policy.

Activity 7.13   Group research and discussion

1   Investigate likely trends in 'school futures' over the next decade in the following areas – divide your group into pairs (or more, depending on overall size) and each focus on a particular strand:
   - curriculum/pedagogy
   - assessment/testing
   - schools' organization
   - teacher education/professional development
   - teacher performance/accountability

NB: investigate recent policy developments, but also look at more 'future-facing' ideas. Look at the work of different policy 'think-tanks' (e.g. Civitas, Institute for Public Policy Research) – this is where politicians frequently turn for their 'next big idea'.

2   Come together as a group and share your findings.

Discuss whether policy in the different strands forms part of a coherent whole, or are there contradictions and tensions in different aspects of reform?

   - How might these tensions play out in the future?
   - What might be the direct implications for schools and for teachers?
     o   What might a school look like?
     o   What technologies will be used?
     o   What might the teacher's day look like?

NB: do not restrict your research to the UK. Look at developments in different countries, different continents. Are there similar trends in reform, or is the 'direction of travel' looking very different?

3   Still in your groups, reflect back on the issues of diversity and social justice addressed in this chapter:
   - How might the future direction of school reform impact on the way these issues are addressed?
   - Are you positive about the future, or do you sense difficulties?

4   Try to identify the visionary, radical educators of today.

Who might prove to be the Illich and Shaw of the twenty-first century and what are *they* saying about the future of schooling?

This chapter has given an introduction to a range of social issues in education that, for beginning teachers, can be particularly challenging to address, and even after reading it you may still feel that these are issues that can wait until you feel more confident in 'getting the basics right'. However, the reflective activities in this chapter have given you opportunities to take a broader view of your motivation for entering teaching – to reflect on the core purpose of education. During your early professional development experiences, the majority of your attention will be focused on the *what* (your subject, the curriculum) and the *how* (pedagogy, the 'craft' of teaching) of schooling. This chapter has given you the opportunity to consider the *why* – the social purpose of education, what we are actually trying to achieve in our work with young people, what kind of society we want to help shape. By using your own life experiences and personal values as the starting point, you have also had the opportunity to see how these impact on your developing professional identity. You can now use this, alongside the sources of guidance and support given in this chapter, to not only challenge and extend your understanding of social justice issues in education, but to have a real practical impact on your teaching.

Critical reading at Master's level

1 Please read the following three articles/chapters, which all theorize the issues relating to social contexts and social justice addressed in this chapter.

Gillborn, D. (2005) 'Education in policy as an act of white supremacy: whiteness, critical race theory and education reform', *Journal of Education Policy*, 20(4): 485–505.

Ball, S. (1993) 'Education markets, choice and social class: the market as a class strategy in the UK and the USA', *British Journal of Sociology of Education*, 14(1): 3–19.

Bauman, Z. (2011) 'Fate of social inequality in liquid-modern times', Chapter 3 from *Collateral Damage: Social Inequalities in a Global Age*. Cambridge: Polity. pp 44–59.

- In order to clarify your understanding, write a short summary of the key points you have taken from each (write these in your own way, as a bullet point list, a short paragraph or diagrammatically).
- What does your reading these writers tell you about the nature of evidence? (None of these pieces of writing draws directly upon first-hand empirical data – although Gillborn's article examines secondary data.)

(Continued)

(Continued)

- What can you learn from these theoretical writings about your developing understanding of researching and writing at Master's level?
- Can you see any common themes across the three apparently very different theoretical perspectives?
- Can you draw any practical or policy-related implications from these theoretical perspectives on social justice issues in education and wider society? What are they?

References

Baker, L. and Credland, S. (eds) (2004) *Listen Up: The Voices of Homeless Children*. London: Shelter.

Ball, S. (1993) 'Education markets, choice and social class: the market as a class strategy in the UK and the USA', *British Journal of Sociology of Education*, 14(1): 3–19.

Bauman, Z. (2011) 'Fate of social inequality in liquid-modern times', Chapter 3 in *Collateral Damage: Social Inequalities in a Global Age*. Cambridge: Polity.

Beattie, J. (2010) '16 of Cabinet ministers went to public school', *Daily Mirror*, 13 May 2010. www.mirror.co.uk/news/top-stories/2010/05/13/16-of-cabinet-ministers-went-to-public-school-115875-22254681

Bhavnani, K.K. and R. Bhavnani (1985) 'Racism and resistance in Britain', in D. Coates, G. Johnson and R. Bush (eds) *A Socialist Anatomy of Britain*. Oxford: Polity Press.

Blair, T. (1999) *Speech to Labour Party Conference*, 28 September 1999. http://news.bbc.co.uk/1/hi/uk_politics/460009.stm

Blanden, J., Goodman, A., Gregg, P. and Machin, S. (2004) 'Changes in intergenerational mobility in Britain', in M. Corak (ed.) *Changes in Generational Income Mobility*. Cambridge: Cambridge University Press.

Bourdieu, P. (1977) *Outline of a Theory of Practice*. London: Cambridge University Press.

Brown, P., Lauder, H. and Ashton, D. (2008) *Education, Globalisation and the Knowledge Economy: A Commentary*. London: Teaching and Learning Research Programme (TLRP).

Burgess, S., Greaves, E., Vignoles, A. and Wilson, D. (2009) 'What parents want: school preferences and school choice', working paper. Centre for Market and Public Organisation, Bristol Institute of Public Affairs.

Butler, J. (1993) *Bodies that Matter: the Discursive Limits of 'Sex'*. London: Routledge.

Callaghan, J. (1976) 'Towards a national debate', speech at Ruskin College, Oxford, accessed online at http://education.guardian.co.uk/thegreatdebate/story/0,,574645,00.html

Cameron, D. (2006) 'Modern Conservatism', speech to Demos, 30 June 2006. www.guardian.co.uk/politics/2006/jan/30/conservatives.davidcameron

Cameron, D. (2011a) *Education Excellence = 'Better Citizens'*, 9 November 2011. www.publicservice.co.uk/news_story.asp?id=17394

Cameron, D. (2011b) Speech on radicalisation and Islamic extremism, 5 February 2011, Munich Security Conference, Downing Street website. www.number10.gov.uk/news/pms-speech-at-munich-security-conference/

Cassen, R. and Kingdon, G. (2007) *Tackling Low Educational Achievement*. York: Joseph Rowntree Foundation.

Coard, B. (1971) *How the West Indian Child is Made Educationally Subnormal in the British School System: The Scandal of the Black Child in Schools in Britain*. London: New Beacon Books Ltd.

Coffield, F., Moseley, D., Hall, E. and Ecclestone, K. (2004) *Should We Be Using Learning Styles? What Research Has to Say to Practice*. London: Learning and Skills Research Centre.

Cohen, G. (1979) *Capitalism, Freedom and the Proletariat*. Oxford: Oxford University Press.

Cole, M. (ed.) (2005) *Professional Values and Practice: Meeting the Standards*. London: David Fulton.

Connolly, P. (2006) 'The effects of social class and ethnicity on gender differences in GCSE attainment: a secondary analysis of the youth cohort study of England and Wales 1997–2001', *British Educational Research Journal*, 32(1): 3–21.

Cundy, J. (2011) *Levelling the Playing Field: Achieving Social Mobility for 16 and 17-year-olds*. Ilford: Barnardo's. www.barnardos.org.uk/barnardo_s_levelling_the_playing_field_full_report.pdf

Curtis, P. (2005) 'Survey shows Oxbridge graduates filling Commons', *Guardian*, 12 December 2005. www.guardian.co.uk/education/2005/dec/12/highereducation.uk

Davies, I., Evans, M. and Reid, A. (2005) 'Globalising citizenship education? A critique of "global education" and "citizenship education"', *British Journal of Educational Studies*, 53: 66–89.

Department for Education (2011) *Performance Tables 2011*. London: HMSO.

Department of Education and Science (1971) *Potential and Progress in a Second Culture*. London: HMSO.

Department of Education and Science (1975) *Educational Disadvantage and the Needs of Immigrants*. London: HMSO.

Department of Education and Science (1981) *The School Curriculum*. London: HMSO.

Department for Education and Skills (2006) *Social Mobility: Narrowing Social Class Educational Attainment Gaps*. London: HMSO.

Dunne, M. and Gazeley, L. (2008) 'Teachers, social class and underachievement', *British Journal of Sociology of Education*, 29(5): 451–463.

Francis, B., Skelton, C., Carrington, B., Hutchings, M., Read, B. and Hall, I. (2006) 'A perfect match? Pupils' and teachers' views of the impact of matching educators and learners by gender', paper presented at the British Educational Research Association Annual Conference, University of Warwick, 6–9 September.

Gaine, C. (1987) *Still No Problem Here*. London: Trentham Books.

Gaine, C. (1989) 'On getting equal opportunities policies – and keeping them', in M. Cole (ed.) *Education for Equality: Some Guidelines for Good Practice*. London: Routledge.

Gender Education Association (2010) *Gender Hysteria: 2010 Examination Results*. www.genderandeducation.com/issues/gender-hysteria-2010-examination-results/

Gillborn, D. (1995) *Racism and Antiracism in Real Schools: Theory, Policy, Practice*. Buckingham: Open University Press.

Gillborn, D. (2005) 'Education policy as an act of white supremacy: whiteness, critical race theory and education reform', *Journal of Education Policy*, 20(4): 485–505.

Gillborn, D. and Mirza, H.S. (2000) *Educational Inequality: Mapping Race, Class and Gender: A Synthesis of Research Evidence*. ED457311. London: Ofsted.

Goodson, I. (ed.) (1985) *Social Histories of the Secondary Curriculum: Subjects for Study*. London: Falmer.

Gorski, P. (2011) *Awareness Activities, Critical Multicultural Pavilion: an EdChange project*. www.edchange.org/multicultural/activities/boygirl.html

Gove, M. (2009) Speech to the Royal Society for the Arts (RSA), 30 June 2009. www.thersa.org/__data/assets/pdf_file/0009/213021/Gove-speech-to-RSA.pdf

Guasp, A. (2009) *The Teachers' Report: Homophobic Bullying in Britain's Schools*. London: Stonewall.

Hagan, M. (2001) 'Educare in the independent sector: a model for the way ahead or the preserve of the elite?', *Irish Educational Studies*, 20(1): 296–309.

Hicks, D. (2003) 'Thirty years of global education: a reminder of key principles and precedents', *Educational Review*, 55(3): 265–273.

Hill, D. (1994) 'Equality, ideology and education policy', in D. Hill and M. Cole (eds) *Schooling and Equality: Fact, Concept and Policy*. London: RoutledgeFalmer.

Hills, J. (2010) *An Anatomy of Economic Inequality in the UK – Report of the National Equality Panel*, CASE report no 60.

Home Office (2006) *Racial and Religious Hatred Act*. London: HMSO.

Hunt, R. and Jensen, J. (2007) *The School Report: The Experiences of Young Gay People in Britain's Schools*. London: Stonewall.

Illich, I. (1971) *Deschooling Society*. New York: Harper & Row.

Independent Schools Council (ISC) (2011) *Sector Statistics 2011*. www.isc.co.uk/Teaching Zone_SectorStatistics.htm#pupil

Jones, K. (1989) *Right Turn: The Conservative Revolution in Education*. London: Hutchinson Radius.

Local Government Act (1988) Section 28. www.legislation.gov.uk/ukpga/1988/9/contents Brighton

Macpherson, W. (1999) *The Stephen Lawrence Inquiry*. London: HMSO.

Major, J. (1992) Leaders speech, Conservative Party Conference, Brighton, 9 October. www.britishpoliticalspeech.org/speech-archieve.htm?speech=138 (accessed 13 July 2012).

Miles, R. (1993) *Racism after 'Race Relations'*. London: Routledge.

Millar, F. (2011) 'Private schools do not understand "public benefit"', *Guardian* 10 May 2011. www.guardian.co.uk/education/2011/may/10/private-schools-charitable-status

Mongon, D. and Chapman, C. (2008) *Successful Leadership for Promoting the Achievement of White Working Class Pupils*. Manchester: University of Manchester Press.

Mulholland, H. (2011) 'David Willetts blames feminism over lack of jobs for working men', *Guardian* 1 April 2011. www.guardian.co.uk/politics/2011/apr/01/david-willetts-feminism-lack-of-jobs

Mullard, C. (1973) *Black Britain*. London: Allen & Unwin.

Nayak, A. and Kehily, M.J. (1996) 'Playing it straight: masculinities, homophobias and schooling', *Journal of Gender Studies*, 5(2): 211–230.

Nordquist, R. (2011) *Essays by George Bernard Shaw: What is Wrong with Our System of Education?* http://grammar.about.com/od/classicessays/a/What-Is-Wrong-With-Our-System-Of-Education-By-George-Bernard-Shaw.htm

Office for National Statistics (2012) *The National Statistics Socio-economic Classification*. www.ons.gov.uk/ons/guide-method/classifications/current-standard-classifications/soc2010/soc2010-volume-3-ns-sec--rebased-on-soc2010--user-manual/index.html

Ofsted (2007) *The Annual Report of Her Majesty's Chief Inspector of Schools*. London: Ofsted.

Olssen, M., Codd, J. and O'Neill, A. (2004) *Education Policy: Globalization, Citizenship & Democracy*. London: Sage.

Osler, A. and Vincent, K. (2002) *Citizenship and the Challenge of Global Education*. Stoke-on-Trent: Trentham Books.

Palmer, F. (ed). (1986) *Anti-racism: An Assault on Education and Value*. Nottingham: Sherwood Press.

Race Relations (Amendment) Act (2000). London: HMSO.

Rampton Report (1981) *West Indian Children in Our Schools: Interim Report of the Committee of Inquiry into the Education of Children from Ethnic Minority Groups*, London: HMSO.

Reay, D., David, M. and Ball, S. (2005) *Degrees of Choice: Social Class, Race, Gender and Higher Education*. Stoke-on-Trent: Trentham Books.

Rivers, I. (2006) 'Bullying and homophobia in UK schools: A perspective on factors affecting resilience and recovery', *Journal of Gay and Lesbian Issues in Education*, 3(4): 11–43.

Skelton, C. (2007) 'Gender, policy and initial teacher education', *Gender and Education*, 19(6): 677–690.

Skelton, C. and Reid, B. (2006) 'Male and female teachers' evaluative response to gender and the implications of these for the learning environments of primary age pupils', *International Studies in Sociology of Education*, 16(2): 105–120.

Social Psychology Network (SPN) (2011) *The Stereotype Game: Understanding Prejudice*. www.understandingprejudice.org/privacy.

Stafford, J.M. (1985) *Public Schools, Private Privilege and Common Sense – A Defence of Independent Education*. Solihull: Ismeron.

Steiner, M. (1996) '"I prefer to see myself as a global citizen": how student teachers can learn to teach for justice', in M. Steiner (ed.) *Developing the Global Teacher: Theory and Practice in Initial Teacher Education*. Stoke-on-Trent: Trentham Books.

Stonewall (2007) *The Experiences of Young Gay People in Britain's Schools*. London: Stonewall.

Sutton Trust (2010) *Education Mobility in England: The Link between the Education Levels of Parents and the Educational Outcomes of Teenagers*. London: Sutton Trust.

Swann Report (1985) *Education for All: Report of the Committee of Enquiry into the Education of Children from Ethnic Minority Groups*. London: HMSO.

Thatcher, M. (1987) 'Interview for "Woman's Own" ("No Such Thing as Society")', in *Margaret Thatcher Foundation: Speeches, Interviews and Other Statements*. London: Thatcher Foundation.

Tomlinson, S. (2008) *Race and Education: Policy and Politics in Britain*. Buckingham: Open University Press.

Training and Development Agency for Schools (2011) *Teachers' Standards*. London: TDA.

Troyna, B. (1987) 'Beyond multiculturalism: towards the enactment of anti-racist education in policy, provision and pedagogy', *Oxford Review of Education*, 13(3): 307–320.

Whitty, G. (2002) *Making Sense of Education Policy: Studies in the Sociology and Politics of Education*. London: Paul Chapman.

Wilkins, C. (2001) 'Student Teachers and Attitudes towards "Race": the role of citizenship education in addressing racism through the curriculum', *Westminster Studies in Education*, 24(1): 7–21.

Woodhead, C. (2009) *A Desolation of Learning: Is This the Education Our Children Deserve?* Brighton: Pencil-sharp Publishing.

GLOSSARY

ability: the quality, skill or power to be able to do something.

academy: a publicly funded school which operates outside of local authority control and receives its funds directly from central government (refer to Chapter 3).

accelerated learning: learning based on strategies which are designed to support the three types of learner – visual, auditory and kinaesthetic.

achievement: succeeding in finishing something or reaching an aim.

action research: a collaborative form of educational research involving teachers and professionals in clusters of schools or other educational units with shared interests. Importance is given to linking theory to practice, through relating theory to the teachers' own experience and observations and through reflection on observations and own practices. Action research maintains a distance between the teacher-researcher and the study and, in so doing, differs from self-study research.

affordances: potential benefits to the learning process through use of a piece of equipment, computer hardware and software or other device.

assessment: the process of judging the validity and worth of students' work in all its various forms.

assessment regime: used to indicate a structure of examinations and other assessment formats that constitute a society's main routes to qualifications.

attainment: something which has been succeeded in, achieved or reached.

attention deficit hyperactivity disorder (ADHD): a term used to describe perceived behavioural problems, most often in children. The main behaviours identified are inattention, hyperactivity and impulsive behaviour.

behaviour management: the various actions and interactions used by teaching staff to enhance the probability of students acting in a productive and socially acceptable manner.

behaviourism: is concerned with: modelling appropriate behaviours; creating environments that enable or condition students to respond in what are deemed appropriate ways; rewarding positive responses; learning through repetition.

'big picture': an overview of what students will learn during the lesson at the beginning of a session and how it connects with prior learning and intended future learning.

blogs: otherwise known as weblogs, these are online journals or filters which allow an individual to post ideas and thoughts, or website addresses they feel are useful for a particular purpose. Other users can add comments concerning the content on the weblog thereby making it interactive.

Bromcom: an electronic system for registering pupils' attendance.

classroom management: the teaching behaviours used by an individual to shape and develop conditions which facilitate learning within a group of students.

coaching: a one-to-one relationship in which a coach offers support that will enable a person to identify their personal strengths and goals, focus on what they want to achieve and plan a course of action to help them do so.

cognitivism: cognitive theory is about thinking and draws on the work of Gagne, Ausubel and Bruner. It assumes that, as learners learn, they draw and build on knowledge they already have, disregarding some prior knowledge when no longer necessary or when new learning makes it redundant.

communities of practice: Lave and Wenger (1991) conceptualized the idea that these communities are everywhere and have a number of characteristics (mutual engagement, joint enterprise, and a shared repertoire). People learn through participating in practice with newcomers learning from longer-standing members and from each other.

concept mapping: a process of building up diagrams which contain a limited number of concepts or ideas with the propositional relationships which join them written on linking arrows.

constructivism: the learner plays a very active role in the construction of his or her new knowledge, skills or attitude. Readers need to distinguish between *psychological* and *social* construction of knowledge, associated with the theories of Piaget and Vygotsky respectively.

curriculum: the group of subjects studied in a school or college or a course of study in a particular subject.

deductive thinking or **deductivism**: a form of reasoning in which ideas are tested before they are accepted formally. It relies on the logical outcomes of current idea or theory, or an imaginative idea arising from that idea/theory. Scientific knowledge for example is built by deduction through the systematic testing of hypotheses. Any observations are directed or led by the original hypothesis.

designated senior person: a senior member of the school's leadership team who is designated to take lead responsibility for dealing with child protection issues, providing advice and support to other staff, liaising with the local authority, and working with other agencies. The designated person need not be a teacher but must have the status and authority within the school management structure to carry out the duties of the post including committing resources to child protection matters, and where appropriate directing other staff (taken from Section 157 of the Education Act, 2002).

differentiation: planning and teaching using approaches to suit the learning needs and prior learning of individual students and to ensure that all are engaged in activities which will challenge them appropriately.

dis-application or **dis-applied**: exemption from participation in certain aspects of the curriculum or statutory assessment processes.

e-learning: learning in which the Internet 'plays an important role in the delivery, support, administration and assessment of learning' (Kirschner and Paas, 2001: 350) (refer to Chapter 4).

e-safety: keeping children safe in their use of the Internet, social media, mobile phones, game consoles, other software or devices used for the creation or transfer of information and educating them about the benefits and potential dangers of information technology (refer to Chapter 4).

Excellence in Cities (EiC): a major government policy designed to raise standards in urban schools. EiC was organized through partnerships, and each partnership included a local authority (LA) and all its secondary schools. EiC had seven key strands:

- support for gifted and talented students
- the provision of learning mentors to support young people facing barriers to learning
- learning support units (LSUs) for students who would benefit from time away from the normal classroom
- city learning centres (CLCs) providing state-of-the-art ICT resources for a small number of schools
- EiC Action Zones enabling small groups of primary and secondary schools to work together to provide local solutions to local problems
- extensions of the existing specialist and beacon school programmes.

free schools: 'all-ability state-funded schools set up in response to what local people say they want and need in order to improve education for children in their community' (DfE, 2011a) (refer to Chapters 3 and 7).

gatekeeper: a gatekeeper is an individual or an institution which controls access to a valuable asset or resource. In terms of schooling, the school acts as gatekeeper to employment and high salaries through its assessment activities.

General Teaching Council of England (GTCE): regulates the teaching profession in England and aims to raise the status of teaching and learning. Similar regulatory bodies exist in Northern Ireland (GTCNI), Scotland (GTCS) and Wales (GTCW).

gifted and talented: a description of young people who have the ability or the potential to develop significantly ahead of their year group either in academic subjects such as maths and English or in practical/creative skills like sport, music and performing arts.

in loco parentis: UK legal term meaning 'in place of the parent'. When parents or carers send their children to school they delegate their authority to the teachers to act in the best interests of the school and the children. A teacher who is supervising or accompanying students on a school trip has overall responsibility for their health and safety and is said to be acting 'in loco parentis'.

inductive hypothesis: this is a thinking process using logical reasoning that a hypothesis can be made because particular cases that seem to be examples of it exist.

inductive thinking or **inductivism**: a way of generalizing from a set of observations to a universal law inductively. It is a process used in one form of scientific thinking/reasoning. Scientific knowledge for example is built by induction from a well accepted (reliable) set of observations.

institutional racism: 'the collective failure an organisation to provide an appropriate and professional services to people because of their colour, culture, or ethnic origin' (from the macpherson report, 1999 as reported in www.guardian.co.uk/uk/1999/feb/24/lawrence.ukcrime7, accessed 31 January 2012).

interpersonal: between people (for example the ability to interact effectively with colleagues in your subject team is an interpersonal skill).

intrapersonal: within oneself (for example the ability to reflect is an intrapersonal skill).

key skills: sometimes known as 'core skills' or 'basic skills', these are areas of schooling that are seen as fundamental to the future performance of individuals in the economy. They include numeracy, literacy and ICT, as well as problem-solving, working with others and managing your own learning.

learning communities: partnerships between different agencies within a community (including voluntary sector agencies) to promote learning. Learning communities can be real or virtual.

learning gain: the gap between that understood by a student before and after a learning encounter.

learning mentoring: providing support and guidance to children, young people and those engaged with them, by removing barriers to learning in order to promote effective participation, enhance individual learning, raise aspirations and achieve their potential.

learning objectives: these specify what you want your pupils to know or be able to do at the end of an activity, lesson or scheme of work (refer to Chapter 4).

Learning to Learn: programmes which seek to give students an opportunity to develop as learners through development of: reflectivity about their learning; thinking skills and ICT.

lesson plan: a framework for the shape and management of learning within a single lesson.

lesson planning: the process involved in developing the structure and activities to be undertaken by students within a lesson and the ways in which their learning will be monitored.

level 3 examinations: these test what might be expected of the notional 16–18-year-old and include for example academic and vocational Advanced level examinations.

literacy: 'the ability to read, write, speak and listen well. A literate person is able to communicate effectively with others and to understand written information' (see The National Literacy Trust website: http://www.literacytrust.org.uk/about/faqs/s1#q4432 accessed 24 May 2012) (refer to Chapter 3).

meta-cognition: a form of knowledge. It is knowledge of one's own cognitive processes and includes both strategic knowledge and self-knowledge. It is acquired through the support of others more knowledgeable than oneself (referred to as scaffolding). It provides the capacity for regulating one's own thinking, so an individual can solve problems or ask questions or model these 'conversations with oneself' based on those previously held with others (teachers or peers).

mind map/mind-mapping: a creative way of organizing material in a visual form that reflects how information is encoded in the brain. A topic or idea is placed in the middle of a page and strands are drawn from it, identifying particular aspects of it. A mind map is usually more systematic than a spider diagram, with the information being organized logically by strands and sub-strands, rather than just putting down ideas in any order.

Neuro Linguistic Programming (NLP): rooted in both psychology and neurology, NLP is based on the work of John Grinder, a linguistics professor, and Richard Bandler, a mathematician, at the University of California at Santa Cruz (UCSC), around 1975. They recognized the importance of eye contact and movement in identifying emotional states and how (rather than what) individuals think. NLP identifies six ways in which individuals perceive information which arrives via the senses. These form the basis of what we now know as 'VAK', the identification of *visual, auditory* and *kinaesthetic* learners and the need to cater for different learning styles in the classroom. NLP also recognizes the importance of non-verbal communication, particularly eye contact, posture, breathing and movement.

observation: the act of recording and noting a classroom experience, predominantly that of another individual.

Ofsted: the Office for Standards in Education, a government agency responsible for the inspection of schools, colleges and teacher training courses.

pedagogy: a generic term for teaching and learning processes.

peer teaching: pupils learning from their peers.

performance data: statistics collected about a school or college that describes the achievements of students in various examinations and other key areas of education. They are usually gathered for purposes of publication to parents, the government, Ofsted and other interested parties.

personalized learning: refer to Chapter 3.

plenary: a review of what pupils have learned (in relation to the learning objectives) during a lesson or part of a lesson (refer to Chapter 4).

professional enquiry: includes several academic and social processes, including engagement with research, and the active seeking of evidence and systematic evaluation by one or more professionals in a professional learning community such as a school, or department within a school.

professional standards: standards for initial teacher training, induction, professional, excellent and advanced skills teachers.

programme of study (PoS): the framework for learning over a prolonged period of time, usually a Key Stage, which might highlight the content and/or skills to be developed.

reflective/reflection: the terms refer to the capacity of an individual to think thoughtfully and deeply, to remind oneself of past events and to consider alternative courses of action.

reflexive/reflexivity: the terms refer to the involuntary or instinctive examination of oneself.

scaffolding: the construction of structures (such as writing frames and bullet point prompts) which support learners in the initial stages of a task or throughout it and which can be gradually removed as a learner gains confidence (see Chapter 2).

schemes of work: a series of lessons focusing on a particular area of a subject, or skill.

school ethos: it embraces the aims, attitudes, values and procedures in the school – the 'intangibles' that come from the spirit within the school and its community, including its students, all staff, approaches to teaching and learning, management of the curriculum and of the school as a whole.

SEF: Self-Evaluation Form completed by schools to evaluate leadership, management and capacity to improve. It is the main document used by an Ofsted team when they plan an inspection.

self-study research: a way of purposefully examining the relationship between teaching and learning so that alternative perspectives on the intentions and outcomes might be better realized. There are similarities and differences between self-study and action research but self-study requires that teachers put themselves, their beliefs, assumptions and ideologies about teaching, as well as their practice, under close scrutiny.

setted: a system where students are put into groups with others of roughly equal ability. The groups may vary between subjects to reflect the different levels of ability demonstrated by any individual student across the curriculum (see Chapter 3).

SMART: an acronym used in target-setting with the aim of focusing on specific goals. A SMART target is specific, measurable, attainable, realistic and time-based. There are a number of variants on the exact wording.

social constructivism: focuses on the cognitive processes that occur as people learn through social interaction such as play, listening to and working with others and how these impact on mental development (see Chapter 2). Vygotsky proposed that learning takes place in the zone of proximal development (ZPD) – a simple way of describing the time and place when two or more people are involved in a learning activity.

social mobility: movement of an individual or a group's position within society.

specification: a detailed outline (or syllabus) of how a course will be examined.

spider diagram: allows you to think about the main idea that, for example, a book is exploring and then how the ideas are seen to be present in many parts of the book. Spider diagrams can combine and extend Venn diagrams to express constraints on sets (ideas) and their relationships with other sets. A 'spider' is arranged as a tree with branches and a trunk, and is used to explore the connection between one set of ideas (the foot of the trunk) and other sets of related ideas (where the branches touch other sets of ideas).

Standard Assessment Tasks (SATs): tests used to assess attainment at the end of a Key Stage.

starter: a quick activity designed to 'hook' students into their learning at the beginning of a lesson (refer to Chapter 4).

statemented: a child who is statemented has a Statement of Special Educational Needs (SEN). This legal document specifies a child's strengths and identifies the support they need in place so that they are able to learn alongside other pupils in their year group.

storyboard: used by film production crews and others in the media. It is a series of sketches and technical notes showing the sequence of key shots in a scene. Storyboards are also used (in simplified form) in English and media classrooms by students to demonstrate their understanding and interpretation of key events or production features of texts they are studying or creating for themselves.

streaming/streamed: a system where students are put into groups with others of roughly equal ability. The groups remain constant across subjects and do not take into account the variable ability of an individual across the curriculum (refer to Chapter 3).

Systematic Synthetic Phonics (SSP): the teaching of reading through understanding the discrete phonemes (sound units) that make up words and their grapheme correspondences (written forms), e.g. that the sound 'ay' can be written in several ways including 'ai' as in daily and 'a_e' as in cake. It is synthetic because learners blend or synthesize phones to create whole words and systematic because learning is broken down into a prescribed sequence of steps. (Refer to Chapter 3.)

unconditional positive regard: an attitude of caring, characteristic of a person-centred approach to client-centred therapy. It provides the climate for change and acceptance of whatever immediate feeling is going on – confusion, resentment, fear, anger, courage, pride. Such caring is non possessive and is not conditional.

value-added: measure of attainment which takes into account levels of improvement when comparing a year group's level of attainment when compared with those in other schools.

vertical grouping: pupils from across an age spectrum are placed in the same form group.

VLEs: virtual learning environments. Software applications which are used to organize, aid and assess learning. They are most frequently accessed through an Internet portal.

wikis: a group of web pages which allows users to add content, while allowing others to edit that content.

Wikipedia: is an encyclopaedia on the web which users can contribute pages to or edit other people's contributions.

writing frames: outline structures or scaffolds which help learners to shape their ideas or arguments, in particular, written forms such as reports, argued writing or responses to texts.

zone of proximal development (ZPD): term first coined by Vygotsky to define the distance between the actual development level of learning and what potentially could be learned through problem-solving either with guidance through that zone by a parent, grandparent, sibling, or other adult such as a teacher, or by collaboration with more capable peers.

INDEX